# EFFECTIVE INTERVIEWING IN SOCIAL WORK AND SOCIAL CARE

# Effective Interviewing in Social Work and Social Care

## A Practical Guide

Gina Allen
Duncan Langford

First published 2008 by
PALGRAVE MACMILLAN
Houndmills, Basingstoke, Hampshire RG21 6XS and
175 Fifth Avenue, New York, N.Y. 10010
Companies and representatives throughout the world

PALGRAVE MACMILLAN is the global academic imprint of the Palgrave Macmillan division of St. Martin's Press, LLC and of Palgrave Macmillan Ltd. Macmillan® is a registered trademark in the United States, United Kingdom and other countries. Palgrave is a registered trademark in the European Union and other countries.

ISBN-13: 978–1–4039–9503–2
ISBN-10: 1–4039–9503–6

This book is printed on paper suitable for recycling and made from fully managed and sustained forest sources. Logging, pulping and manufacturing processes are expected to conform to the environmental regulations of the country of origin.

A catalogue record for this book is available from the British Library.

A catalog record for this book is available from the Library of Congress.

10   9   8   7   6   5   4   3   2   1
17   16   15   14   13   12   11   10   09   08

Printed in China

2|10

To Madeleine . . .
she knows why

# Contents

# Preface

Why a book on interviewing?

Some years ago a social worker was asked to visit a young mother whose child was suspected of being at risk. The worker visited regularly, always found the house clean and tidy, and felt that over several months he had built up a very good relationship with the mother. However, he never saw the child. Every time he asked after her, the mother apologised, and usually explained her absence by saying 'She's with her father today'. Eventually, after three months, the social worker's supervisor insisted that the child must be seen. So, when on the next visit the social worker was told that the child was with her father, he demanded the address. Then, and only then, did it emerge that the father had moved back to Ireland six months before (where the child turned out to be happy, and very well cared for). Her mother would probably have welcomed social work visits indefinitely.

Of course, there could have been other, more sinister, reasons for that failure to produce the child; but underlying the whole issue was a more specific problem: the worker's basic failure to challenge and probe. By handling the initial interview appropriately, the interviewer could have learned at once that the child had moved away.

What might have caused this failure?

Let's consider the possible background. While social workers and social care workers are perceived to be professionals, they are also, by definition, individual human beings, with accumulated life experiences, one of which is basic communication with others.

So it is likely that a new interviewer's perception of 'communication' has been based on talking and interacting with friends and family. For this reason, it is understandable that this will be the 'default' model they bring to personal interaction in the social care setting, rather than a substantially different 'professional' approach, which should be acquired during training.

A *personal* approach may be exactly what a service user will be expecting, and indeed, to some extent this is justified. In their interactions with service users, social workers look for unique strengths and abilities, and attempt to equalise power relationships. In talking about personal matters, service users are likely unconsciously to model their behaviour on family relationships, or on a close and trusted friendship. This means that a social care worker or interviewer may well be perceived as a trusted friend – with all that this implies.

It is therefore clear that, from the outset, an interviewer should be careful to make their professional boundaries quite clear to a service user – and to be clear about limits themselves. Failure to do this will almost certainly lead to serious problems in their attempts at professional interviewing.

In the example mentioned earlier, the social worker probably started the initial interview using an approach that was familiar to them, and most likely to the service user, too – one that the worker had evolved and used with success in the past, when meeting new people in a social setting. Such an approach by an interviewer who is new to social work is understandable; however, despite their name, 'social work' interviews are emphatically not 'social'. For example, getting to know someone socially will not normally be accompanied by the need to complete a list of personal questions.

Inevitably, then, if an interviewer takes a 'social' interview approach, their requests for information cannot be direct. In particular, it will be extremely difficult for a novice interviewer to ask for information that a service user may be reluctant to give, and the interviewer will be tempted to avoid asking for it.

Therefore social work interviewing needs particular expertise; familiar social communication skills are not sufficient, and may even be counterproductive. Without special training, a social care interview is unlikely to be either effective or successful.

It should be borne in mind that social workers may have to deal every day with situations that may be – and all too often are – both distressing and stressful. An interviewer must, while empathising with the problems of service users, still be able to keep some emotional distance from them. This is crucial: any interviewer who is unable to resist these work pressures is likely to experience professional 'burnout'.

> Burnout is a state of mental and/or physical exhaustion caused by excessive and prolonged stress.
>
> (Girdano et al., 1996)

However, it is important to appreciate that burnout does not occur at random. It happens, not because social care interviewers are poor at their job, but because they are human.

Here, knowledge of professional interviewing techniques may be especially helpful. By understanding how to conduct an interview in a professional manner, a social worker is better able to retain emotional distance, and preserve their objectivity – essential qualities in all professional social work.

The need to preserve emotional distance does not imply that a social worker or social care worker should be completely without emotion. Clearly, workers need to be aware of – and sensitive to – the emotions of their service users, and in touch with their own emotions. However, as professionals they need the knowledge and ability to deal with distressing and emotional interviews without being overwhelmed; and, if necessary, to do so repeatedly.

Clearly, then, in order to become an effective and productive interviewer in a social work or social care setting, a social worker must learn and then practise a variety of new techniques.

There are various ways in which to accumulate the necessary interview skills. The traditional approach was to throw the interviewer in at the metaphorical deep end. The new worker would be given details of a service user, and told to go and interview them. With luck, the social worker would learn from their resultant accumulated and inevitable mistakes.

Such an approach has obvious and very real dangers, especially for those who as yet have little or no practical experience – social work students, for example, or perhaps new practitioners. Even if they already appreciate that the social work interview will be a primary tool in their future work, they will certainly need initial help and advice in how to define – and carry out – an effective interview. This is, of course, what this book aims to achieve.

Today, gaining insights through reading is likely to be a particular asset, because, due to the competing demands of twenty-first-century social work education, practical opportunities involving 'live' interviewing experience are never likely to feel sufficient.

Even in student placements, where the focus is on gaining practical, face-to-face experience with service users, a practitioner inevitably faces considerable paperwork and other 'overheads'. In reality, the amount of time available to be spent with service users may be only around half of what is theoretically available. In these circumstances, it is clearly important to make the very best use of limited contact.

This book, therefore, looks at examples ranging from straightforward one-to-one interviews between worker and service user, to complex interviews involving several different agencies. It looks in depth at interview planning, and considers how interviews may be best structured. It 'deconstructs' the interview. It describes a range of core skills and techniques that you can use to best effect, and a chapter is devoted to what may go wrong in an interview, and to suggested strategies for recovery.

The book takes as its starting point the discussion of core communication skills, and some basic techniques. For this reason, we have not discussed in depth some more complex interviewing situations, such as investigative interviews. In the same way, we see the topic of interviewing young children as outside the scope of this book, although there is reference to work with young people.

Many 'real-life' illustrative examples have been included. Essentially, varied social work practice has been condensed into a practical guide containing a wide variety of useful information and relevant strategies.

While intended mainly for social work students, *Effective Interviewing in Social Work and Social Care* should undoubtedly help any social work or social care interviewer to think about their practice and gain knowledge.

## THE TEXT

Chapters begin with pointers to National Occupational Standards in Social Care Key Roles that are particularly relevant to that chapter. They end with a summary of the main points dealt with in the chapter. There are also some relevant questions addressing chapter material; these chapter questions are intended both for class discussion and private study.

Throughout the book we have added information 'boxes', containing definitions and practice examples. The first time a specialist term is used, we have tried to accompany it by a 'definition' box; when a good-practice issue is discussed, it will often be illustrated by an example taken from practice. References are given throughout; full details of the cited texts may be found in the Bibliography and References, which also contains a selection of relevant sources that have not been quoted directly.

# Acknowledgements

We acknowledge with thanks permission to use material from the following sources:

Liz Stone, Total Communication Officer, MENCAP; Joyce Boaz, Executive Director, Gift From Within; Karen Cook and the Diversity Project Group, Northern Ireland; Robert Currington, of Royal National Institute for Deaf and Hard of Hearing People; Lyn Nock, Manager Publishing and Services, British Association of Social Workers; Dr Frank Ochberg; Skills for Care; Social Care Institute for Excellence.

Also, grateful thanks to friends and colleagues who have helped the progress of this book, especially Cordelia, Maggie and Rosalind, whose support at all times was much appreciated.

# Introduction

*This chapter introduces the topic of social work or social care interviewing, and emphasises its importance. After exploring the meaning of a social work interview, we briefly describe the contents and arrangement of the book.*

## A STARTING POINT

We begin by considering this statement:

> Interviewing skills are the central skills on which all components of the social work process depend.
>
> (Kadushin and Kadushin, 1997, p3)

That is certainly a pretty fundamental pronouncement. If it is true, then an understanding of successful interview techniques and skills is essential for all social workers.

But is Kadushin and Kadushin's statement in fact true? At first, you may well find their assertion rather hard to accept. After all, the words 'social work' actually describe what is, today, an extremely large field. Moreover, it is a field with multiple facets, employing many different professionals to carry out a huge assortment of tasks in a wide variety of settings. Yet, despite such diversity, everyone who works in the field almost certainly considers themselves to be employed in 'social care' or 'social work'. Could all this hugely varied activity really be constructed upon 'the interview'?

Well, yes; it could. Put simply, by definition all social work deals, in one way or another, with the social needs of individuals. Consequently, an ability to understand and respond to people's needs is essential for any practitioner. We can therefore accept, as a fundamental assertion, that an insight into the needs of individuals is basic for social work professionals.

So, social work and care professionals must be able to understand the needs of individual service users. That certainly sounds a reasonable statement; but, if we accept it, another important question arises: exactly how do we *get* this essential information?

We are living in the age of information technology; so, in theory, it might be possible to interrogate the Internet, or to access electronic records, or to link with electronic data stores. Or we might perhaps investigate and hunt through official and unofficial paper files, or even try to search for clues by studying local newspapers. Certainly, all these approaches are possible – if hypothetical – paths to understanding the needs of service users.

However, these paths are also indirect, and very complicated. Is there perhaps a more straightforward approach? Fortunately, yes. There can be no doubt that the best way to understand the needs of individual service users is simply to ask them: uncomplicated, but effective.

All that is left is to clarify the skills that a practitioner will need for talking with a service user. Appropriate training and practice will equip a social worker to properly perform this information-related task – which we will call an *interview*.

Clearly, in order to make their interviews productive, all social workers will need an understanding of successful interview methods; but there is another reason for learning interview skills. While personal communication is probably the best method for discovering personal information, it is also a very effective tool for passing on information.

Naturally, if we wished merely to make a service user aware of material that might be necessary or useful to them, we could send them a letter, or perhaps put a note through their letterbox, or leave a message on their answering machine. But, unless there is a specific reason why the data should be delivered in one of these ways, much the most straightforward and effective method of getting and giving information to a service user is simply to meet them, and talk.

## MEETING PEOPLE, AND TALKING

It's surprising how often core practice in social work essentially means meeting people, and talking. It might seem to an outsider that an interview is a simple encounter between two or more people, with the associated interaction. Simple it may appear; but, as this book will show, recognition of significant layers of complexity, together with considerable skills, are needed before a 'simple meeting' can evolve into an effective professional interview.

In addition, as concerned practitioners, we may well decide on personal interviews as the most appropriate way to forge a working alliance with our service users. We cannot, however, assume that people will understand all that may be needed, or be able to give full answers if they do. Furthermore, clients may have special communication needs. Finally, a service user may, for a variety of reasons, provide us with information that may be misleading, or even incorrect.

For all these reasons, we must, as professionals, engage in these key personal interactions with service users having acquired some skill in understanding the processes of the interview, and having learnt to handle its complexities.

As an interviewer, you must be clear about what you are doing, and why you are doing it; then become able to interact personally with service users in a productive and professional manner. You must learn how best to plan and manage the interview, and be able to cope with the range of emotions and reactions that may arise. You must be able to listen to the person, understand the various pressures on them, and be capable of encouraging an appropriate response – while at the same time allowing them to react naturally. Later, you will be trying to engage them in some change in themselves or their environment.

This may sound a complex task. It will certainly be helped if, before meeting and interviewing service users, you have already practised or thought about a range of suitable communication skills and interview techniques.

This book is written not simply to describe, illustrate and demonstrate many of those communication skills. By exploring the entire interview process in detail, we hope also to demystify the process of social work interviewing.

In summary, therefore:

- Interviewing is the key task in social work.
- Service users need social workers who understand the principles of good communication skills and the processes of interviewing.

## DEFINITION OF A SOCIAL WORK INTERVIEW

A dictionary definition of 'interview' is 'an exchange or meeting between two or more people, face to face'. A further definition we use is 'an interchange or conversation with a purpose, commonly between two people'. This definition begins to emphasise the role of the other party, the service user in our case, in the process of interviewing. How you view the service user, as a partner, as someone with whom you can make a helping alliance, should be at the heart of your interaction.

Kadushin and Kadushin describe an interview, at its simplest, as 'a conversation with a deliberate purpose that the participants accept' (1997, p4). And, as we have suggested, a social work interview will normally be for the collection or exchange of information, or for therapeutic purposes. Of course, this is a wide scope; and social work interview objectives can be complex. Social workers, and social care workers, are called upon to evaluate the information they receive, and may then have to make judgements about risk or safety to the person, or to a third party in the plans made together.

More formal social work definitions refer to interviews as a special kind of conversation or discussion (Trevithick, 2000, p69). Although on one level the information exchanged in a social work interview may seem quite straightforward, the interview *processes* will probably be much more complex. These processes include history and information about people's lives and relationships, which are rarely simple, and may well come loaded with emotional freight.

Another definition of a social work interview comes from Coulshed and Orme:

> An interview is a process which involves a combination of social psychology and sociology, where theories and information about people in their social circumstances, their motivations and their responses in interpersonal relationships can be used to help the worker understand the individual in their situation, and to gain relevant information and offer appropriate support.
>
> (1998, p69)

Clearly, a 'social work interview' will need time. It is important to give people sufficient space in which to respond. So, in order to respect people's feelings, to carefully check out cultural or diversity issues, to explore their views and make mutually agreed plans, an interview will need adequate time.

## WHERE ARE SOCIAL WORK INTERVIEWS HELD?

Settings for social work interviews differ. The location for your interview may be official, as in an office setting, or it may still be official, but held within a service user's home. However, not all social work interviews are necessarily formal – some interviews may be more relaxed, for example interactions in day centres on a day-to-day basis, or perhaps at residential homes. Of course, in a few social work and social care situations, there may not even be a face-to-face meeting at all; telephone interviews also have their place.

## INTERVIEW – OR MEETING?

How many people are present in a social work interview? When might an 'interview' become a 'meeting'? Social work interviews are not necessarily limited to the two people essential for an exchange of views: the service user and practitioner. As is discussed later in this book, sometimes the service user will want a third party to be present at the interview, or joint interviews, sometimes in association with other professionals, may need to be arranged.

Once the number of people present is larger than four, however, it becomes more difficult to view the interaction as an 'interview', unless you have more specialist skills, such as in family therapy. You may need to employ the same communication skills, but other 'meetings' skills may be needed. This remains the case even if the purpose of the meeting is identical with that of a one-to-one session, and similarly focused on the needs of the service user.

As will be seen from this exploration of the term, social work interviewing includes many variables, and may consist of many different elements. Although Coulshed and Orme's definition needs keeping in mind, for the purposes of this book we felt a more straightforward term was appropriate. We therefore consider the social work interview to be 'an exchange of information or discussion with a purpose, focused on matters of importance to a service user'.

## ORIGINS OF THE BOOK

It is possible to discuss the actual practice of social work and social care from a wide variety of theoretical perspectives, with the potential benefit of many different theoretical models. We do, of course, accept the importance of interviewing theory, which is discussed in detail in Chapter 2.

It follows, though, that in social care, interviewing theory must always inform practice. Practitioners know that, as well as theoretical models, first-hand interviewing experience will, over time, allow the gradual accumulation of tried and trusted techniques. These are built upon the individual skills and experience of the worker, and assist their practice (Hargie and Tourish, 2000, p76).

As this book is intended as a practical guide for social work practitioners, it is important to stress that we have included material based not only on theory, but also on real examples, and wide-ranging practice. Such hands-on skills are the raw materials for this book.

The aim is to describe and illustrate methods and experiences from which you, as a practitioner, can learn, incorporating the knowledge into your own practice.

## IMPORTANCE OF STRUCTURE

It is possible to carry out interviews casually, without prior thought and with no consideration of either anticipated outcomes or the handling of results; but such an approach is unlikely to produce an effective conclusion. At best, an unplanned and disorganised interview will generate unplanned and disorganised results, and, more importantly, distress service users. It will probably have to be repeated, which is normally rather difficult for both sides.

At worst, too, the results of a lack of planning may be unexpected:

| Practice issue |
| --- |
| A student, working on placement in an inner city Social Services office, was asked to talk to a single mother over serious childcare issues. However, when the supervisor was shown a write-up of the interview, he was so incensed at its poor quality that the student – after an uncomfortable period of expedited learning – was sent out to undertake the interview again. However, the mother's rather possessive boyfriend had been unhappy with the first visit, and unfortunately misunderstood the reason why another call had been made so soon. |

With today's workload and time pressures, doing the same piece of work twice is to be avoided. You should also (for much the same reasons) extract the maximum information possible from every interview. This will mean careful planning, together with a degree of skill in the handling of the interview itself.

Finally, it should not be forgotten that almost all social work interviews have two different outcomes. First, they should ideally accomplish the tasks planned. Second, they will have to provide an adequate written record of what has been attempted, and fulfilled.

Looking more closely into what is needed, a social care interview may have three distinct planning stages:

1 Before
2 During
3 After

The first stage is that of *pre-interview planning*. The decision on whether an interview is actually necessary, and appropriate, should be carefully considered – and never merely assumed. Should an interview be decided upon, then plan the most suitable approach and initial objectives. This does not rule out considering what the service user's goals might be, even if you cannot clarify them until the interview.

The second stage concerns the *interview process* itself. You will need to consider its dynamic management, and select any special modes of communication. Both spoken and non-verbal communication will need to be taken into account at this planning stage.

Finally, prepare for the *recording* of the interview. This is an area of social care/social work interviewing that people often regard as unexciting and time-consuming, and which in consequence may not be given its due importance. However, adequate and apt recording of an interview is essential. All social care interviewers should understand that, should there be no correct record of their interview, that interview is unlikely to have been a professional one.

## CONTENT

The content of the book has been planned so that, although each chapter can be read in isolation, overall learning is best experienced by reading through the chapters in order.

### Chapter 1: Values and anti-discriminatory practice

Chapter 1 argues that the working alliance or the relationship is the keystone of the interview. We look at the source of the principles we bring to interviews with service users. Whether they are personal or professional, these values set the scene for the interaction. The chapter then goes on to examine anti-discriminatory practice in social work, and major oppressions and discriminations in society faced by service users, such as disability, race or gender.

### Chapter 2: Theory: its place in interviewing

Chapter 2 considers why there is a need to incorporate thinking on interview theory into practice, both in preparation for an interview and in the interview itself. It argues that if theory and evidence-based knowledge are not used, then the interviewer will be open to less rational ways of thinking; which could, for instance, prove discriminatory. As we know, social workers and social care workers have to deal with a wide cross-section of people, so they need to develop professional ways of relating to people that are capable of supporting non-judgemental involvement.

## Chapter 3: Types and purpose of interviews in the agency context

A social care worker may need to examine the 'frame' of their involvement with service users. What they do should be put into the context of their employer's role, and their particular role within the organisation. Understandably, given the wide range of interviews that are carried out under the broad heading of 'social care', each will be different. Therefore reflecting beforehand about *each interview* is important. What may be a sound communication method for one service user could well not be suitable on another occasion. A further section of this chapter looks at joint interviewing with other professionals, and interviewing on the telephone.

## Chapter 4: Preparation and pre-planning

Chapter 4 discusses the pre-planning and thinking necessary before an interview is undertaken. It considers the interviewer as a reflective worker, aiming for the best possible outcome for the time they spend with the service user. Consequently, as a first step you should reflect on time, location and duration: essentially, once you take the decision to hold an interview, think through where and when it would best be held, and how long it should last.

We also discuss how to review information that may already be available to the agency, and give thought to what information to offer the service user. This section covers what interview planning is necessary, up to the first contact with the client.

Finally, the chapter suggests, it is also well worth taking time to consider who should be included in the interview. This should cover not only whom to include, but also, importantly, whom it may be appropriate to *exclude*.

## Chapter 5: Questions and interview techniques

Chapter 5 moves on to examine a range of skills in questioning and use of silence that may be helpful in working with service users – building what is, essentially, an interview 'toolkit'.

As there is always a changing dynamic with the service user, so demands on you will be constantly changing – sometimes dramatically! This dynamic means that no one technique will be appropriate throughout every interview

– you have to retain flexibility to suit service users. The range of possible interview communication skills discussed in this chapter therefore consists of a wide variety of mostly spoken methods – questions, comments, humour, silence and challenges. We also look at non-verbal communication: how people employ body language and other non-verbal cues, and how that can tell us more about the processes of the interview.

Finally, the chapter directly addresses some issues that may arise: how, for instance, should you respond to frustration, or to racist or sexist remarks. Service users may request confidential information, or personal information: both situations may involve some judgement.

## Chapter 6: General and specific communication skills

Chapter 6 studies further ways in which an interviewer and different service users may establish effective communication. It looks at some important skills drawn from counselling, such as use of paraphrasing and summarising. It goes on to address issues of special communication needs, whether these are sensory or cultural. Specific problems may occur when interviewing through an interpreter, and we look at issues in language interpreting and signing.

Chapter 6 also briefly considers some pointers for working with young people and adolescents.

## Chapter 7: The stages of the interview

Chapter 7 first addresses how you might make initial contact with a service user. It discusses some issues of safety when working with strangers, and refers to some dilemmas that may arise.

The chapter then looks at the opening stages of the interview, not forgetting the initial introductory phase, and discusses how you may proactively help to set the scene for an effective interview. We note the use of open questions at the beginning, before discussing ways of moving the interview on to the middle section, where questions change to become more focused and precise, and where the major work of the interview is accomplished.

We make no bones about restating that an interview is a complex, dynamic process, calling for you to retain flexibility especially when dealing with service users' emotional responses.

Finally, we mention the significance of endings, often a difficult area, as well as noting factors relating to 'disengagement' from relationships made with service users.

## Chapter 8: Thinking and interview handling

In Chapter 8 we begin by discussing the *thinking* involved in an interview. This analysis asks you first to identify your strong points in interviewing. Importantly, you need to have insight into what your personal and professional strengths may be.

This chapter then looks more closely at ability to handle changes in an interview. As interaction with the service user progresses, it may take the interview in unforeseen directions and cause you to rethink the path you planned to take. We consider the need to be adaptable, and to modify any plans to reflect service users' needs. You must keep your emotions and thinking processes under review, so that, even if you feel disconcerted, you can still work with the service user to reach shared objectives.

## Chapter 9: Potential pitfalls

It is tempting to talk about social work interviewing by describing good practice and skills that you can use for effective interviews. However, addressing only positives ignores the real world: not all interviews go smoothly. Whether these are minor issues, or disasters, any practitioner will recognise problems with interviews as – if not a familiar experience – an occasional occurrence. Learning how to change and do things differently on future occasions is a useful skill.

We divide the problems into four groups. The first set relates to *planning beforehand* – aspects of the interview concerning pre-interview arrangements and preparation. Specifically, this includes discussion on questions such as, 'You arrive without essential facts' and 'You arrive well prepared only to discover you have actually prepared for a different type of interview'.

The second set deals with the interview itself – these are situations that generally relate to your attempt to reach planned *objectives*. Sample questions addressed are: 'You become aware of the need to obtain further, external, information when well in to an interview. Without this information, you cannot carry out an effective interview.' What to do? Or, perhaps, 'Something serious that had not been foreseen has arisen during the interview. It has become essential to seek specific advice.' Again, the chapter considers these and other related 'real-world' issues, and seeks possible solutions.

The third set covers other possible issues that may arise in an interview, from the struggle to achieve a joint agenda, to issues of long-windedness. This section also considers some aspects of time management within an interview, and about ending an interview early but respectfully.

The final set includes issues that may occur at any time – situations of perceived *physical risk* to the interviewer. The risk of violence always needs to be assessed beforehand, in order to lower that risk, but sometimes aggression occurs. It is important to know the risk factors, to be able to recognise warning signs, and to understand how to respond.

### Chapter 10 – Recording an Interview

Recording an interview is sometimes seen as merely a footnote to the interaction. However, there may be legal and principled issues for this, such as accountability, so confirmation in writing of what happened in the interview is an integral part of the process. We refer to the British Association of Social Workers' (BASW) Privacy, Confidentiality and Records section in their Code of Ethics (BASW website). We discuss the underlying principles of recording, and the need to consider the Data Protection Act.

The chapter then looks at the focus required for that staple of student learning: the process recording, and moves on to deal with the area of how to practise skills. The chapter describes methods that you can attempt without running the risk of harm or damage to service users.

## CONCLUSION

Social work is undoubtedly a challenging profession. One of its ambiguous pleasures is to be involved with a variety of people, service users, from many backgrounds. Such direct work with people may well be the reason that most practitioners enter the social work profession.

For upcoming interviewers in the field of social care and social work, day-to-day contact with service users will be an important part of their training and experience. There is also much to learn from the experiences of other practitioners. Within an interpersonal skills model, wide practical knowledge, informed by theory, can enhance professional interviewing, and be invaluable in developing and improving robust professional practice. Acquisition of the information included in this book will be important to the development of any new practitioner, although we believe the contents may benefit experienced interviewers, too.

Our hope is that this book will provoke thinking about interviewing, encourage and accelerate learning, and will help practitioners be more reflective and engaged in their direct work with service users.

# Chapter 1

# Values and Anti-discriminatory Practice

## NOSSC RELEVANCE

The material in this chapter relates to the following values, defined as part of the National Occupational Standards for Social Care (NOSSC).

Social workers must:
a.  Have respect for:
    *   users and carers, regardless of their age, ethnicity, culture, level of understanding and need
    *   the expertise and knowledge users and carers have about their own situation
b.  Empower users and carers in decisions affecting them.
c.  Be honest about:
    *   the power invested in them, including legal powers
    *   their role and resources available to meet need
d.  Respect confidentiality, and inform users and carers when information needs to be shared with others.
e.  Be able to:
    *   challenge discriminatory images and practices affecting users and carers
    *   put users and carers first.
                    (General Social Care Council website: topssengland)

*This chapter considers values and attitudes in social work, and in particular the central importance of anti-discriminatory practice, qualities at the heart of communication and interviewing. You must be alert to the values and attitudes of service users, as your attitude will influence whether they will want to 'engage' with you and be advised or assisted by you.*

## INTRODUCTION

Social workers are called upon to interact with a wide variety of people, and often with individuals or in groups that have been marginalised by society. This responsibility calls for special qualities in your dealings with the public, both in how you initially present, and how you respond to and interact with people and situations. The problem is that, although basic situations may be similar, each person, their history and their influences (personal and social) are individual. These constitute their individual values, of which you must be continually aware in your professional involvement, balancing the issues within individual situations.

The values that we as workers bring to social work and social care are formed from a powerful mixture of influences. These influences are likely to be fluid and changing, for we operate within society, where the prominence of certain issues and themes may change throughout our working life. For instance, responses to the Victoria Climbié Inquiry are changing social work with all groups, and not just work with children and families.

The influences that form our values will probably include:

- personal philosophies,
- professional values, defined by the General Social Care Council and Skills for Care,
- cultural customs and shared commonalities, and
- structural forces and values in society.

All these have an impact on the types of relationships we can make with service users, and they are likely to be expressed during our social work interviewing – whether consciously or not. Kadushin calls this

> the communication bridge between people. Messages pass over the bridge with greater or lesser difficulty, depending on the nature of the emotional interaction between people.
>
> (Kadushin, 1972, p41)

A discussion of values within relationships will lead us on to issues of anti-discriminatory practice, with associated issues of power within the interview situation.

## VALUES IN SOCIAL WORK INTERVIEWS

During your life, and especially in the course of your professional work, you will undoubtedly meet a great number of families, carers and individuals. These people will come from many different backgrounds – not only are there likely to be cultural, racial and ethnic differences between them, but there will also be diversity dependent upon age, sexuality, background, life experience, and other crucial factors (Jones, in Davies, 2002, p7). This inherent variability means that social workers and social care workers must learn to relate to a wide variety of people in appropriate professional ways.

Any social worker will consequently need to be equipped with the knowledge and skills to relate with sensitivity and **empathy** to people from any kind of background, and then be able to help the service user examine their predicaments in a culturally appropriate way.

> **Definition**
>
> **Empathy**
>
> Empathy is a quality of emotional thinking. It is a way of putting yourself into people's experiences on a feeling level, without necessarily identifying with those feelings.

Naturally, on occasions it may well be difficult to be non-judgemental about some service users. Although our training will help us understand the forces that lead to circumstances such as drug dependence, and other situations that some sections of society routinely condemn, sometimes it is genuinely hard to be involved. As a fundamental part of the job, social workers are regularly asked to visit people who have only a marginal stake in society, or are socially excluded. This is why the reflective and **reflexive** aspects of working are so important: they enable you to reflect upon difficult situations, leading to further insights on structural and interpersonal factors, which will help your skills to evolve (Payne, 2002, p127).

> **[Reflexivity]** demands that workers continually consider the ways in which their own social identity and values affect the information they

gather. This includes their understanding of the social world as experienced by themselves and those with whom they work.

(Burke and Harrison, 2002, p231)

The emphasis on understanding in this definition is significant.

Given such complexity, what helps social workers to deal respectfully in an interview with such a diverse range of people, in a way that does not discriminate, oppress or show prejudice? What kind of attitudes is it important to convey to the people and families social workers meet? How may your intervention encourage service users to empower themselves and gain confidence and control in their lives?

## Definition

### Reflexivity

Reflexivity is a way of working that grows from reflective practice. It is a circular process, of meditating upon the involvement you have with service users, and the changing interactions between you and them. It takes into account the structural forces (such as power and oppression) inherent in the interview situation, as well as examining the psychological issues that may also have an impact on the process. You then evaluate and examine your and others' reactions, to see how future involvements may be changed.

## PERSONAL PHILOSOPHIES

As we have said, the values brought consciously or unconsciously into the interview by a social worker are likely to have several sources.

First, let us consider the values that many people in the helping professions bring from their personal life to their work. If people who hold religious beliefs, follow a Humanist tradition or Marxist philosophies seek employment in social care or social work, their views are important to their work, and will inevitably contribute to the environment in which they and their social work colleagues operate. Individuals may express their beliefs as 'wanting to make a difference', seeking a fairer and more equal society, or making a mark on life. Biestek expressed this as the 'social worker as an instrument of divine providence' (Biestek, 1979, index).

In addition, there is the impact of life experience. Whether your childhood was a happy one, or perhaps less so, there may be a resultant determination to either use or offset these personal experiences in an altruistic way. Such use can hold good for later life experiences as well, often expressed as 'putting something back into society'.

It is hoped that what social workers as individuals bring to their work and profession will form a basis for working with people of all back-grounds, from all areas. Of course, the reality is rather more complicated than that. Some people may not yet have the breadth of experience to relate easily to everyone, while of course we are all drawn to different areas or agencies within which to work. However, the general precept still holds good: you must be open to working with as wide a range of people as possible (Lishman, 1994, p8).

## FORMAL VALUES

This section focuses on the explicit values available from professional social work sources, including Skills for Care, the National Occupational Standards for Social Care (NOSCC), and the General Social Care Council (GSCC). We also consider what supporting policies may be available to practitioners through their employer.

Skills for Care, the national training forum for social work, has formu-lated general standards it considers to be appropriate for social workers engaged in working with members of the public:

> The standards come from a detailed analysis of what social workers do, through consultation with employers and practitioners. Standards include service users' own statements of their expectations of social workers.
>
> (GSCC/Skills for Care website)

The NOSCC specify five qualities, which were detailed at the beginning of this chapter. The NOSSC emphasise that these qualities should always be kept in mind when dealing with service users, and with the public in general. These attributes are also referred to as 'values', and, of course, are essential to good practice within the United Kingdom. It is important to stress, however, that while they form an excellent foundation, they are only the bare essentials; exactly how these values are confirmed through interviews and action is a much more complex matter.

The professional frames of conduct set out by the GSCC are also of considerable significance in establishing expected professional behaviour. Social work underwent a profound change with the introduction of the

GSCC. Now, in common with longer-established caring professions, it possesses an organisation external to employers for standards, complaints and information. With the establishment of the GSCC has come the need for qualified social workers, and those working within the profession, to formally register with the Council. An important part of the registration process is to confirm that the values and standards set by the GSCC are and will continue to be a part of a worker's professional practice.

The standards by which social workers (the GSCC talks of 'social care workers'; both terms apply) should judge themselves when dealing with members of the community fall under six outline headings:

1  Protect the rights and promote the interests of service users and carers.
2  Strive to establish and maintain the trust and confidence of service users and carers.
3  Promote the independence of service users while protecting them as far as possible from danger or harm.
4  Respect the rights of service users whilst seeking to ensure that their behaviour does not harm themselves or other people.
5  Uphold public trust and confidence in social care services.
6  Be accountable for the quality of their work and take responsibility for maintaining and improving their knowledge and skills.

(Reproduced with permission of the GSCC)

All six standards – and particularly the first four – are highly relevant both to the interview and to an interviewer's objectives.

Skills for Care (formerly the Training Organisation for the Personal Social Services – TOPSS), in parallel with the introduction of a new degree for social work training, has also established a series of National Occupational Standards in social work practice. To become a professionally qualified social worker, a student will need to show that they are not only conversant with 21 standards within six key roles, but are also practising them.

Skills for Care has additionally identified six central values. Looking specifically at these 'values in practice' that student social workers are expected to meet, we find again that they are highly relevant to the interview process.

The Skills for Care values are:

---

1   Awareness of own values, prejudices, ethical dilemmas and conflict of interest and their implication on practice.
2   Respect for, and the promotion of
    a.   each person as an individual
    b.   independence and quality of life for individuals, whilst protecting them from harm
    c.   dignity and privacy for individuals, families, carers, groups and communities.
3   Recognise and facilitate each person's use of language and form of communication of their choice.
4   Value, recognise and respect the diversity, expertise and experience of individuals, families, carers, groups and communities.
5   Maintain the trust and confidence of individuals, families, carers, groups and communities by communicating in an open, accurate and understandable way.
6   Understand and make use of strategies to challenge discrimination, disadvantage and other forms of inequality and injustice.
                    (Reproduced with the permission of Skills for Care)

---

As well as a national code of conduct for social care workers themselves, there is now, also through the GSCC, a national code of conduct for *employers*. This special code supports the code for social care workers, and reminds employers of their responsibilities to deliver services of quality to service users.

As the GSCC employers' code is, in the main, related to the behaviour of social care workers within their employ, in the context of interviewing, knowledge of the employers' code can be helpful.

To meet their responsibilities in relation to regulating the social care workforce, social care employers must now:

---

■   Make sure people are suitable to enter the workforce and understand their roles and responsibilities;
■   Have written policies and procedures in place to enable social care workers to meet the General Social Care Council (GSCC) Code of Practice for Social Care Workers;
■   Provide training and development opportunities to enable social care workers to strengthen and develop their skills and knowledge;

■ Put in place and implement written policies and procedures to deal with dangerous, discriminatory or exploitative behaviour and practice; and

■ Promote the GSCC's code of practice to social care workers, service users and carers and co-operate with the GSCC's proceedings.
(Reproduced with the permission of the GSCC)

These responsibilities are understandably more distanced from the values of the individual social practitioner working within the organisation, except in so far as employers are expected to 'promote' the GSCC Code of Practice. They have a responsibility, as well, to police 'dangerous, discriminatory or exploitative behaviour and practice'.

An employing agency may also have its own ethical guiding principles, such as 'whistleblowing' policies, or service standards. Such agency-related values can help to clarify to social workers what actions are expected of them.

Values and codes of conduct need to be kept in mind when:

■ thinking about the type of relationship to be established with service users,
■ planning the interview,
■ planning what you want to achieve,
■ planning how to achieve it, and, of course, within day-to-day interviewing situations.

As well as statutory Codes of Conduct for social workers, there are additional forms of support from other professional bodies. The primary such body in the UK is the British Association of Social Workers (BASW); their Code of Ethics is available from the BASW website. In the same way as the professional guidelines we have described, it highlights ways for social workers to behave, without being specific about individual interview situations. It therefore inevitably leaves many questions unanswered, and thus when it comes to a difficult interview, may not be as much help to you as you might wish (Shardlow, 2002, p35).

Shardlow also deals with the historic influence of Biestek (Biestek, 1979) on the type of relationship that you might wish to establish with service users. Biestek outlined seven values, including confidentiality and non-judgemental attitudes, that he deemed important to interaction with clients; Biestek's principles are discussed later in this chapter.

---

### Practice issue

Talitha acknowledged that she had been in the sex industry in her youth. Perhaps in consequence, her views on sexuality were widely at variance with those of Peter, her middle-aged, male social worker, making it difficult for the worker to be objective and non-judgemental in interviews about Talitha's present situation. Peter resolved to raise this issue in supervision, as a check on how prejudice might be influencing him; and also to seek clear feedback from Talitha on his role.

---

In circumstances like Peter's, it helps

- to be conscious of the dilemma, and bring it to the front of your mind, so that it can make less of an unconscious impact,
- to keep to relevant discussion areas,
- to talk the issue over with someone, such as a supervisor,
- to understand the service user's life choices and history from their viewpoint: to empathise.

## CULTURAL INTERNALISATION AND SHARED VALUES

Here we look at the wider, social psychology issues that may affect the way in which we conduct interviews.

As individual members of society, we grow up within a way of life, within which we have *internalised* thoughts and values from the influences on our being. This scenario has a parallel to Thompson's place of culture in the theoretical frame of understanding discriminatory behaviour (Thompson, 2001, p23).

Cultural groups carry with them the potential for many qualities: defining the outsider, promoting the cohesiveness of its members, ascribing to certain personal or societal values. From your own knowledge of the groups to which you belong, you can surely add to this list. You will see that some values are indeed positive attributes, whilst a number are neutral, and others negative. Some attitudes you encountered earlier in life you may now reject as incompatible with your professional values. However, all such accumulated 'baggage' has the potential to make an impact on the process of an interview, and your part within it.

## STRUCTURAL FORCES IN SOCIETY

Perhaps some of the most powerful influences in service users' lives come from the structures in society, and the power that is inextricably allied to them. As

Thompson argues (Thompson, 2001, pp16–35), certain sections of our society are given and maintain conscious and unconscious status. The main such divisions are often connected with class, and with money. However, there are other significant differentiations, for example those based on gender, race and ethnicity, age and disability. These differences may lead to assumptions and prejudices, and to discrimination against certain sections of society.

## ANTI-DISCRIMINATORY PRACTICE

In all social work interviewing, we need to consider and explore the nature of anti-discriminatory practice, and the concept of oppressive practice. An awareness of these concepts is fundamental to good, reflective work (Thompson, 2001, p10).

In this section, we therefore examine the conceptual framework of anti-discriminatory practice, and discuss why, when interacting with service users in an interview, it is important to be aware of the structures in society that contribute towards inequality, lack of influence, and powerlessness.

One way to do this is to think of an interview as dealing with society's issues at a micro level: the people you meet will be individuals to you, and you will see how their temperaments, psychological factors and family will influence the partnership work you can do together. You will find that a structural analysis of society and its institutions can also inform your work with people.

> **Definition**
>
> **Anti-discriminatory practice**
>
> Anti-discriminatory practice (ADP) is reflective social work practice that takes into account how personal, cultural and especially structural influences and attitudes may cause oppression and discrimination for individuals in society. ADP seeks to make people aware and more confident about change and challenging attitudes, thus engendering power in individuals. The need for practitioners to challenge prejudice and discrimination is a given. ADP also ensures that interactions and services are culturally apt and sensitive to the individual within their culture.

Different practitioners, though, will put different stress on the part that structural forces play in the work they do, and their practice is likely to reflect that difference (Thompson, 2003, p51). Perhaps in this context you should reflect on how rigid or flexible your working is, and how open you are to considering new insights from others.

After examining the theory supporting anti-discriminatory practice, we will focus specifically on how anti-discriminatory practice relates to interview planning and recording. We then look at how it relates to the interviewing process, identifying potentially sensitive issues.

Social work values (explored at the beginning of this chapter) are unlikely to be explicitly stated during the course of an interview. Nevertheless, they form an essential foundation of the interview process, expressed through non-verbal means as well as verbal exchanges. They should underpin your view of the interview exchange: stressing respect for the person as an individual, and communication that should also encourage trust.

Prejudice and discrimination are part and parcel of human experience, but some groups are especially vulnerable. The process starts from the differences within society that are inescapable, but lead to a complex array of consequences. These major differences are of race, class, disability or illness, age, gender and sexual preference (Burke and Harrison, 2002, p232). Other differences, such as religion, poverty or even geographical location, can also contribute to discrimination. And, of course, there may be multiple discriminations, such as those outlined by Norman (1985) as a 'triple jeopardy': the experience of growing old, being of a different race, and living in a second homeland.

If you are on the alert, social differences and consequent discrimination may become clear through individual statements made during an interview, but you will find that the causes of such inequalities are deeply entrenched in society. Individuals, people in groups, or the workings of institutions and other structures with which services users interact can express a lack of equality. The Stephen Lawrence Inquiry, for instance, found the police to be 'institutionally racist' (Stephen Lawrence Inquiry website). There are admitted inequalities in health provision and outcomes, highlighted by the Acheson Report (1998) (Acheson Report website).

Because social work is a profession frequently concerned with individuals and their transactions with powerful institutions, such as state bureaucracies, the issue of discrimination will inevitably become a key issue for you, and for the individuals you will interview.

Thompson's model of how discrimination works, and how it can be examined, is based on looking at three levels of interaction in society: the personal (**P**), the cultural (**C**) and the structural (**S**) (Thompson, 2001, p21–39).

At a personal level, psychological influences and reasoning have a part to play. In communication theory, people are conceptualised as routinely assimilating information about their interaction with others. Individuals have internal rules for assimilating information, however, leading to *selective perception* (Payne, 1997, p165). Selective perception allows us to look for sense and patterns in our social interactions, as well as choosing to focus on certain phenomena. Selective perception may therefore lead to bias, favouritism or discrimination.

In considering the cultural base for discrimination, Thompson examines the 'shared meanings' that people absorb throughout their lives, looking at discrimination and prejudice from a viewpoint of social psychology, and identifying the culture that people absorb by the groups they inhabit. Patterns of behaviour and the norms that define us in communities may be prejudicial, or ignore the rational. (For some examples, see National Aids Trust website.)

While Thompson depicts all influences in concentric rings, with the personal contained within the cultural and the structural surrounds, it is too simplistic, as he argues, to separate one sphere from the other two. Personal factors will have an impact on cultural influences, which may in turn overlap with structures of society, so that the experience of a one-parent family, for example, will not be separated from the beliefs of common stereotyping, or state policies that support single parenthood.

Thompson goes on to maintain that social work has not always addressed social stratifications and the consequent power imbalances in an adequate way, especially not to the satisfaction of the groups and individuals who have experienced discrimination and oppression. Anti-discriminatory practice is a way of actively challenging such power inequalities, and leads to action in changing the status quo.

Putting anti-oppressive values at the centre of social work practice helps practitioners to recognise and challenge prejudice and discrimination. These issues are enmeshed within the complex power relationships that minority groups may have with people having authority, or perceived as having authority.

Power and power relationships have always been a central issue in social work, and, by extension, in the interviewing situation. The dilemma is that social workers are, inevitably, part of the structure of these powerful bureaucracies. A social work interview can be seen as a forum where individuals may play out many roles and processes; and power issues are not excluded. Service users, understandably, often perceive or invest power in the professional social worker; while, in reality, workers are unlikely to have that control. Such perceived power is therefore not necessarily related to *actual* power; but awareness of an apparent power differential may generate responses that are just as strong as those based on reality. This is part of the reason why considerable emphasis has come to be laid on openness, empowerment and partnership working in social work (Leadbetter, 2002, pp200–206; Thompson, 2003).

Social work as a profession has made an effort to consider the balance of power in a typical social work interview. Practitioners have responded to criticisms about their lack of awareness of ethnic, cultural and feminist, disability, and other issues. The serious reception given by social workers to such criticisms largely arose from an acknowledgement of failure; in an increasingly multicultural society, social work was found to be lacking in knowledge of the oppression experienced by minorities.

A prime example lies in the mental health arena. Although reports over a period of years have highlighted the problem, mental health services are still cited as an area where there is a concern about racial and cultural sensitivity (see 'The Costs of Race Inequality', Sainsbury Centre for Mental Health website).

Of course, there may sometimes be genuine power issues. For instance, social workers may on occasion need to act as 'gatekeepers' for scarce resources, while an interviewer's conclusions on social assessment court reports can make a very real impact on people's lives. The Climbié Inquiry reminds us that the issues of culture and belief should always be considered in the context of professional knowledge about what is acceptable treatment towards children (Climbié Inquiry website).

Another important consideration for social workers concerns their own individual attitudes and feelings. It may be difficult to appreciate that you may not be totally 'colour-blind', or completely free from prejudice. If individuals are not actively tackling discrimination, whether conscious of bias or not, then they may well be part of the problem (Thompson, 2001).

The main discriminations in society are experienced through class, race, gender and disability. While we accept that for some people other types of discrimination may in practice be as important, we deal with these four as typical examples of anti-oppressive practice. The intention of this analysis is to assist you in an interview situation to identify these types of discrimination, and others, too.

## Class

It is a truth generally acknowledged that people who are users of social services are drawn mainly from the lower socio-economic classes (Jones, 2002, pp7–18). This is not to say that all the people you will interview will be from the working class. Indeed, it is an important point to appreciate that, in the complex situations with which we deal, other factors may well take precedence. But why should **class** feature at all?

Class is strongly linked with poverty, which in turn is linked to other aspects of deprivation, such as unemployment or poor neighbourhoods (Joseph Rowntree Foundation website). Poverty also affects groups in unequal ways: for instance, proportionally, more old women are poorer than old men (Age Concern, 2004, p7). There is interplay of class with economic and other inequalities – such as health and health provision.

> **Definition**
>
> **Class**
>
> Although there are many arguments for different definitions of 'class', here we take class to be the socio-economic categories in society.

In interviews, you may well find that class is a factor. You may come from a different class, and have different standards of life from service users. You may need to make judgements about whether a way of life is acceptable, or if it perhaps forms a risk to the functioning of any vulnerable members of the family or group.

Most of all, you may need to be aware of your language. Accent, vocabulary and way of talking all have an effect on the interview situation, and may reinforce a power differential instead of encouraging working towards partnership.

### Race and ethnicity

The area of race and ethnicity is one whose complexities and subtleties have increasingly occupied professional social work. As NOSSC guidelines make clear, social workers today need to be equipped to function effectively in a multiracial society. As there are indications that people from different ethnic backgrounds have specific deprivations – educational achievement, higher unemployment for black teenagers, for example (Statistics on Race/Guardian website) – it is likely that poverty, ill health and cycles of deprivation will bring about a continuing need for social services.

It may be necessary to emphasise that the concept of 'race' is a socially constructed notion. We are all one 'race', in that we all belong to the human race; differentiations emerge from within our societies. 'Racist' behaviour does not depend on colour, but on prejudices and stereotypes. These labels reinforce the power of influential factions against the diminished power of minority groups – defined as those who do not conform to the look or behaviour of the dominant parties (Thompson, 2001, p65–9).

Since social workers are part of the predominant culture, and consequently may be less aware of power issues, our training cautions us to be alert to the possibility of racist behaviour, and to challenge that behaviour should we experience it. In interviews you will therefore need to monitor yourself for assumptions and prejudices, as well as appreciating the effects of powerlessness on service users.

## Gender

Feminist social work emerged in the 1970s and 1980s, from a growing real-isation that women, and particularly women who are represented as social service users (one-parent families, older women, women with mental health issues), suffer oppression in our culture and society (Orme, 2002, p218). This is because the orientation of power in society has been towards men, and in particular men from white and middle-class backgrounds.

As with other types of oppression, you should be aware that the women and men you meet in interviews may need to challenge your ideas (Dominelli, 2002, p104). This may be in the way they consider their prob-lems: is it actually an individual issue, or is it something that has grown from societal norms and pressures? It might also be useful to challenge language, or biologically based stereotypes (Thompson, 2001, p18), as well as your own assumptions. (For example, how often do you assume a doctor is 'she' rather than 'he'?)

## Disability

One of the major discriminations faced by people in society is that caused by attitudes to disability. An *impairment* may have many causes, such as acci-dent or chronic disease. Impairment especially includes people with mental health issues or learning difficulties. However, people are *disabled* and disad-vantaged because they live in a society with structures that function for the benefit of the non-disabled majority. Consequently, power and confidence are eroded for those people with impairments, and they become oppressed. Able-bodied people in society may be unconscious of the effect, do not understand it, and may avoid (and consequently not challenge and correct) the oppressions this causes to people with a disability (Thompson, 2001).

Rather than being reduced to individual 'tragedies', a view that feeds into the medical model of disability, a more recent model of 'disablism' recognises that the discrimination comes from societal structures. Society needs to be challenged, and to be required to examine and change its attitudes towards people with a disability. An example might be, in the spirit of **normalisation**, to modify transport arrangements or employment policies, so that people with impairments can participate more in society and lead full daily lives.

Oliver (1987) criticises professionals who 'know best' about what to provide to people with disabilities, considering this attitude as patronising, or, worse, causing people to become 'passive recipients' of services.

In interviews, you can counteract such thinking by sharing professional

> **Definition**
>
> **Normalisation**
>
> The principle of normalisation addresses the needs and rights of people who have an impairment (especially mental impairment) to do things that people without disability take for granted as normal patterns of living: in work, leisure, housing. This may mean challenging both the assumed unimportance of everyday routines and the avoidance of risk.

knowledge with service users; sharing power, by encouraging people to write reports themselves and by concentrating on working in partnership (French and Swain, 2002, p398). Partnership may also entail supporting people to challenge the disabling structures of society.

## WORKING RELATIONSHIPS WITH SERVICE USERS

In working with individuals and families, there will be differences in the depths and types of relationships. It is important to state that flexibility in tolerating different types of relationship needs to be learnt – service users would justifiably not welcome a standard approach to their individual situations. In any professional relationship, there are many possible variables. Some differences in relationships will relate to the personalities involved, while some may be based upon how frequently the service user is seen; and some interactions will be affected by the method of intervention followed. For example, if you work in a children's mental health unit, your mode of working is likely to be more psychologically based than that of a welfare rights worker in a community centre.

However, it should be possible to identify a common 'core' to our interaction with service users. This core relates to our common values, and may be expressed in how we engage and relate to service users, and with the respect with which we strive to treat people.

As an individual, you need to find a method of working effectively with service users that will also fulfil the functions of the agency for which you work. However, an important factor to bear in mind is: what does the service user expect or need from the agency – and from me? Relationships are led by the needs of service users.

---

### Practice issue

Mrs York had used up her capital in fees for residential care in a home where she was happy and felt well cared for. She then had to approach the Social Services Department for financial assistance. Mrs York came from a middle class background, where throughout her life family money had usually allowed her to be independent of welfare benefits. Luckily, she saw a sensitive care manager, to whom she could express her negative feelings about requesting financial aid. While she participated in the assessment process, Mrs York was relieved when her need for support over the fees was agreed, and she could disengage from visits from the care manager.

---

To some extent, Mrs York must have thought that the interaction and interviews with the care manager were an administrative but necessary pain, an emotional price she had to pay for financial help. Consider how the same practitioner's relationship with other service users might differ from the one they made with Mrs York. In situations where an emotionally closer relationship may be forged, such as support through a period of bereavement, you are likely to develop quite a different relationship from that with Mrs York.

The question 'How does [the service user] perceive me?' is always a very useful reflective question for you to ask yourself. If appropriate, this query might also be introduced into the interview, especially if there appears to be some block to the relationship. Asking this question, in whatever form, may well lead to further insights, more honest communication – and at the very least to clarification of roles.

## What does 'engaging' someone in the relationship mean?

Many social work interviews, such as duty interviews, or information-giving sessions, will be naturally limited to a single transaction between the social worker and potential service user.

This constraint may very well suit the service user being interviewed. They may be under a misconception about what is involved in the interaction with the agency, and need this interview to clarify their expectations. They may need thinking time to digest the information given them, or perhaps they may have second thoughts, once the parameters of agency involvement are explained in more detail.

A first interview can therefore be a good opportunity for resolving misconceptions, allowing service users to evaluate whether a commitment to the worker or the agency will prove a useful investment for them (Coulshed and Orme, 1998, p72).

While there are also, of course, situations that entail a certain degree of compulsion, for example youth justice schemes, even with these the service user needs to feel the time spent with the social worker is useful, while establishment of an effective working relationship is just as important.

For most social work interventions to be successful, then, time and effort from both you and the service user will be needed. To plan and follow through on aims and objectives in a working alliance can normally be accomplished only over a long period of time. It may take considerable commitment – on both sides – to undertake a course of action involving a major change in a social situation, or in personal functioning. Even where a degree of compulsion in the interaction with a social worker is involved, change can only take place when individuals are willing to try out new ways of thinking or action.

In such a process of change, feelings may be uncomfortable, and a service user's positive relationship with you may often be crucial in moving forward. The Social Care Institute for Excellence (SCIE) highlights this issue as social workers needing to

> recognise the loss of dignity people experience when approaching social services for the first time – the 'cost' in this – and respond sensitively.
>
> (SCIE, 2004, p14)

For a social worker, establishing a relationship is the positive initial step in making a personal association with the service user. The purpose is, of course, to facilitate aid; but it is also to demonstrate that the service user is valued, and will be treated with respect and honesty. It should also begin a process of trust between the people concerned.

It should be kept in mind, though, that people might understandably find it hard to engage in a relationship that will lead to changes about which they have anxiety.

---

### Practice issue

Mr Milton has long-term mental health issues. He lives at home with his wife, who has developed heart problems, and can no longer easily manage all his care; so she has requested help. But Mr Milton fears being 'put away', and sees any help, even in his own home, as a first step in this process. His anxiety and consequent agitation mean that the care manager cannot on a first visit address any support to change the situation. Ideally, the care manager would like to come back two or three times, to see if this would build up enough trust to overcome Mr Milton's reluctance to discuss any change to his situation.

You may decide that some situations of reluctance are important enough for you to make an effort to help a person work through their disinclination. This approach is really the basis of getting a service user to 'engage' in the furtherance of a helping relationship that is intended to benefit them.

### What is the basis of the relationship made with service users?

Although individual relationships may differ, some common elements are recommended in the social work relationship with service users. The value base of social work describes, in general terms, the type of relationship to be striven for in interactions with service users (this was discussed earlier in the chapter). The relationship you make with a service user should be an inter-connection, intended to show a willingness to enter into a partnership with the person in order to seek change.

Biestek (1979) outlined a 'casework relationship'. He described and analysed the basic points of what he saw as a helping relationship between social worker and service user. Biestek's seven principles were:

- Acceptance
- Client self-determination
- Individualisation
- Controlled emotional involvement
- Purposeful expression of feeling
- Non-judgemental attitude
- Confidentiality.

While these are still factors worthy of consideration, the frame and ethos of social work has evolved and changed significantly since Biestek was writing. Nearly twenty years later, Lishman (1994, p45) looked at skills in building and maintaining 'helping relationships', and identified six:

- Genuineness
- Warmth
- Acceptance
- Encouragement and approval
- Empathy
- Responsiveness and sensitivity.

These skills correlate closely with the qualities Carl Rogers (Rogers, 1942) identified for therapists in person-centred counselling:

■ Congruence (genuineness and honesty)
■ Empathy
■ Respect (acceptance, unconditional positive regard to the client).

Egan (2002, pp69–70) is also concerned with the quality of the relationship, and put forward what he called a SOLER model of non-verbal skills, which was intended to enhance and communicate a 'respectful, empathic, genuine and caring mind set'. He called it 'the skill of visible tuning in to clients'.

SQUARELY  face the client (put your body in a position that shows inter-est and attention).
OPEN  gestures (to be congruent with relaxed listening).
LEAN  towards the other (to show interest).
EYE  contact (paying attention).
RELAXED  or natural in these behaviours.

Lists of qualities such as the above have been criticised for vagueness and malleability (Timms, 1983; Shardlow; 2002), but there is nevertheless surely a need to define *somehow* the basis for interaction between service users and practitioners. Even today, research into what consumers want still maintains that one aspect to good communication in relationships is to 'build trust, empathy and warmth' (SCIE, 2004, p14).

We suggest that the essentials for effective and productive interviews appear to be:

■ an emotionally warm attitude, with genuine feeling,
■ an ability to be non-judgemental,
■ an ability for empathy with service users,
■ respect for people's individual situations, within their culture and community,
■ an ability to be confidential, while prepared to be honest.

What earlier models of social care interaction do not necessarily stress is the ideology of partnership and empowerment, a central issue that has emerged from a growing awareness of discrimination and continuing inequalities in people's lives.

### Preparation for the interview

Because discrimination can happen unconsciously, it is important to examine in advance relevant factors that may have an impact on your interviewing.

In preparation for an interview you need to have considered those elements of the service user's situation that may lie outside your usual knowledge and awareness.

> The wisest course is to be humble when considering the extent of one's own knowledge about different 'cultures' and to take advice whenever it is available.
>
> (Climbié Inquiry website)

One effective method of expanding your understanding is for you to read material designed for, or by, a service user. This has the additional advantage that it will enable you to pick up language that is relevant to the service user. Other useful information may be gained by talking to more experienced colleagues, or – while maintaining confidentiality – perhaps with members of the same ethnic community.

## Feedback/checking things out

To be able to summarise and ask the service user if you have understood their situation correctly is an immensely powerful 'tool'.

It is never sufficient for you to assume that your understanding of a service user's situation is clear, unless you have first confirmed your understanding with them. Any assumptions or conclusions that you may make about an individual's circumstances will need to be proactively explored, together. While always important, checking assumptions is particularly valuable when you and the service user are from culturally different backgrounds.

*An occasional phrase such as: 'What I hear you saying is . . .', or 'What I am understanding is . . . Is this right?' should show a service user that the social worker wants to understand their situation, and also that what service users are themselves saying is being attended to.*

Seeking confirmation in this way also has the valuable function of setting you back on the right track, should your understanding have gone astray.

The practitioner is present as an agency representative. This 'power' role must inevitably have an influence on the interview, and will need to be taken into account. For instance, those interviewers who ask their questions in a non-threatening tone are more likely to elicit more helpful information. The interviewer needs to be alert, and sensitive to any power imbalance that service users may feel; and, of course, to be aware of the impact a perceived power imbalance may have on relationships in the interview.

| **Consider this** | |
|---|---|
| Jamaica, a single parent, has been forced to ask for help from a social worker in sorting out her benefits. This is especially difficult for Jamaica, as in her teens she spent several years in care, and was left with a residual feeling that social workers tell you what to do, but do not do enough to help you. She does not vocalise this feeling, but her social worker is conscious of unexpressed anger. | What might the worker do to examine the power relationships, and try and get this interview onto a more equal footing? |

Alongside the concept of anti-discriminatory practice, a philosophy has evolved in social work of *consumerist* and *empowering* models of intervention. These are models where the service user is made aware of choices, and is actively involved in the processes selected to make changes in their circumstances. It also draws on people's strengths, rather than focusing on negatives.

How might this approach affect an interview?

What have evolved are essentially partnership models of intervention, where (as the values and standards described above explain) social workers promote and seek independence, and work *alongside* their clients to achieve this. Such an approach may be expressed not only in the non-verbal process of the interview (for instance, how seating is arranged, where you sit in relation to the service user), but in addressing the *goals* of the intervention, and ensuring that they are service user focused.

### Racism in the interview – responding to racist or sexist statements/questions

Social workers must appreciate that not all those with whom they may have to deal will possess socially acceptable views and opinions. Some questions or statements should not be answered, but nevertheless may need to be acknowledged; however, it is seldom (if ever) appropriate for a social worker to enter into a political argument with a service user. How, then, should we challenge when an service user asks a prejudiced question, or makes a remark that we cannot accept – but to which we cannot respond, either?

The simplest response to this situation is also the most faint-hearted – it is just to carry on, and pretend that you have not heard anything untoward. While this reaction may (perhaps) work, it is unfortunately more likely to encourage an even more extreme statement, used in an attempt to force a reaction from the interviewer; and refusal to comment will certainly affect a service user's view of their interviewer.

Clearly, some sort of response will be needed – but agreement with a racist remark is equally clearly not appropriate. We need to be able to disapprove of the comment, without being seen to be agreeing with it. One approach, which has been proven to be effective, is simple acknowledgement:

SU:  Immigrants; they're all useless, aren't they?
SW:  I hear what you say.
SU:  Don't you agree with me? All immigrants are bloody useless?
SW:  I hear you.

Of course, it should be that you are not prepared to give even tacit support to views that may be abhorrent to you. In this case, a mix of body language and response may be effective:

SU:  Immigrants; they're all useless, aren't they?
SW:  [holds up hand, palm outward]
     You're entitled to your opinion, but I'm afraid I am not prepared to listen to this.
SU:  Don't you agree with me? All immigrants are bloody useless?
SW:  I am not prepared to listen.

Another possible approach is to make clear the impact that the language has on you. You can say that it is offensive to you, and that you consider it to be discriminatory.

As a general rule, if given a clear and consistent response, in a calm an unemotional manner, even the most difficult of people will eventually get the message. So, if you are neither intending to accept their views, nor prepared to enter an argument about them, you should say so consistently; but be prepared for it to take a while.

## CONCLUSION

In this chapter, we discussed:

- The values in social work: personal, formal and professional.
- Anti-discriminatory practice and its importance.
- Major oppressions (class, race, gender and disability) that you need to be aware of in the interview.
- Qualities of the relationship with service users, and the flexibility needed for different situations.
- Issues of practice ('checking things out', responses to offensive language).

## QUESTIONS

1   Mr Green was a heroin user until he had a stroke at the age of 46. Since then, he has used alcohol freely. His GP has said that he is showing signs of severe depression, and warrants a social services assessment of his needs.

    What prejudices or preconceived notions might you have about Mr Green's situation?

    When you go to see Mr Green, how do you plan to minimise their impact?

2   A youth offender presents you with his sexual orientation at the beginning of a first interview.

    How do you respond? Why?

3   A mother complains that she is not getting help because available money is going 'to all those asylum seekers'.

    What do you say in reply?

4   What 'multiple jeopardies' can you list?

## FURTHER READING

Adams, R., Dominelli, L. and Payne, M. *Social Work: Themes, Issues and Critical Debates*, Chapters 2, 3 and 8.
Egan, G. *The Skilled Helper*.
Thompson, N. *Anti-Discriminatory Practice*, 3rd edn, all chapters.

*Chapter 2*

# Theory: Its Place in Interviewing

**NOSSC RELEVANCE**

The material in this chapter relates to the following National Occupational Standards in Social Care:

- **Key Role One,** Unit 3. Assess needs and options to recommend a course of action.
- **Key Role Five,** Unit 14. Manage and be accountable for your own work.
- **Key Role Six,** Unit 18. Research, analyse, evaluate and use current knowledge of best social work practice.

*This chapter looks at the importance of knowledge, theory, evidence-based work and research outcomes in interviewing situations. It considers how to work towards incorporating into good practice the range of theory, knowledge and perspectives that relate to social work interviews.*

**WHAT IS THEORY?**

The concept of **theory** in social work is complex and multi-faceted. It may help in understanding its place in your interviewing practice to begin with a general dictionary definition of theory.

This dictionary definition emphasises origins and explanations, or general laws; and laws which may be simple to correlate with causes where the facts and the situations are straightforward. However, life is rarely uncomplicated:

we live in complex societies and shifting groups. So, when we come to study and evaluate social situations in order to help our interviewing practice, what role may be played by theory?

## THEORY IN SOCIAL SCIENCE AND SOCIAL WORK

Once you begin to consider theory in the context of human behaviour, the situation rapidly becomes intricate. This is because interactions within human society can be extremely

> **Definition**
>
> **Theory**
>
> Theory is a scheme or system of ideas or statements held as an explanation or an account of a group of facts or phenomena; a hypothesis that has been confirmed or established by observation or experiment, and propounded or accepted as accounting for the known facts; a statement of what are held to be the general laws, principles, or causes of something known or observed. (*Oxford English Dictionary*, 1979)

complex (Cree, 2002, p276). In today's society, people come from different social and ethnic backgrounds, and a high degree of social mobility is to be expected. In twenty-first-century Britain family composition and structure varies widely, and influences from society upon family members can be very diverse, with consequent unpredictable responses. As a result, theorising about society, its cultures and its institutions is a subtle process, with many potential variations and differentiations.

A qualification should be made here: in any approach to theory, you may need to consider the impact of unconscious values. Specifically, it can be argued that cultural differences may underlie traditional theoretical understandings and interpretation. Theoretical perspectives that originate from a Western Judeo-Christian culture may therefore, in a modern multi-ethnic society, be open to criticism (Payne, 1997, pp7–13). People from different cultures within the UK may well hold cultural norms that are not only at variance with Western culture, but with one another, bringing a need for understanding – as well as potential for tensions and conflict between underlying beliefs.

> **Definition**
>
> **A cultural norm**
>
> An underlying value in a society (or group) that may be implied or expressed, but that does not necessarily have supporting legislation. Such values may be positive (ideals) or negative (prejudiced). Cultural norms can be internalised within a group, and will then inform the customary interactions between individuals within that group.

Social work falls within the field of social science, and accepted knowledge in social science is drawn from a variety of disciplines, adding considerably to the complexity of social work

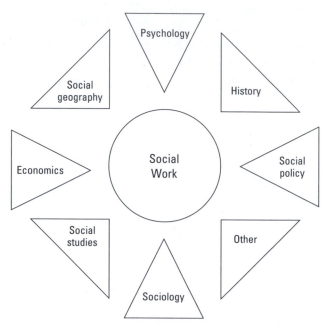

**Figure 2.1** Disciplines contributing to social care theory

theory. Essentially – taking 'social science' to be the examination of individuals in society and of their relationships to (and within) society – studies in social science may include information from the disciplines of economics, social geography, history, social policy, psychology, social studies and sociology (see Figure 2.1) – and this is by no means an exhaustive list.

In social work, therefore, the term 'theoretical knowledge' inevitably carries a broad definition and wide interpretation. While it should certainly encompass knowledge that explains, informs and may even predict people's behaviour, it is also knowledge that will provide frameworks for our interventions. The meaning of *theory* in the context of social work interviewing may consequently be widened to embrace academic research, insights into institutions, knowledge about groups with whom you are working, and the psychology of individual functioning.

Theoretical knowledge is also generally taken to cover the methods of intervention that you engage in with service users. Examples might range from task-centred practice to Egan's three-stage problem-solving counselling method (Egan, 2002).

To work effectively, you will need to accumulate knowledge from informed reading and thinking, as well as from practical experience. Any of the areas contributing to social work may make helpful contributions to interview practice. However, given the potentially enormous range of available information, it is clearly not easy to select information that may be most useful and appropriate for specific interviews.

---

### Practice issue

Jojo had been to see Paula, a young girl with cancer whose life was being severely affected by panic attacks. Jojo discussed with her supervisor suitable approaches to take, finally deciding to engage the service user in a cognitive behavioural anxiety management approach. Jojo had read about the effects of Paula's cancer, and about how to structure the sessions, as well as researching the usual support networks for the ethnic group to which Paula belonged.

---

## CAN WE MANAGE INTERVIEWING *WITHOUT* THEORY AND KNOWLEDGE?

In an interview, you are likely to be looking for information, whether verbal, non-verbal, practical, or on a feeling level; basically, your target will be data that are valid and appropriate to the task. However, while you may be able to collect information, how can you know that it is actually suitable and relevant?

In everyday life, we are constantly being presented with information – far more than we can possibly absorb. We therefore employ a form of filtering process, so that information we acquire is usually understood and evaluated by being related, consciously or unconsciously, to our existing knowledge.

When we come to conducting an interview, our existing knowledge may include previously formulated and relevant concepts, together with experience from earlier interviews; learning from our reading; and perhaps also information from formal and informal discussions about issues of social work interviewing.

Reference to such previous knowledge is likely to be of considerable support to you, because people generally need a 'conceptual frame' on which to structure their thinking – although such a frame will probably not prevent you from sometimes feeling 'all at sea'. Where does the frame originate? A 'conceptual frame' may sometimes be slowly and painfully built up from repeated personal experience, but its creation and effectiveness in professional practice can be greatly boosted by reference to elements of interviewing theory.

> Even if a framework is not used deliberately or explicitly, it is inevitable that our actions will be guided by sets of ideas and assumptions. The idea that we can have practice without theory is therefore a fallacy. A theory does not have to be a formal or 'official' theory as found in books or academic journals. Theory can refer to any ideas or frameworks of understanding that are used to make sense of our everyday experience and practice situations.
>
> Theory is therefore inevitably applied to practice, but, if we do not apply such theory explicitly or deliberately, we are relying on untested assumptions and therefore leaving a lot to chance.
>
> (Thompson, 2002, p237)

Once formed, 'conceptual frames' can be of great support to an interviewer, particularly in challenging situations. One aim of social work education is to enable you, whatever the interview circumstances, to bring about a 'good enough' interview outcome. This is perhaps analogous to learning safe and effective driving techniques. Once you have acquired these, whatever the weather conditions, you should have safe and reasoned skills – the ability not put yourself or other drivers at risk.

## THEORY IN PRACTICE

Are links to theory minimal in social work practice – and in those communication skills needed for interviews?

A timely review of the literature (Trevithick et al., 2004, p13) groups 'theory for social work' into three areas: *psychology and counselling theory*, *communication and learning theory* and *other theoretical perspectives*. Some of the review's conclusions, however, suggest a degree of uncertainty in establishing the meaning of common terms, and identify a need to establish much clearer links between theory and practice.

So, given such a complex background, what emphasis should we give to theory in interviewing practice? Hearn (1982) (in Payne, 1997, p48) counsels against seeing theory and practice as being two opposing ends of a spectrum. Rather, he feels that the two concepts weave in and out, intertwining and always relating to each other. Thompson, however, considers theory and practice differently: he views them as two ends of a continuum, with the purely practical or the rigidly theoretical extremes being seen as 'destructive/unhelpful' (Thompson, 2002, pp234–6).

In reality, for most practitioners there is likely to be a complex interplay between theory and practice. Using tested methods of intervention should provide you with an effective structure for your interventions; and you can be more confident of results when your interaction is based upon good principles in communication, well grounded in research. Also, of course, should things go wrong, theoretical frameworks may help you to analyse a situation and identify possible causes.

However, theory is not the only path: you will certainly learn valuable skills by observing more experienced practitioners, or by practising with a colleague or supervisor.

The approach we recommend is to integrate both concepts into a **reflective practice**, whereby practice will benefit from theory, while theory will be tested and enriched by practice.

This book takes a pragmatic approach, and leans towards discussion of the practical side of interviewing and core skills. While theory to underpin interventions is always important, our main objective is to consider workable communication skills and techniques in planning, questioning, communication and recording – practical skills that will directly help you to be more effective in your professional practice.

> ### Reflective practice
>
> **Definition**
>
> A method of monitoring your performance in interviewing, and then, afterwards, reflecting critically on the issues in that performance (especially non-discriminatory practice), so that in future you can modify your actions to be less discriminatory and more effective.

To summarise: when you, as a social worker, are interviewing service users, we see it as important to have some understanding of, and insight into, the theoretical bases and perspectives that inform your interactions with others. Such an understanding will help provide consistency in working towards good, reflective practice.

When someone is new to interviewing situations, they are understandably more likely to feel out of their depth. Questions such as 'What is happening?' 'How do I make sense of it all?' 'Did I miss something?' are almost certain to run through your mind. For this reason, it can be all the more important to have acquired a general understanding about theoretical perspectives, and especially why social care interviews are carried out in certain ways, and not in others. For example, we do not maintain the rules of a social conversation in a social work interview: the balance of speech is weighted towards service users; it has a purpose.

Theoretical knowledge is particularly relevant when service users themselves may be uncertain about what is happening in the interview, or what may be needed from it. While you can have a good relationship, and get along with one another, *someone* needs to know about the task in hand, and its accomplishment (Kadushin, 1972, p43).

Should you have been interviewing for some time, you may well have already assimilated theory into your work, and so not be immediately aware of how much your practice refers to underlying concepts. If this is the case, it should be possible to become consciously aware of the use of theory in your work, and then think reflectively about changes, should you wish it.

## KNOWLEDGE FOR SOCIAL WORK INTERVIEWS

As we have said, it can be difficult to decide just what frameworks and theorising will be helpful to you in an interview situation. In addition, there are very many strands in a social work interview for you to reflect upon, observe and analyse:

> any analysis of the interview is complex, since the process itself is influenced by a large number of impinging personal and contextual factors.
> (Hargie and Tourish, 2000, p71)

The time-line of an interview's verbal progress is not the only characteristic to be considered. During the course of the interview, you will be constantly presented with all sorts of information. Some of it will be non-verbal, while you will also be listening to comments and assessing reactions from service users, and simultaneously using empathic skills to foster partnership work – plus, of course, thinking about future plans or questions. Interviewing can be an exhausting business!

## ANALYSIS OF RELEVANT KNOWLEDGE

For the purposes of this book it seems most helpful to categorise relevant social work interviewing knowledge by looking first at the overall frame of the interview, before examining communication skills. We then move on to models of assessment, including structures to evaluate judgements and risks, and finally investigate potential theoretical frameworks for social work intervention.

In summary, we will be examining:

- theoretical models of how interviews operate,
- communication theory and skills,
- models of assessment, and
- therapeutic interventions.

Possession of such information will assist you in guiding lines of questioning, in thinking about the non-verbal processes of the interview, and will also help you to retain a sense of the direction the interview is taking. Essentially, the application of interviewing theory can help make sense of all the jigsaw pieces – or to hear the individual orchestral instruments more clearly.

In everyday life any individual may have selective perception, and consequent bias. However, a professional social worker should not allow any preconceived notions to affect their interactions with what will inevitably be a wide range of people, coming from very different backgrounds.

For example, in social situations, first impressions, especially non-verbal first impressions, are important, even though they may easily produce a **halo effect** that gives them an inaccurate bias (Dennis and Strickland, 2002). However, as a trained professional dealing with people all the time, you cannot afford to be influenced by immediate impressions: you need to be aware that first impressions can be wrong, or potentially prejudicial, and be able to reflectively reassess your initial judgements.

> **Definition**
>
> **Halo effect**
>
> The tendency to judge someone favourably on a first meeting, based on only one or two positive characteristics – the assumption being that all their other characteristics will be similarly positive.

## Theoretical models of how interviews operate

An interview is normally an interaction, at a fixed time, and within a fixed space, between two or more people. To that extent, it has a settled and solid existence. However, how we have initially *conceptualised* the exchange will affect our interpretation of the real events within it. Basically, how we view the interview will colour our understanding of what is going on within the interview.

In practice, the difficulty with this model is that there are a welter of different ways of conceptualising the interview. Hargie and Tourish (2000, pp71–87) make a useful résumé of some of the key ways in which an interview may be interpreted.

First, it can be viewed as a type of **transactional analysis** (Berne, 1964). This

> **Definition**
>
> ### Transactional analysis (TA)
>
> A type of psychotherapy based on an awareness of the interactions (transactions) between patient and therapist and between patient and others in the environment. It focuses primarily on ego states, principally the parent, adult and child.

approach may be particularly useful in examining how an interview has been conducted. Remember, though, that different participants are likely to have differing views of the roles. You may think that you are acting and responding within an 'adult-to-adult' frame. However, service users, perhaps more conscious of power relations, may – if they are asked – perceive your involvement rather as a 'parent/child' exchange. Transactional analysis may also be used within a counselling frame, to help people to understand and reframe their interactions.

A second way of imagining an interview is as a place for dramaturgical roles, where the performers use a theatre/drama frame to perform a script (Goffman, 1986). In this, a variation on a normal role theory, participants in an interview are thought to unconsciously use scripts that assume their taking of a particular 'role' (moral guardian, carer, etc.) and that, once assumed, will steer them through a series of scenes and finally to the interview ending, or curtain. Within such a frame, you and the service user will have assumed roles and associated scripts that both need to understand and follow.

Although elements of these theoretical perspectives can be helpful in individual situations – perhaps to aid you in having a greater understanding of motivation, or perhaps aiding insight into the dynamics of a particular exchange – a further way of looking at an interview is to see it as an **interpersonal skills** model: learning skills in communication.

The third approach (Hargie and Tourish, 2000, pp71–84) depends very much on both parties having goals that they wish to pursue in the interview, and being prepared to work out

> **Definition**
>
> ### Interpersonal skills
>
> Skills in relating to people. In social work, they build on communication skills, often drawn from counselling, and include such skills as assessment, risk and evaluation.

in the joint arena how to accomplish those objectives. The quality and solidity of these objectives, as well as the *mutuality* of the goals, are all contributors to the individual dynamic nature of a specific interview. This model follows a behaviourist pattern. Feedback from either party will have an effect on the perception (to include any mediating factors), and on responses.

Personal factors are taken into account, and might include:

■ gender,
■ appearance,
■ personality,
■ age,
■ cultural background, and
■ the setting in which these goals are discussed.

Other theorists have worked from a *counselling* basis. This suggests that one way to view an interview is as a form of reciprocal interaction, in which the participants either match verbal and non-verbal behaviour, or substitute a reward or encouragement – to make up for the counsellor, say, not disclosing the same amount of personal information (Hargie and Tourish, 2000).

Egan (2002, pp23–25) outlines a different approach. He poses a three-stage method of counselling, involving a problem management approach. Service users are encouraged to be specific about their issues, and then to explore opportunities. Egan suggests that this approach can potentially help service users:

■ clarify the key issues for change,
■ decide their goals, where they want to go, and
■ devise strategies to get there.

Egan's theoretical model is flexible enough to adopt alongside other interview models (for instance, methods of intervention) because the principles will be very similar. It is also a framework that practitioners have identified as helping them (SCIE, 2004, p7).

Yet another useful way of understanding interviews is to see them as a five-stage process (Nicholson and Bayne, 1984, p31–52). These stages are:

1   Preparation, or the pre-stage before the interview.
2   Exploration and definition of the issues, as well as the commencement of an interpersonal relationship.
3   Understanding and testing a service user's awareness to consider new thinking.
4   Action.
5   An after-stage, or the recording of the interview, and further thinking about avenues to explore.

In this approach, 'preparation' relates both to the practical knowledge needed for the interview, and to the state of mind of the practitioner. Within this model you need a range of skills suitable to each of the stages, with an emphasis on general communication and relationship skills.

## Summary

Even in this brief survey, it will have become clear that models of interviewing within social work are extremely diverse. The most engaging, however, seem to stress the complexity of each individual exchange within a defined overall framework. They also emphasise that the quality of the relationship between service user and practitioner plays an important part within the interview.

## Communication theory and skills

Communication theory and skills are central to our understanding of the processes of the interview. Communication theory in social psychology comes from a body of research evidence concerned with how people relate to each other, and associated patterns of behaviour (Payne, 1997, p165). At its simplest, communication can be one person sending information, to be received and interpreted by another person. In the field of social psychology, this simple process becomes much more complex, with rules – often culturally sensitive rules – that may enhance or deter communication.

Communication skills in social work are normally seen as the effective use of verbal and non-verbal forms of communication, as employed by practitioners. Communication skills also include the sensitive use of language, written skills, information-gathering or investigative skills, and interviewing skills (Trevithick et al, 2004, p116).

Interviewing skills have traditionally been seen as a sub-set of abilities within the sphere of communication skills (Lishman, 1994; Koprowska, 2005). Developing communication skills, practising them, seeking feedback and learning new communication expertise consequently form essential components of interviewing.

## Models of assessment

Initial interactions in social work are largely based upon **assessment**. You may find that the assessment process itself may be led and defined by an agency's need for completion of assessment paperwork as much as the needs of the concerned service users.

Assessment frameworks are often tied in to the theory behind them. For instance, cognitive behavioural assessments will target antecedents, behaviour and consequences (Cigno, 2002, pp186–7). Therapeutic interventions based within a health setting may well have an emphasis on disease diagnosis and medical history (Bögels, 2000).

In contrast, Sutton and Herbert's ASPIRE assessment framework (Sutton, 1994) is more generalised.

ASsessment
Planning
Intervention
Review
Evaluation

This, like Egan's model of intervention, takes us well beyond the first period of an evaluation interview, and into interventions.

> **Definition**
>
> ## Assessment
>
> A process of coming to an understanding, evaluating or making a judgement about a person's situation. This may include looking at the **risks** in the situation, the **strengths** and the **needs** of the individual or family. It is important that the assessment should be completed in partnership with the service user, with regard for their input. Assessments may be completed over time. They may be limited to one sphere of functioning, but are more likely to be comprehensive, complex and concerned with the whole person. The question of evaluation of risk, whether it is in families with children, or individuals' situations of risk, may form part or the whole of an assessment. Assessment may involve wider enquiries and observations beyond the interview itself.

### Therapeutic interventions

In the next chapter (Chapter 3) we examine the types and purposes of interviews. It is important to keep in mind that, in an individual interview, it can be very difficult to separate one purpose from another. However, in that chapter, we will see that one function of an interview may be for therapeutic intervention.

So, if in an interview you are using a social work intervention that does not fit into a generalised model (such as Egan's three-stage model, or the ASPIRE framework), you are likely to be working to a model within a specific area of social work. We now briefly examine some major models of involvement and intervention.

### Brief therapy

Brief therapy is a time-limited involvement intended to help people identify where they want to change, and help them work towards it. It is sometimes called 'solution-focused' therapy, because it is goal directed, and concentrates on the future rather than an exploration of the past. Significant elements are: use of 'scaling' ('Where do you put yourself on a scale of one to ten? What will help you move one place up the scale, towards getting where you want to be?'); identification of 'exceptions' to the norm of individual behaviours; trying something different; and 'the miracle question' ('If you could wave a magic wand . . .?'). It is an approach that works well within a collaborative and empowering framework, as it focuses on a person's strengths, and builds on what has worked for them in the past (O'Connell and Palmer, 2003).

## Cognitive behavioural approaches

Cognitive behavioural approaches, also called cognitive behavioural therapy (CBT), is the term describing short–term involvements that help people understand their unhelpful or negative behaviours, and then seek to work with them to change the cognitive model of their actions (Sheldon, 1995; Cigno and Bourn, 1998). This approach lends itself well to working with people to effect changes in attitude and feeling, as well as changes in environment.

## Task-centred practice

Although the concept of task-centred practice as an approach has been established for many years, it remains in favour, perhaps because the approach has clarity of concept. Goals can be identified and worked on in partnership with service users, and may be adapted to different settings, even where there is an element of coercion. Its method is to identify objectives to be accomplished (not necessarily practical goals) and then to distinguish the steps needed to achieve them. Goals are to be accomplished within a clear time framework, and service users are deliberately involved through the making of contracts (Marsh, 1991).

## Person-centred counselling

Person-centred counselling has its roots in Rogers's exposition of counselling and the associated counselling relationship (Rogers,1942). Counsellors' attention to interpersonal skills has particularly influenced social work, as has their account of the client/worker relationship. Even if the context in which we work (such as a statutory agency) precludes our being able to practise in a person-centred way, the concepts drawn from counselling continue to resonate in social work practice. The ideas of empathy, warmth and acceptance (discussed in Chapter 1) are still important features of the social work vocabulary.

A central element of most of the above interventions is their foundation in research, and in working towards evidence-based practice. Originally developing from medical care, evidence-based practice has transferred to the social care arena, and is especially significant in work with children and their families (Research in practice website). This approach works well alongside the model of working in partnership with families or individuals, since reasoning for decision making becomes more transparent, especially when options and outcomes have been recorded appropriately.

## Summary

Whatever synthesis is constructed for use in an interview, it must have relevance to the exchange between the service user and you, and be pertinent to your role within your organisation.

Two examples may reinforce this point: when the focus of the interview is a person with learning difficulties, then you will clearly need some specialised knowledge and skills; and these skills will be different from those needed when working with someone from the deaf community.

Second, Brown and Harris (1978) cite the lack of a confidant as a major factor in vulnerability to depression. Learning in an interview if a service user has someone with whom they can share worries and feelings will therefore add to your relevant knowledge of the service user's situation. Identifying the *lack* of a suitable confidant might alert you to the possibility of depression. Such a conclusion might then merit further questions, before, it is hoped, leading to a more productive exploration of the emotional issues.

Social workers may also bring with them various theoretical perspectives. These personal frameworks may well be different, even between workers within the same agency. Here we must stress the need for practitioners to be flexible, and to consider additional theoretical viewpoints for 'making sense' of situations: one theoretical frame does not necessarily fit all.

## TWO-WAY PROCESS

An objective is always for you to be able to consistently carry out a competent or 'good-enough' interview. Although in principle more practice at interviewing builds greater skill and confidence, this gain must not be at the expense of the service user. It is important to acknowledge that every interview is, every time, a two-way communication. For this reason there will be times when even an experienced social worker may not feel they have performed at their best, or might feel they have 'blown' an interview. The reason may not be because they are ill, or the venue is not right. It may simply be that, at that particular day and time, in that setting, the individual human variation between interviewer and service user conspired against a favourable conclusion.

Conversely, of course, 'good interviewing is the result of the complex interplay of the interviewer, interviewee, purpose of the interview, and setting in which it is conducted' (Kadushin and Kadushin, 1997, p391).

So, should an interview prove unproductive, don't despair. In social work interviewing, very few things are set in stone. After reflecting critically on the event, talking it over with your supervisor, and perhaps actively rehearsing how you plan to aim for a better outcome, you can return to the fray, ready for improvement.

## LEARNING FROM INTERVIEWS OUTSIDE SOCIAL WORK

Interviewing is a skill not confined to social work. When people are asked to consider what an interview is, they may often think of job interviews, or interviews for entry to school or college. Even within the caring professions, there is a wide spectrum of interviewing. Apart from social care interviews, psychiatry, medicine and allied vocations all use interviews professionally.

You can usefully learn practical techniques of interviewing from other disciplines. The channels for this learning may be wide; for example, a television programme on the training of doctors can give valuable insights into how to make – or not to make – introductions; the Internet may have recorded mp3s of interviews (website: mental health TV), while a joint interview with someone from a different professional background can extend your interviewing skills.

---

### Practice issue

Seb, a new social worker, was unsure how severe Mrs Fiddler's short-term memory loss was, and how much it affected her life. The Community Psychiatric Nurse needed to carry out an assessment interview, so Seb sought permission from both parties to join it. He observed how the nurse asked Mrs Fiddler questions about memory and her everyday routines. He found it helpful to incorporate these questions into later interviews with other service users.

---

A comprehensive assessment interview from another discipline will nearly always have at least some overlap with social work, and may well contain approaches and questions that you can place within the context of your own interviewing.

## CONCLUSION

This chapter looked at the place in social work practice of knowledge and theory, and made the following points:

■ Interviewing has often been seen purely as a practical skill to be learnt 'on the job', but there is a wide range of theoretical knowledge to bring to interviewing.

■ Theory and practice learn from each other. We discussed the importance of knowledge and reflection to the practice of social work interviewing.

■ We discussed theoretical frameworks for
   (a) Conceptualising the interview. You can model the interview as a social transaction, as roles both play, as interpersonal skills, or as a problem-solving activity.
   (b) Communication theory and skills; how these add to the confidence and expertise of social work practitioners.
   (c) Assessment of social situations, and models to consider.
   (d) Interventions: we looked briefly at some therapeutic models used in practice, such as brief therapy, CBT, and task-centred work.

## QUESTIONS

1   What theoretical perspectives might you use for understanding/interpreting an interview with a couple who wish to become foster parents?

2   Think about an interview that you have recently undertaken, or observed. Explain to a friend, or jot down, the range of reading, research and theory that you may have consciously or unconsciously used in the interview. Were there any gaps?

3   What do you understand by the term 'conceptual framework'?

## FURTHER READING

Berne, E. *Games People Play*. Still useful in analysing relationships.
Lishman, J. (ed.) *Handbook of Theory for Practice Teachers in Social Work*, especially Chapter 6 by P. Hardiker and M. Barker.
Payne, M. *Modern Social Work Theory*, especially Chapters 6 and 7.

# Chapter 3

# Types and Purpose of Interviews in the Agency Context

**NOSSC RELEVANCE**

The material in this chapter relates to the following National Occupational Standards in Social Care:

- **Key Role Four,** Unit 13. Assess, minimise and manage risk to self and colleagues.
- **Key Role Five,** Unit 14. Manage and be accountable for your own work.
- **Key Role Five,** Unit 17. Work within multi-disciplinary and multi-organisational teams, networks and systems.

*This chapter begins by considering the preliminary steps needed before an interview can be planned and then carried out. This includes placing it in the context of an employer's responsibilities – the 'frame' of the interview – as well as professional values. We then describe the types and purposes of interviews. We look at the particular needs and approaches relevant to joint interviews, before concluding with an examination of telephone interviewing.*

## WHAT IS THE INTERVIEW *FOR?*

The decision to meet a service user should not necessarily be an automatic one. Before arranging any interview, you will need to first be sure of the purpose in meeting, and have set out the objectives, as we discuss in Chapter 4. However, even when objectives and purposes are both clear to you, it is still necessary to see whether the interview needs to be carried out in person, or whether a telephone interview could replace it.

> **Definition**
>
> **Communication skills**
>
> Communication skills are the range of learnt techniques that help social work professionals to communicate clearly, warmly with a wide range of people, even those who may have impaired communication, or whose first language may not be English.

Additionally, you should keep in mind the range of possible interview scenarios; for an effective interview, some choice of **communication skills** may have to be made.

In thinking about the methods you plan to use in an interview, consider the needs of the service user, your abilities, and the individual circumstances of that specific interview. Key variables are likely to be your level of experience, the service user's priorities, and the complexity of their situation. Of course, these initial choices should not be inflexible; Chapter 8 discusses how to monitor the course of an interview, and dynamically assess any need to amend your initial plans.

## AREN'T ALL INTERVIEWS BASICALLY THE SAME?

To an inexperienced social worker, perhaps studying job advertisements, it may appear that in social work we all face tasks that are broadly similar. Of course, this is a misapprehension; responsibilities can be different, and often are very different, as anyone who has worked in the area of social care for any length of time will be able to confirm (Adams, 2002, p251).

Even when professional responsibilities may at first appear to be identical, a job in social care or social work involves working with people – and, because people are different, they will inevitably respond in different ways.

Whatever the interview setting or purpose, a satisfactory outcome cannot be achieved without successful communication. So, while the surroundings in which social workers are employed may differ – and the roles they take may be very different – an ability to communicate effectively is always fundamental to the job. Even after you have built communication and interviewing expertise and become a more skilled practitioner, you will still need to look afresh at each interview (Hargie and Tourish, 2000, p84). This is because, in practice, the 'human element' (on both sides!), as well as other variables, will always mean even apparently identical tasks will vary in their demands on you. Due to the human element, there can never be a standard interview technique, to be carefully rehearsed and used with every service user on all occasions (Kadushin and Kadushin, 1997, p391).

## GENERAL AND PARTICULAR KNOWLEDGE

In Chapter 2, we saw that different levels of knowledge and skills are involved in social work interviewing. There is an obvious need for *general* knowledge, concerning the business of interviews and relationships within them.

However, it is important to appreciate that such *general* knowledge will always need supplementing by *particular* knowledge, focused on the detailed needs and demands of that specific interview. Pertinent information may be available from studying case files, or perhaps talking to a previously involved worker.

For example, if you are having an interview with Mrs Green about child-care, general knowledge about the needs of young children could usefully be supplemented by particular information about the specific needs of Mrs Green's children. Concentration on just one or the other would be too narrow. This is because, to interview effectively, attention to both specific and general needs is required.

We therefore have a situation in which even a skilled practitioner cannot assume that their meeting with a new service user will present the same interview environment as an earlier interview, however apparently similar the circumstances may be. This is an important issue, and one that will crop up repeatedly as we examine interviews from a number of different perspectives.

While a steady accumulation of skills and experience throughout a career will build up your personal and professional resources, your ability to select appropriate priorities for individual interviews will still be needed. However experienced you may be, there may still be occasions when fresh knowledge will be required.

## RESPONSIBILITY TO AGENCY

When you are planning an interview, in addition to considering the primary needs of the service user, there are also two other important points:

■ to keep in mind your own personal and professional standards,
■ to be aware of the position of your employer.

An interviewer who is being paid to carry out an organisation's work should always have a clear understanding of the requirements of the business. This means that, when you are working for an agency, you need to understand how your task has been defined, and to appreciate how your employer, or the employer's representative, feels you should best undertake it.

These two points are probably fairly obvious. However, what may be less obvious is that an agency's policies, while clearly important, should always be supported and balanced by the professional principles of the social care workers *themselves*.

What this means is that any request or instruction that you receive should always be considered in the light of your own professional standards. If, as a result of this internal questioning, a request is found to be at odds with your professional standards, the request should, at the very least, be subject to further discussion. Such a response is in line with the GSCC's guide to employers' and employees' responsibilities (GSCC website). Reflecting upon possible 'dilemmas' in working with people, and taking steps to resolve them, is an integral part of professional practice.

An example may make this clearer:

---

### Consider this

An anxious SSD manager responded to an increasing rate of referrals by allocating cases regardless of the ability of particular social workers to handle them, or the number of cases that had been already allocated. It was considered sufficient that a case had a named social worker, even if sheer pressure of work meant the service user could not be visited or interviewed.

A newly appointed worker, faced with picking up an existing and already very large case load, asked to be excused the allocation of new assessment interviews until they were up to speed on existing cases.

Should we consider this a reasonable request?

And, if we were the new worker, would it be appropriate in these circumstances to actually refuse to accept cases involving further interviews?

If you're unsure; would it help you to decide if you considered what might happen should one or more of the new cases allocated to you – and as yet unassessed – reach crisis?

---

Consider too a further related issue, taken from a different area of social work:

| Consider this | |
|---|---|
| Mrs T works in residential care home. Abbey, a visiting social worker, learned while interviewing a resident that her service user had been an accidental witness to Mrs T abusing another resident. However, due to mental frailty, Abbey's client was not a reliable witness. Should Abbey report Mrs T? She is not Mrs T's line manager, just a social worker. | What do you think Abbey should do? What do you consider are the important issues here? |

Social work concerns itself with the complexities of life, and perhaps issues are seldom clear-cut, which means simple solutions or outcomes may be rare. So what *should* happen is that, before acting – or not acting – the worker concerned needs to be able to justify to himself or herself whether *they* feel action or inaction is appropriate. They then need to be able to justify their proposed response, in consultation with their manager or supervisor.

## AGENCY 'FRAME'

Let us now assume that we have considered whether the proposed interview meets personal and professional standards, and conclude that it does. The next stage in the interview process will be to think about the *purposes* of the interview. Before arranging an appointment, you need to be sure why you are planning to interview someone, and what you hope to achieve by doing so. First, however, you need to identify the 'frame' of the proposed interview – and to weigh up what is expected of you in your current working role.

## THE INTERVIEW 'FRAME'

By the 'frame' of an interview, we are referring to three main characteristics:

■ the nature of the interviewer's agency, or employer,
■ the agency's objectives, and
■ the agency location within which the interview will take place.

While there may well be additional influences, these three points should provide the general context, or 'frame', of an interview. As we will see, in order to make a working alliance with service users, we must first identify which of several – potentially different – work-related 'frames' are relevant to a particular interview. This is a task that you can complete early. Thus the professional or agency background to an interview will have an effect on the way it is held.

For example, a large local authority may employ social workers who will variously interview people at home, in offices, in residential homes, hospitals, and so on. Each of these different settings will require a modification to the interview plans to reflect the particular needs of that setting, and, more importantly, the needs of a service user who is within that setting. You can combine your forward thinking with the interview setting to create work-related 'frames'. Over time, you will increase your knowledge of the work-related 'frames' that are likely to be relevant to your interviewing – a frame is certainly capable of a broader application than to just a single interview.

Once the 'frame' is defined and understood, you then should identify specific needs – and possible constraints – that may impinge on the interview.

### What influence on the interview does an employer have?

In the field of social care there are major employers, such as local authorities with Social Services Departments (LASSDs). These authorities may each define how they expect their social workers to act. Even within one authority, there is no easily defined single social care role. As a social care worker, you cannot anticipate being given just one solitary, clearly defined task; instead, you would expect to be asked to fill a potentially wide range of different roles, each of which might need a variety of responses.

Whatever disadvantages there may be to this, on the positive side it does mean that one of the rewards of working in the field of social work is that the job is seldom likely to be boring. As we have already suggested, continuing interest – or lack of boredom! – largely comes about because the job involves dealing with people in society. You may remember a recent social work advertising slogan – 'It's dealing with people – as simple and as complicated as that'. However, what are the specific demands that an employer might *legitimately* make on you?

### Social work employers

In recent years the range of social work employers and settings has become more diverse, and liable to change. You can categorise employers of social work interviewers by client group (such as children, young offenders, older people) or the setting (day services, residential care, hospitals), or the purpose (assessment or providers).

We feel it may be helpful to look also at the principal categories by role, and this is done below.

## 1 Local authorities with social services departments (LASSDs)

An LASSD is a government agency established by legislation, with the legal status of a corporate body with an independent legal existence. A County Council is a statutory body; so is a Metropolitan Borough Council. The responsibilities of a statutory authority are, by definition, detailed by statute, so social workers employed there will have both delegated powers and delegated responsibilities. There are essentially two types of statutory powers and responsibilities: *mandatory* – the authority must enforce these; and *permissive* – the authority may decide for itself whether or not to act.

Social workers have the delegated responsibility of their authorities and therefore act for the authority. There are exceptions where they act as independent professionals, notably in mental health.

## 2 Specialist charities

A specialist charity is a legally incorporated non-profit organisation that operates for the public benefit, usually by promotion of health, relief of poverty or distress, and other purposes that benefit the community. They tend to be funded through contributions from the public. In the UK it is unlawful for charities to solicit financial contributions without first being registered with the Charity Commission.

Social work for a registered charity has much in common with work for a voluntary agency – work is likely to be closely focused on a particular geographical area, or more probably a specific area of work. In practical terms, because of their reliance on voluntary funding, charities are likely to have limited funds, which may mean that social work resources may not be plentiful. However, you are unlikely to be expected to take on a role with public and legal duties.

## 3 Other non-governmental organisations (NGOs)

Voluntary associations and voluntary agencies need less compliance with formal statutory procedures than other social care agencies, and are therefore probably less intimidating to service users. However, they do not exist as legal entities separate from their members. This means that individual committee members increase their risk of personal liability. It is also possible that, because of their less rigid structure, other agencies may regard a voluntary organisation as less stable, or perhaps even less professional.

In practice, a voluntary agency may be at least partially funded by a Social Services Department, and is likely to have a fairly tightly defined remit. In consequence, such an agency will almost certainly specialise, again, in either a particular geographical area or a specific area of social work practice – for instance, fostering children with challenging behaviour.

## 4   Private agencies

Private agencies, although they may contract services to LASSDs, are run for profit, and have their own policies and terms of employment. Their role may be similar to NGOs, but individual practitioners may find varying expectations of their role.

Each of these agencies is likely to have differing requirements for its social work staff, so interviewers need to be aware of the particular role taken by their agency.

### Context of client group

The final point about the interview 'frame' is to consider your current specialisation in social work and its detailed needs and demands. Essentially, your organisation will expect you to address specific issues in your work, and you will therefore be expected to include relevant aims and objectives in your interviews. (For example, if your task is to assess and write a report for a Court, then this has to be your interview priority, even though you and the service user may have other priorities.) These 'work' objectives may vary, depending upon the nature and aims of the employer, but you will always need to have them in the background of your work.

There is also the locality to consider: some settings in social work are much more relaxed than others. 'Secondary settings', that is places that are not the home environment, may sometimes be quite formal, as for example hospital surroundings; or much more informal, as in coffee bars (Lishman, 1994, p141). With more informal, day-to-day exchanges, the boundaries of what is a conversation and what can be called 'an interview' may become more blurred. Disclosure of some risk factor in these settings may therefore be more surprising to you, just because you may have to 'switch' from one role to another very quickly. This is one reason why it can be useful to think about and make clear your agency role. Are you a 'friend'? Or does the relationship need defining a little more closely?

Here is an illustrative example about the influence of an employer on a social work interview:

---

### Practice issue

Chitra was newly appointed to the job of Fostering Officer for a local authority. Part of her job was to seek out new foster parents, and, when following up one lead, she visited Mr and Mrs Teal. The Teals were clearly experiencing serious relationship stresses with their children. Chitra, who had previously worked in a Family Service Unit, knew she would be able to help the couple, and therefore planned a series of interviews with them.

However, when she discussed the Teal family with her supervisor, Chitra was concerned to find that, while her supervisor agreed that the work she had planned with the family was necessary, it was not thought to be appropriate for her. With their agreement, the family were instead referred to a Family Support team; and Chitra was encouraged to continue her search for other potential foster parents.

---

Finally, the particular *sector* of social care work within which the interview will take place can also affect its conduct. Essentially, a social care worker will be expected by their organisation to address specific issues in their work, and, as we have said, expected to set relevant aims as clear objectives in their interviews. In practical terms, this means that, while you might as an individual be trained, experienced and competent to address particular issues or approaches, it may nevertheless still be inappropriate for you to do so.

Another example points up such an effect.

---

### Practice issue

As a simple illustration, think about the same social worker being asked to handle two interviews – one with prospective foster parents, the second with a young offender subject to a Youth Court Order. Once aware of what is needed from these situations, and while being mindful of the values that inform the relationship, the *same* worker would handle each interview differently.

---

The important point here is to see whether the intended method of intervention or assessment is *outside* your current role. This may be the case, even if the issues to be addressed may otherwise appear broadly relevant for the agency.

We are now able to identify three issues that you will need to consider in framing an interview.

1   If you keep in mind the diversity of the 'human element' in social care, all interviews should be seen as potentially different. There is no 'one size fits all' interview technique: there are too many variables for that.

2   You need to understand the relevance of employment 'frames', or your roles within an agency. You also need to identify which 'frame' will be the most applicable for a proposed interview.

3   Check that there is a need for a face-to-face interview before actually arranging one.

## TYPES AND PURPOSES OF INTERVIEW

Having set the scene, it is time to move on to consider what types of interviews there might be. Two important points should be repeated here: there is probably no such thing in social care as a 'typical' interview, simply because there is such a wide range of possibilities. Second, although an interview may have a primary purpose, this does not prevent it from fulfilling more than one function. Therapeutic interviews may also provide information, and vice versa.

So a single interview may have multiple and overlapping purposes. To analyse and discuss them, however, we are going to separate out the different functions, although we acknowledge that this is an artificial way that would not be reflected in a real-life interview.

Kadushin and Kadushin (1997, pp14–15) look at types of interview by their purpose, and see them as:

> ■ **Informational** (To gather information or to make a social report, such as for court or for doctors, or an agency.)
> ■ **Assessment** (To arrive at an understanding, an appraisal or an evaluation. This may be for services, or suitability, such as to be foster parents.)
> ■ **Therapeutic** (To effect change within a service user's personal functioning, or within their environment.)

However, Kadushin and Kadushin approach the purposes of an interview from an American viewpoint, within a very different system of legislation and culture to that of the UK. Although they qualify their categorisation by stating that purposes merge, there does seem to be a strong overlap between informational and assessment interviews, while *investigative* interviews are sidestepped. (Although investigative interviews are beyond the scope of this book on core skills, in the scheme of things they are a significant type.)

Trevithick (2000, p70) looks at interviews from the point of view of their purpose, but directed towards the outcome:

> ■ Formal interviews (protection 'investigations' whether in child care or adult services; mental health or community care assessments).
> ■ Less formal interviews (where 'everyday' problems may be presented).

This can be a useful way of thinking about your role in the interview, although it perhaps underestimates the complexities of certain situations, where purposes and roles may perhaps be more subtle. Assessments under the Community Care Act 1990 may be formal – but can present informally too.

There are some other ways of describing functions of social work interviews, too, as shown in Table 3.1.

As can be seen, categories merge and overlap. However, despite this, it can aid you to identify the interview's *main* purpose. This is because without a view of the interview's objectives, it is unlikely that you will be able to define an outcome, far less reach it (see Chapter 4).

## I  Investigative, exploratory and assessment interviews

First, any assessment, exploration or investigation should be based on an understanding of the service user's situation. It should also work within a frame of service user consent and confidentiality. Within these forms of interview, there are sub-divisions, mostly concerned with information. These sub-divisions are discussed below.

**Table 3.1**  Categories of interview

| Type of interview | Example |
| --- | --- |
| 1  Investigative, exploratory and assessment | Adult protection. Court Report |
| 2  Goal-directed | Help/advice to single parent under pressure |
| 3  Statutory | Reviews, following a care or supervision order |

### Information-gathering interview

Information gathered in this type of interview may be *visual* information, *verbal* and other *aural* information, or *emotional* information – and quite possibly all four.

Characteristically, someone will hold an initial information-gathering interview to find out whether further social work involvement is appropriate or necessary. Remember that this could mean that the *service user* screens the agency, as well as the other way round. You may arrange later information- gathering interviews in order to update your knowledge, or possibly to discover answers and information on specific issues. An interview for information collection generally gathers facts that will help you later in understanding and analysing (for instance, an interview might collect information that could subsequently be shared at a case conference).

The information you obtain may well go towards further evaluation. All types of information are a key part of the process of assessment. This process may include other features, such as observation (seeing how a person's non-verbal behaviour reflects their mood, perhaps), or seeking information from other parties (such as health professionals or other social work staff involved with the family).

In an information-gathering interview, your main role will be to observe and respond to all you hear, see and experience. Monitoring all the non-verbal channels of communication (so important in conveying interpersonal feelings and emotions) can be difficult to do continuously (Cook, 1971, p66).

### Information-sharing interview

An information-sharing interview is most commonly carried out in association with representatives of other agencies. In the interview itself the service user is likely to be interacting with two (possibly more) professionals, where each participant may need to ask questions. This type of interview helps decide the level of involvement appropriate for different agencies with a particular service user. The inherent complexities both for the service user and for other participants in this type of meeting are discussed later in this chapter, in the section dealing with inter-professional interviews.

It is worth making clear that while information is certainly shared in a case conference meeting, a formal case conference is *not* an information-sharing interview. A case conference is essentially a forum to present information that has already been gathered, and its function is to make decisions based on that information.

## Information-giving interview

An information-giving interview is likely to be a straightforward meeting, in which you offer specific information to a service user, either in written or in verbal form – or both. The information given may be about the agency itself, or may include any other items of information pertinent to the service user's situation.

The provision of information is of course an important aspect of social work (Lishman, 1994, p78). It is also likely to be of central importance when working in partnership – the knowledge and power equilibrium can be affected by how and what information we share with service users.

## Information evaluation interview

An evaluation interview enables decisions to be reached during the interview itself. Typically, when the interview is concluded you will decide whether service users are eligible for certain support. This may be practical services, such as support workers, or less tangible assistance, such as regular social work visits.

Whatever the setting of an information evaluation interview, it will involve some kind of *appraisal*, and this will normally be one that helps the agency come to a decision about policy, services or action.

This type of interview will not be carried out frequently, but, if it does recur, is likely to do so at regular intervals. This will generally be to monitor the progress of your involvement, or to re-evaluate a situation following a change in circumstances. Such later interviews may also be called 're-assessment' or possibly 'review' interviews, and could well be scheduled some time in advance.

An *investigation* interview is a specialised type of evaluation interview. As this book concentrates on core skills, investigatory interviews lie outside its focus. However, it is worth making clear that the communication skills needed in any assessment and evaluation are basic to more specialised interviewing.

## 2   Goal-directed interviews

Goal-directed interviews are those in which, in partnership with the service user, you identify an objective. An example of a goal could be support to a single parent under pressure, or helping a young offender stay away from crime.

A therapeutic interview is a kind of goal-directed interview. The priority here is to effect change collaboratively with service users, whether in their personal functioning or their social situation (Kadushin and Kadushin 1997, p17). There is also the implication that therapeutic interviews have a theoretical framework, to which both are working (discussed in Chapter 2).

*Goals* (achievements), *aims* (plans to do or achieve something) and *objectives* (aims or goals) have interconnected definitions. There can therefore be some confusion about the terms; in social work they are not always clearly defined. It is useful to consider objectives as long term, or at the end of the process of involvement. Short-term aims or steps contribute to the overall objective(s).

## 3   Statutory interviews

Statutory interviews almost invariably concern practitioners who work within LASSDs. Under specific legislation, a statutory agency has mandatory and/or permissive responsibility for social care involvement and services. Interviews arranged under statutory powers are parallel to Trevithick's 'formal interviews'.

Although the fabric of social work agencies is changing, and there is a wider range of smaller and informal agencies, many staff continue to work within LASSDs. Their role, however, is likely to be more authoritative, as mandatory powers carry reference to risk and harm.

Now we consider a slightly different viewpoint. If you have constantly to handle a mixture of types of interview, this can be positive. A variety of experiences may actually prove a benefit – there are advantages to diversity, and a variety of interviewing experiences can often provide job satisfaction.

---

### Practice issue

A team leader, running a team of intake social workers, found that one of the chief positives for team members answering the phones was the impossibility of knowing what would happen next. While all telephone calls and visits to the office inevitably resulted in an interview of some kind, a wide range of both people and issues meant that intake interviews were diverse. In order to be effective, intake team workers were constantly kept on their toes. Because the techniques they used in interviews often needed to be different, their skills and confidence grew as they dealt with a wide variety of situations.

## INTER-PROFESSIONAL INTERVIEWING

There has been an increasing trend for separate professions to share common elements of training, particularly at postgraduate level, and, in some situations, for the lines between different professions to become blurred (Barr, 2002, p269). In the UK, the government is anxious to encourage 'joined-up' working with service users, expressed through concern for a client-centred approach, efficiency, and consciousness that failures in communication between professions are costly – in all senses (Victoria Climbié Inquiry website).

Social work has undoubtedly become more complex, and there are now substantial budgets for social care. Legislation, such as the The NHS and Community Care Act (1990), specifically states that NHS and social services personnel should jointly assess complex needs. In a changed social climate, today's expectation is that even individuals with complex needs will be supported in the community, with more 'joined-up' working.

Of course, joint visits have always been undertaken, but well over a decade of closer inter-professional training and working has emphasised the importance of developing closer working relationships. In childcare, considerable adjustments are under way, with joint departments of Education and Childcare Services forcing a pace of change to closer joint work.

What underlies good joint working is a respect for the other professionals and their viewpoint, and an understanding of their role. It certainly helps to make individual links, perhaps through the team, and to spend time with colleagues from other agencies, getting to know them on a personal level.

### Definition of inter-professional interviewing

An 'inter-professional' interview implies that two workers from different professional backgrounds need to interview the service user for similar purposes. The need for two people to be involved will usually arise because both agencies need to evaluate the position before making shared decisions with the service user (SCIE, 2004, p8). It could also be that the service user's situation is so complex or urgent that another professional's opinion or advice would be beneficial – arranged, of course (unless there is risk of harm) with the service user's prior permission. In certain circumstances it may accordingly be right for workers from different agencies to interview a service user together.

---

### Practice issue

Adhiambo was the mother of four young children. She lived alone in temporary council accommodation, was experiencing considerable stresses, and as a consequence had asked for her two older children to be looked after. Her social worker suggested a joint interview with both himself and a Housing representative, with the intention of clarifying her housing in relation to childcare issues.

---

## With whom will you be working?

The role of a social worker overlaps with a number of other professional roles. Professionals from the Health Service (for example, doctors, nurses, health visitors, occupational therapists) may be involved in working with social workers, but other professions and administrators (such as Housing Officers, the Probation Service, Education Department personnel, or Department for Work and Pensions officers) are also frequently concerned with service users.

In situations where it is proposed that two – or even more – professionals should jointly talk to a service user, it is important first to decide with service users whether this is necessary for or beneficial to them. To be interviewed by two or more people, however well intentioned this may be, could be stressful and unsettling to service users. Sometimes the service user may not previously have met one of the interviewers. Would these interviews be better carried out separately?

We have said that the service user should agree to the joint visit. Essentially, this means that you should fully explain why you think it is a good idea, discuss it with them, and seek their cooperation. Only when the service user has given their agreement should the workers concerned move forward to plan their joint interviewing.

It will then be necessary to decide which workers from which agency will participate in the interview. Take, for example, a situation where a service user is in hospital. Although they may currently have high nursing needs, they could well be returning to the community. Would it be more appropriate for a social worker to jointly interview with the ward nursing staff, or with the district nurse?

It is perfectly possible for an assessing social worker to take both professionals' views into account, along with the views expressed by the occupational therapist and physiotherapist. What needs clarification is who are the appropriate people to join an interview with a particular service user.

The individual workers concerned may not, of course, have the power to decide. In many parts of the country there are likely to be local protocols in place, intended to help in just such situations. If they exist, local procedures may well define which people should be involved in the interview.

## Where the service user's main needs lie

The choice of which other professionals to include in a meeting with a service user may be clear from the available initial information. However, this cannot always be assumed; preliminary information sometimes lacks precise detail. In such an event you may need to judge the service user's individual needs, and decide which should take priority. It may only be after this, and after discussion with the service user, that you can identify the best person to take the lead in the interview.

---

### Practice issue

Cindy has had multiple sclerosis for some years. Recently she has become depressed, having had to give up her job, experiencing childcare problems and getting behind with the mortgage. Her social worker discusses with her which of the issues is her main concern, and together they arrange a joint interview with the community psychiatric nurse, to discuss her main priority.

---

## Decision on lead interviewer

You have reached a decision to hold a joint interview and you know the professional(s) to include. The next step is to decide on which professional will take on the role of **'lead' interviewer**. Sometimes this decision is left until the interview itself, or even overlooked altogether, which can cause confusion.

One possibility is that whichever agency has responsibility for the service user's priority needs will be the lead worker. That person would obviously have the greatest need to ask questions, and to make the major contribution to the discussions. However, the choice of lead worker could also reflect the relationship of the worker to the service user – if the service user is already familiar with one of the professionals involved, and trusts them, that familiarity is obviously likely to help the service user. Should neither of the professionals know the service user, this is likely to

**Definition**

### The 'lead' interviewer

The interviewer who will take the principal role both in talking with the service user and in seeking information.

create an especially sensitive situation for all participants, particularly if the issues that need discussing are very personal and important.

## Confirm the arrangements beforehand

Agreeing interview arrangements in advance may seem an obvious precaution. It is, though, important to confirm practical details with the service user, and whether they need the support of anyone, such as their carer, for the joint interview. Try to discuss the process of the interview itself in advance with the other interviewer too. Even if only a brief discussion on presentation and role is possible, don't overlook the opportunity: a service user's perception of the outcome of the interview may well depend upon each worker being aware of a shared and mutually agreed agenda.

In essence, such advance planning means that you will have a chance to discuss any areas of potential dispute beforehand. Advance discussion also allows you to plan together how you can best structure the interview for the service user's benefit. Will its length and intensity tire the service user?

## Be clear about introductions

Having more than two people present at the interview will inevitably add to the complexity of the interview process, and consequently to the possibility of the service user's confusion. As we have said, with inter-professional interviewing there is always the possibility that one of the interviewers may be unknown to the service user; their role and responsibilities may consequently be equally unknown. For this reason it is even more important to be very clear and careful about introductions. In this case, an introduction should not only include the names and the roles of those people concerned, but also details (preferably written) of how they may be contacted.

Towards the end of the interview, the professionals may need to spend time on clarification. For instance, will planned actions be joint, between agencies, or the responsibility of a single agency? Even if you agree decisions during the interview, the options may have to be ratified later by a manager. Finally, whatever the outcome of the interview might be, you should aim to decide in advance how the outcome can most sensitively be relayed to the person concerned.

## Where and when to negotiate

In joint working, there is always the possibility of a need to negotiate, particularly about areas of difficulty between agencies. Typically, you may need to debate and agree the use of resources from either agency. While you may start from a position that this negotiation could be done with the service user, there may be occasions when either or both interviewers believe it would be damaging to challenge opinions or 'bargain' for resources in front of the person concerned. To hammer out a joint decision may take time, and the process of effective negotiation may call for plain speaking. Although partnership and honesty should be at the front of your mind, in some circumstances you may need to make space for a private interlude with the other professional.

---

### Practice issue

Mrs Motton is in a hospice, but wants to go home to die, with her children around her. Ada, the social worker, and the community nurse have to work out their respective services, especially since budget cuts have recently led to tighter controls. Ada explains to Mrs Motton that they would like to discuss 'who does what' outside, and plan to come back with joint ideas for her support.

---

If major disagreement is imminent during a joint interview, it is perfectly acceptable to seek 'time out' to discuss the situation in more detail with your colleague. Check that the service user does not mind. Phrases such as 'I'd like to talk to you privately for a minute' or 'I think I need to check something out with you. May we discuss it outside?' may raise questions in the service user's mind, but these may be preferable to open disagreements. Of course, leaving an interview even temporarily in this way does exclude the service user from the decision-making process, so it may therefore be a difficult choice.

### If you don't agree . . .

There will be times in joint interviewing when the colleagues concerned do not agree on the outcomes, or perhaps not on the exact support services to be put into place. They may not agree between themselves; or the service user may not agree with their views. In these circumstances, it may be sensible, rather than feeling the interview has been unproductive, to see first if there is any agreement that *can* be negotiated – even if it is only a step towards the anticipated goals of the interview. Such shared negotiation also helps to frame a situation of mutual positiveness, in which other issues may be worked on.

In explaining decisions to the service user, it is good practice to make these clear *jointly* at the conclusion of the interview. One reason is that there could be issues not previously expressed that the service user would wish you to take into account. Second, information on how a service user could challenge the professionals' decisions is best given at this time.

### Who takes the lead on planning and timescales?

When concluding a joint interview, a final important point for the professionals is to summarise the decisions they have reached. You can then confirm *for each issue* the person who will be responsible for ensuring that decisions are implemented.

Shared training can undoubtedly help with both planning and undertaking joint interviews (Barr, 2002, p270). The agencies involved should initially have provided policy guidance on major issues. While in theory this should happen, in practice people move on. Knowledge can be lost. Even if the organisation has a rolling programme of education in place, people who are new in post may understandably have gaps in their knowledge.

It is therefore sensible to adhere to good guidelines on clear communication, and never assume that the other professional will be knowledgeable about the workings of agency systems, and their responsibilities.

## TELEPHONE INTERVIEWING

Straightforward telephone calls to a service user to clarify a piece of information can hardly be classed as an 'interview'. An interview implies that questions will range over several areas of interest and concern, and it will certainly take time. While it is usually preferable to carry out an interview in person, inevitably there are occasions when a personal visit may be difficult, or impossible. In such circumstances using the telephone may allow you to carry out an interview that could not otherwise take place.

Sometimes – if you are a duty officer taking referrals from the public, for example – interviewing by telephone is inevitable. A telephone interview may be appropriate if the agency feels the level of assessment can be adequately decided over the phone. A telephone interview may also be preferable if time factors mean that coordinating a personal visit is not going to be possible; or perhaps you just need to complete a form-based interview (Payne, 2000, p91). In addition, sometimes people may be too far away to be visited very often.

Telephone interviews for assessment purposes also allow the agency more easily to 'keep at a distance'. If a person does not fit eligibility criteria, then the use of a telephone for an initial interview means neither side has invested much time – or nervous energy – in the transaction, and not too many expectations will have been raised.

However, the process of interviewing by telephone is emphatically not the same as in a face-to-face interview. While the objectives may be similar, skills will differ.

### Differences when interviewing using the telephone

Some noteworthy differences between face-to-face interviewing and using a telephone for interviews include, not in any particular order:

- Practitioner/service user communication is limited to the verbal, intonation and use of silences.
- It is impossible to observe facial expressions or body language.
- Lack of visual cues may lead to misinterpretations and misunderstandings.
- Use of the telephone may be interpreted by the service user as a lack of commitment on the part of the social worker.
- Simple personal interactions, such as 'Here's my card', are not possible.
- Communication issues, such as deafness, become more significant.
- An interviewer is safe from physical risk.
- Travelling is eliminated. The time needed for each interview is potentially reduced.
- More frequent 'visits' are possible.
- Multiple activities, such as checking the file, may be carried out simultaneously – 'Hold on, and I'll check . . .'

### Simple telephone interviewing

As we have said, telephone interviews can save time, but for this very reason it is important to consider their use carefully; and, specifically, to consider when they should *not* be used. What are the purposes of this interview – and can these goals be achieved by a necessarily restricted telephone interview?

| Consider this | |
| --- | --- |
| *Interview with Mr Smeeth*<br>Objectives:<br>Discuss his recent fall; discuss increasing support from daughter; discuss possibility of rehab; if necessary, request financial details. | Does this list of objectives make the interview with Mr Smeeth suitable for a telephone interview? |

## Analysis

This interview has a potentially high emotional content. Discussing his possible loss of independence is likely to distress Mr Smeeth, so you will obviously need to be sensitive to this possibility. You would not want to go directly from discussing his recent fall to mentioning a possible need for a rehabilitation care unit, without first seeing his level of mobility. While it may be appropriate to keep the possibility of rehabilitation in reserve, and acceptable to Mr Smeeth – additional support at home may be sufficient. The attitude and responses of Mr Smeeth himself will be very important to this decision; balancing his abilities with his wishes has potential difficulties, too. In such circumstances, you are likely to need all the additional observation and non-verbal input a personal interview makes possible.

### When is a telephone interview appropriate?

Dealing with emotional issues, and issues that are likely to raise emotions, are the key factors in deciding if you can use a telephone interview. An interview principally aimed at exchanging practical details and information, or fact-finding, with a service user already known to you will be more suitable for a telephone interview. The dilemma in telephoning is that emotional issues may arise, and then you will not have the important face-to-face contact to deal comprehensively with them.

Situations where a telephone interview could work include:

- initial screening by an agency that has clear eligibility criteria,
- simple assessments, or reviews, where the form used can be clearly communicated over the telephone,
- exchanging of simple practical details or information.

As always, the best approach is, to consider *in advance*, each interview individually. Work pressures may mean that you have to use telephone approaches more than you would like, but it is always possible to record your rationale for doing so in case notes.

Situations where a telephone interview would not be appropriate include:

- when the service user has communication difficulties,
- when you need to interview more than one service user or carer,
- when you need to observe the service user's interactions with others,
- when the emotional content is expected to be highly charged,
- where the interview is likely to be complex.

## Before the interview

The most significant difference between a face-to-face interview and one carried out using a telephone is obvious: you will be forced to handle it without any of the usual *visual* cues. Recalling the power of non-verbal cues over verbal messages (Kadushin and Kadushin 1997, p289), you need to put preparation and forethought in to counterbalance the lack of important information – on both sides.

## Arranging the interview

A first step is to arrange the *time* of the telephone interview with all concerned, by telephoning or contacting people beforehand to ensure that they will be able to come to the telephone. At this stage it is important to warn people how long the interview is likely to take, and to set limits that fit with the needs of service users (such as choosing a time when they are likely to be least tired, and not needing the toilet). It is important, too, to confirm where their telephone is situated, and ensure that privacy is guaranteed. With advance notice, there is a better chance of this.

At your office, arrange (if at all possible) for a quiet room in which to make the call, and request no interruptions. Leave time after the telephone interview, before other appointments.

This should help relax you, and, if you are relaxed, that will be reflected in your tone of voice, and so communicate itself to the service user. If you have no need to hurry somewhere, there should be no sense of rush about the proceedings, either.

## The interview itself

We now move on to consider the practicalities of carrying out a telephone interview.

Telephone interviewing allows you to make a written reminder or checklist beforehand, of points to cover in the interview. Normally you would base this on the list of interview goals, but revise it for limited communication channels.

You can consult this list of interview goals throughout the telephone interview. It not only allows you to view each item, but also makes it far easier for you to maintain a balance between the items. For instance, if there are four issues to be discussed, it will become visibly apparent if too much time is spent on just one of them.

As in any other interview situation, you need to apply your communication skills, especially in clear speaking and accessible language. You should proceed at the service user's pace, and listen actively. These points will be discussed in later chapters.

As there are no visual cues for the interviewer to rely upon, it is particularly important in a telephone interview to check frequently that the person is following your communication. Regularly asking the service user to feed back their understanding is doubly important in a telephone interview as is **active listening**.

**Definition**

### Active listening

A state of heightened attention on the part of an interviewer in an interview. It describes the non-verbal and verbal cues, phrases and interchanges that tell the person being interviewed that the interviewer is concentrating on them, and making sense of their story.

### What if a telephone interview is not appropriate, but ...?

It is important to be realistic. In the real world, you will sometimes conclude that a telephone interview is less than ideal; but, despite this, there may be no time – or resources – to carry out a face-to-face interview. What should a worker do then?

While each situation must obviously be considered on its merits, in such circumstances it is generally best to extract from your aims just those subjects that *are* suitable for a telephone interview, and cannot wait, and deliberately to leave others for a later, personal visit. Knowing that a personal visit is firmly scheduled can help a service user to cope in the meantime. Certainly such a 'blended' approach is more likely to be appreciated by the service user than would a telephone call alone.

However, occasionally there are issues that are both unsuitable for a telephone interview, *and* that cannot be postponed. In such cases, these aspects should considered very carefully, and without haste. Only the essentials should be addressed, combined with the assurance that you appreciate the difficulty of dealing with such matters over the telephone, and will of course be visiting in person as soon as possible.

### Telephone interviews with other professionals

Particularly when taking referrals, a worker may be called on to talk to other professionals. A cardinal rule here is always to confirm the identity of a caller. This precaution will obviously be particularly important when discussing sensitive information, but it should be considered as good practice in any event. If necessary, call them back on a known switchboard number. It is not advisable to use a number given by the caller for a confirming callback. Instead, even if it takes longer, you should look up the number of the organisation to which they claim to belong.

A cautionary example illustrates this point. Some years ago an intake team were involved in handling what became a high-profile child care case. A telephone referrer wanted to discuss the case, claiming to be 'from the surgery'. When challenged, though, the 'referrer' turned out to be a tabloid reporter.

Once you have established their identity, a professional is probably (but not always) easier to speak to than a member of the public. The professional language that you share, and the 'jargon' common to you both, can ease communication. You may also find you can phrase questions more directly.

A word of caution, however. Responsibilities between agencies are not clear-cut. It is not unknown for one agency or professional to misunderstand or deny responsibility. It is therefore good practice to make sure that, at the end of the call, you summarise and confirm what has been said, and accurately record it. Remember, too, that you may need management approval for some commitments.

## CONCLUSION

In this chapter we discussed the starting points for social work and social care interviews, the 'frame' of the interview.

- We emphasised the importance of establishing the interview context by clarifying the needs of the agency. Your role may vary, but you must meet your employer's expectations, and take professional responsibility.
- We looked at types and purposes of interview: informational, assessment or therapeutic, or some mixture of the three.
- We looked at the special needs and approaches relevant to joint, or inter-professional, interviews.
- We considered telephone interviews as opposed to face-to-face interviews, and when they could be used to advantage.

## QUESTIONS

1   Consider an assessment worker in a busy city Children and Families office, and a specialist adoptions worker. What similarities might there be in their approaches to interviewing? What might be the differences?

2   Out of the blue, a locum manager asks you to request an Emergency Protection Order on a young person you have not seen, from a family you have never visited. How might you respond?

3   What do you understand by *inter-professional interviewing?*

## FURTHER READING

Kadushin, A. and Kadushin, G. (1997) *The Social Work Interview*, Chapter 1.
Trevithick, P. (2000) *Social Work Skills*, Chapter 4.

# Chapter 4

---

# Preparation and Pre-planning

---

## NOSSC RELEVANCE

The material discussed in this chapter relates to the following National Occupational Standards for Social Care:

- **Key Role One,** Unit 1. Prepare for social work contact and involvement
- **Key Role Two,** Unit 4. Respond to crisis situations
- **Key Role Six,** Unit 20. Manage complex ethical issues, dilemmas and conflicts.

*This chapter focuses on the preparation and thinking processes needed before an interview is undertaken. You will naturally want your interviews to be productive, but how might you arrange matters in advance to optimise your chances of successful interactions with service users?*

*The answer is, of course, to ensure time for preparation, which will normally include:*

- *considering anti-discriminatory factors of power and difference,*
- *goal setting,*
- *arranging practicalities,*
- *deciding on whom to include in the interview,*
- *anticipating any constraints.*

As discussed in the Introduction, a social work interview can be considered as a 'conversation or discussion with a purpose'; this purposeful conversation is, of course, the normal foundation of the majority of interactions between any service user and practitioner. Naturally, how the interview is carried out is important; but, before discussing specific interview techniques, we perhaps need to answer the question: Why should you, as a busy social work practitioner, spend valuable time thinking in advance about an interview, and planning what might happen during the course of it?

## WHY IS IT NECESSARY TO THINK ABOUT THE INTERVIEW?

Perhaps the easiest way to respond to this question is to consider what would happen if you did *not* plan an interview. In such a case, success is unknown. If you are not clear about what needs to be achieved when you begin the interview, how can you possibly know at the end whether the interview has been successful?

Put another way, you should think about interview groundwork in advance because, when there has been a thoughtful and careful preparation, with the service user firmly at the centre, you will have worked out beforehand the *aims* of the interview. By identifying goals in advance, there is clearly a greatly improved chance of the interview being productive, and accomplishing the objectives of the interaction (Trevithick, 2000, p73).

## REASON FOR THE INTERVIEW

We suggest that a period of planning before an interview is a key activity. (A planning flowchart is presented in Figure 4.1.)

- It will confirm that you know *why* you are to undertake the interaction.
- It identifies – and clarifies – what you expect or hope will *happen* in the interview.
- It enables you to make best use of what information is available.
- It allows preparatory work, such as telephone calls, likely to ease the course of the interview.
- Advance planning considerably improves the chances of an interview meeting both the service user's and your objectives.

So, when an interview is first proposed, the first planning stage identifies why you feel an interview is necessary. Should this be a first meeting, the service user's own agenda may as yet be unknown. Studying the relevant

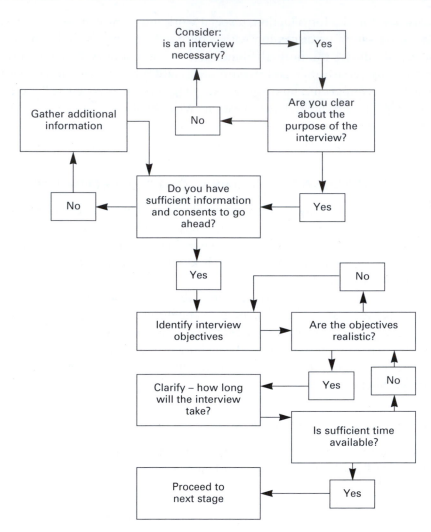

**Figure 4.1**   Interview planning flowchart

details from whatever information is available (perhaps a referral letter, or a file) may help you to theorise in advance about the situation of the service user, and to consider potential interview issues and outcomes.

As well as attempting to see a situation from the service user's viewpoint, you might usefully focus on what that individual might wish to gain from an interview. A useful way of putting this, and probably the best way to clarify the purpose of an interview, is to identify what both service user and practitioner should have gained by the *end* of the interview that they did not have when it *began* (Kadushin and Kadushin, 1997, pp77–9). Of course, there could be a wide range of objectives from which to choose. In practice, variation within these objectives may also be possible.

In every interview, initial objectives will primarily depend on the needs of the service user and of the agency. Goals can also vary depending upon when the interview occurs in the course of social worker and service user intervention – for example, first interviews are more likely to have as their objectives information gathering and understanding the service user's perspective; or perhaps clarifying structural power issues for the individual that may have led to their current situation. In contrast, later sessions may focus more on empowerment and change, and necessary strategies for their accomplishment.

## INTERVIEW GOALS – TWO PERSPECTIVES

Interviewer and service user may share an interview, but they may have very different perspectives on the interview's objectives. Here is an illustration of potential goals viewed from these different perspectives:

| | |
|---|---|
| Find out if this social worker can give me the information I need. | Find out how the service user thinks, and what they need. |
| Get some practical services to help my situation. | Discover whether they are eligible for social care services. |
| Relieve my feelings by talking them through. | Find out whether they are more depressed than when last seen. |
| Help me get re-housed. | Help with debt advice and re-housing application. |
| Help get my child back home. | Gather information for report to a Court. |

Such a list can be extended almost indefinitely, but the differences in approach should be clear.

In order for an individual plan of objectives to be prepared, you will first need to consider *possible* objectives, and then identify preliminary aims, or stepping-stones towards these objectives. It may be better, however, for you to leave your initial plan defined only in *general* terms, and for you to be prepared to be flexible about its exact contents. Interviews, because of respect and empowerment issues, must not be too rigid.

It may be that an initial reflection process also generates a longer-term plan (objective), which may include additional short-term aims. In that case, your future interview planning should incorporate consideration of the established 'long-term' list of goals, in addition to your current objectives.

It is at this early stage of planning the interview that you will need to address issues of anti-discriminatory practice. As was discussed in Chapter 1, you will need to be aware of difference: in age, gender, race, or indeed anything else that may have an impact on the interview.

When considering anti-discriminatory practice, you may wish to focus on the most appropriate *method* for communication. Is there any reading, or perhaps talking to members of a minority community, that might help you better appreciate the service user's experience? Neil Thompson's writings are useful texts to consult here: his book *Anti-discriminatory Practice* (2001) is standard, but *People Skills* (2002) is also well worth investigating.

## COMMUNICATION ISSUES

While the issue of communication is discussed more fully in Chapters 5 and 6, it is also relevant as an essential part of the interview planning stages. It is usually helpful to ask questions about communication, including:

- What is the service user's preferred method of communicating with people?
- Will the service user hear what I say, and clearly understand spoken communication?
- Will I be able to hear the service user, and understand them?
- Would it be sensible to take a pad and pen, for written comments?

Any contact beforehand with the service user (or a carer) should seek to clarify whether basic communication will be possible. If, as a result, you feel that communicating with a service user is likely to raise problems, some prior organisation will be necessary.

You may need to set up physical aids, such as amplifiers; or perhaps enlist other people – interpreters are the obvious example – to ease communication. Of course, arranging for special aids to communication may take time, so the sooner the arrangements are in place, the sooner an interview date can be confirmed.

## PRACTICAL PREPARATIONS

The next stage in the interview planning process is to think about, and then make, any practical preparations that may be needed before the actual meeting with the service user is arranged.

'Preparation', in this context, does not simply mean keeping time available in your diary for an appointment – and not merely gathering together any forms that may need to be completed, either. Interview preparation needs to be a much more proactive process.

Interview plans involve forethought, especially in considering the *practicalities* of an interview. We have already considered the possible need for help with communication. Other questions might include:

- What is the best location for the social worker to meet with the service user?
- What is the most appropriate day in the week for the interview to be arranged, and the best time of day to hold it?
- Will the service user be too tired?
- Are their children at school?
- Will they be alone?

Deciding on the optimum length of an interview should be thought about in advance – and from the service user's point of view, not just from your own perspective.

## DIRECT PLANNING

After completion of the preliminaries, the process of forward thinking can move on to planning the interview itself.

First undertake some analysis of how the interview might progress, perhaps considering potential reactions from the service user to the introduction of various topics you plan to raise. Advance thinking here might also include a decision about the theoretical assessment and intervention perspectives you intend to apply to the situation.

To summarise planning issues:

- Prepare proactively; planning is not simply form collecting.
- Think about the practicalities of the interview.
- Decide the approximate length of the interview.
- Examine theoretical approaches or methods of intervention.

## REVIEWING INFORMATION ALREADY AVAILABLE

It is helpful, before an interview, to find out what written information may already be available, and to make yourself familiar with it. Such 'information seeking' is especially useful when preparing for a first interview.

Even in a first interview, the service user is likely to have an understandable expectation that you will already know something about them; it is, fortunately, very unusual for a practitioner to have to interview a service user without knowing anything about them at all. If this does occasionally happen – most usually on duty visits – it can create a very uncomfortable feeling. It is worth holding on to that feeling, as it provides an insight into how service users may feel about the unknown 'official' who is coming to see them.

Should a visit be necessary, and there is no one currently in the office who may have personal knowledge of the service user, there is usually at least minimal paperwork available, and often much written information available for you to consult – if you are prepared to look for it.

In some ongoing family situations, however, there may be too *much* paperwork. Some complex family situations generate extremely thick files, and, without spending considerable time on the task, it can be difficult to make a useful synopsis of all the information they contain.

### Analysing a file

An agency file may be packed with information that you really should read and analyse before contact. Analysis of a bulky file can be intimidating, but there are approaches that may help. One useful method is to code relevant entries with sticky coloured 'flags', according to topic. Perhaps p19 of the interview notes contains factual notes about the relationship between mother and children, with more entries on mother and child interaction on p25 and p66. Flagging these pages with a coloured marker, or Post-It note, and marking other entries with different colours (risks could, for example, be denoted by red markers) will help make sense of the material. As a bonus, such methods are likely to prove useful in any later report writing.

Building a **genogram** from the information on the file could also be another useful advance task; this might also provide an agenda item for the interview (Burnham, 1986, p25).

A high priority for any initial file search should be to discover if there are any references to violent or challenging behaviour. If so, this should not simply be noted. You will need to start an immediate dialogue in the office about any safety measures that might be appropriate. If these are felt

---

**Definition**

**A genogram**

A genogram is a visual way of describing family relationships and emotional closeness in graphic or diagrammatic form. It looks at the relationships between generations, and describes patterns of behaviour, or links between people.

necessary, you must ensure that proper safeguards are considered, and in place, *before* there is any significant contact with the service user.

However, you should regard the information recorded on file with some caution. It may not be accurate, and may also be out of date. (Accuracy can often be judged by close reading of the referral information, as contradictions can sometimes show up.)

Familiarisation with a service user's situation in advance of an interview will obviously depend on what information is available in the agency, but at a minimum it is likely to involve looking at any previous notes about the person already held by the organisation. If there is a chance to discuss the family situation with a worker who may have had previous contact, this can often be very helpful.

## Referral study

When there is no previous information and a service user is unknown to the agency, at the very least you should look critically at the referral information. A referral should not be accepted uncritically: note where the information originated, and assess its reliability, before using the referral facts to make tentative notes of the family structure.

When properly completed, referral information should contain basic details about the person or family involved. It should tell you the address, individuals' ages, and whether (on information currently known) the family is a single- parent one. A referral is also likely to give ethnic background, and will often disclose who the next of kin might be, and the GP with whom the service user is registered. The Victoria Climbié Inquiry made it clear that, for a social care worker, knowing a person's GP is *essential information* (Victoria Climbié Inquiry website). It would be most unusual, therefore, for an interviewer to be expected to make contact with someone without the opportunity of first knowing a little about their situation. With increasing experience, it will usually be possible for you to tentatively theorise about the scenario you may be visiting, even when only very limited information is available.

In addition, when forming initial judgements based on referral information, you need to consider the role – and perhaps bias – of the person who made the referral. If it is a **'third-party' referral**, then that person may perhaps have his or her own perspective and feelings about the referred service user. Even when it is accurate, such a third-party agenda may not parallel the view of the person referred; and, of course, it may not *be* accurate.

An informative referral should indicate how the person referred views the referral, and whether they consent to the agency's involvement.

<table>
<tr><td>

**Definition**

**A 'third-party' referral**

A referral coming from a person other than the individual named as the service user or client on the referral. It could also come from an organisation involved with the service user, such as a community centre or housing advice office. A good referral makes clear if the service user is aware that they have been referred, or, if not, what risks justify the referral.

</td></tr>
</table>

Sometimes, of course, there may be situations of risk and potential harm, where permissions or approval have to come into a practitioner's evaluation of a situation. A judgement about the need for consent to involvement, and the referred person's ability to consent, may then need to be made. Such a judgement will need careful thought, possible consultation, and certainly thorough recording.

An initial referral, then, provides a first base. From this, you can begin considering what the person to be interviewed might need, and what you may need to accomplish together.

### How to get more information before an interview

Even after evaluating the referral and any previously written records, a further important step should be taken before conducting an interview. In this – the final part of the information-gathering process – you consider whether any additional information will be needed before you see the service user; and, if this is the case, what permissions may need to be sought.

Should the referral be from an outside agency, such as a Housing Department, or a voluntary agency, who may not be familiar with the referral needs of your organisation, it may be necessary to go back to the referrer and request more clear or precise information.

Other relevant information may not directly involve people. For example, it is possible to research some aspects of a client's situation by reading up on their special needs, or perhaps checking relevant websites. Data on rare diseases, or knowledge about resources for specific cultures, are two such instances.

However, advance information does not just come from files, a referral, or the Internet. Preparation for an interview, especially a first interview, can also include contacting other people for information or advice. While prior information can be useful, there is always the important issue of confidentiality to keep in mind. It should be understood and accepted that the service user has a fundamental right to privacy. As has been mentioned, unless there are situations of considerable risk or harm, the service user's consent should be obtained before third-party information is sought. If you feel further information is essential, but it is *not* practicable to obtain this consent, you might perhaps consider exploring information with outside agencies in *general terms*, preserving a service user's anonymity.

| **Practice issue** |
| --- |
| After reviewing information about the family available from the referral and file, Davina, the social worker, realises that current information about a decision from the Housing Department appears very relevant to the problem. Davina thought it was worth a phone call to the prospective service user seeking permission to contact a Housing Officer, before going out on the interview. |

There are both advantages and disadvantages to this method of work.

On the positive side, it may be possible to accomplish far more in an initial interview if you have been able to access relevant information from other sources. You will then have been able to incorporate this information into your initial review of the service user's position, and in planning your possible involvement.

However, there is an associated risk. Should the service user realise that you have sought further information, he or she may interpret this action as meaning that they are no longer at the centre of the assessment. Such a perception might well lead to loss of trust in you, which in turn could bring about an adverse change in the positive relationship you will be hoping to establish. Think carefully, therefore, about where and how you might collect additional pre-visit information.

**Interviewing without information**

Despite the very considerable advantages of gathering relevant information before an interview, there may be times when you might deliberately decide to go into an interview 'blind', without making yourself familiar with all the available information.

This might be a valid approach, for example, if it were designed with anti-discriminatory practice in mind, in order to avoid a risk of bias or prejudice at first contact. In such a situation, you may perhaps have learnt that different parties hold strong and conflicting views about the individual concerned; perhaps they have described the person in emotionally derogatory terms, such as 'manipulative', or 'egotistic'.

In such cases, there is a danger that even before meeting the service user you will have assimilated negative opinions expressed by third parties, and form a view based on these opinions; or it may be that some previous opinions –

including those written in a file – might be prejudiced. Being aware of such views in advance of the interview may well result in bias about the service user – and adversely affect plans for the interview.

---

### Practice issue

A hospital social worker was asked to see a pregnant mother on a hospital ward. Mrs B. only spoke Punjabi, but had been accused by another mother on the ward of stealing. She was also not eating. The social worker was asked to go and talk to Mrs B. With the help of an interpreter, it was discovered that Mrs B. had in fact wanted to borrow a knitting pattern, to knit a matinee coat for her baby. Communication difficulties had led to this action being interpreted in a negative light. The social worker also discovered that Mrs B.'s vegetarian diet, supposedly catered for by the hospital, had been spoiled because the cook had put gravy all over her food.

---

Clearly, if in this example the social worker had accepted the initial negative description of Mrs B. as being fact, the interview may well have gone very differently.

In general, however, only after considerable thought about the total situation should you make a decision to deliberately avoid reading or accepting available information. This analysis should involve weighing up the merits of considering more detailed information (but with the risk of potential bias) against going into the interview with less information, but with a potentially less biased attitude. Criticisms are certainly more likely if you have not apprised yourself of the background (Trevithick, 2000, p74). Service users may also wonder that you did not do your homework (Kadushin and Kadushin, 1997, p77). The essential point for you to establish is that the position has been thought through, and discussed with your supervisor.

---

### Consider this

Rosie was allocated a new duty referral that stated that Mrs Lee's housing worker saw her as 'loud and bossy'. Rosie felt that the statement was making a value judgement about the service user. Rosie did not want this opinion to cloud her initial assessment of Mrs Lee's situation, so wanted to hear Mrs Lee's own views. After discussion with her supervisor, she therefore deliberately chose to talk first to Mrs Lee, and read other file information later.

What do you consider are the advantages in Rosie's approach?

Do you feel there are any potential risks? If so, what might they be?

---

In general, therefore, review information beforehand:

- What do I know about this person's situation?
- What else do I *need* to know, before making contact with them?
- How can I locate this information?

## GATHERING INFORMATION TO TAKE TO THE INTERVIEW

### Paperwork

Most agencies have forms, particularly assessment forms, which will need completing with the service user, so an important part of advance planning for an interview is to ensure that all the relevant agency documentation you may need is at hand. If possible go through this beforehand. Such study can be surprisingly time-consuming, and time is not always an abundant commodity. This stage of 'documentation study' may seem tedious, but you do need to appreciate that being familiar with documentation is useful, as written information backs up what you may say.

In planning, you will also need to look at forms to be filled in *during* the interview. For both parties, form filling can often give rise to understandable anxiety, especially if this is the first contact a service user has had with a social worker.

Carefully going through forms in advance of the interview is good practice. It is likely to empower the service user and reduce anxiety if you are able confidently to share information, and establish that you can understand and explain forms.

If you are new to an agency, you will obviously be unfamiliar with their 'relevant paperwork'. Sometimes, to ensure that they do not miss anything, inexperienced practitioners may feel that they need to direct an interview in order to complete the required forms. However, even though your agency's assessment form may have a set pattern, it is not always a good idea to follow it slavishly. When you are new to interviewing, you may worry that you will forget to ask for some relevant and important information; so you should remind yourself that, even if you do miss something, you can always go back, or check by telephone.

In contrast, once forms have become familiar, an experienced worker is likely to take a much more relaxed approach to form completion. Rather than allowing its completion to direct the course of an interview, a skilled worker will extract what is needed for the form from a less obviously controlled interview.

Forms are a visually obvious symbol of a large organisation, so it is not surprising that, if not properly used, they may not only be off-putting to service users, but may also be perceived as bureaucratic and unnecessary. For this reason, completing forms during an interview may sometimes get in the way of making a direct, personal relationship with a service user, especially if they perceive you as concentrating on paperwork. Such a perception may raise emotional barriers surprisingly quickly, as it can appear that you are concerned with your employer's (or placement's) needs over theirs.

In more informal settings, any paperwork may appear intrusive, but you nevertheless are usually charged to make some evaluation of need. Keeping the intrusion of paperwork to a minimum, and explaining in advance what needs to be done, can both be helpful, as can sharing the forms with the service user.

### Must forms be completed?

You can accomplish interviews, even assessment interviews, with a service user without any forms being completed *at the time*. There are certainly situations (for example, if a service user is not sure that they actually want involvement with the agency, or they appear particularly anxious) when it may be useful to be flexible, and dismiss all plans to fill in forms. However, it may take a great deal of confidence – and familiarity with the forms – to build up to this point.

What if you are in doubt over whether to fill in forms during an interview, or, instead, spend time on establishing a better relationship with service users? In such a case, it is almost always wiser to rely on taking brief notes, and to focus on the relationship. These 'brief notes' should allow necessary forms to be completed later – perhaps when you have returned to the office. To carry out this notes-to-form approach successfully, it can be useful to jot down, in advance, reminders of areas you need to cover, so that the official form, and on what page you will need to write information, will not be particularly obvious. This less focused approach is likely to be more time-consuming, and will take more effort, but it is usually well worthwhile in establishing a working alliance with a service user.

### Giving information

In any interview, information flows in both directions. In making practical plans for the interview, you should therefore prepare by bringing together in advance any information that you may need to *give* to the service user. The range of such information is potentially wide – for example, there might be practical or benefits-orientated pamphlets, information about the agency, details of resources, other agencies, and so on.

In a first interview, it may not be possible to do more than guess what information the service user may need.

---

### Practice issue

Ethan, a social worker, has an appointment to see Jane South, a woman in her twenties with a learning disability, who is still living at home with her parents. The daughter is not known to the local specialist day care facility. The referral has come from her parents, who have developed health problems.

Ethan looks out general information, and also specific information on respite care and the local day facility, in case either daughter or parents show an interest in learning more about support services.

---

### Complaints

If the interview is likely to raise strong feelings or negative emotions in service users, complaints information may have to be given out. While this is unusual on a first visit, it may follow the conveying of unwelcome decisions, perhaps about the allocation of resources. If a leaflet about how to complain needs to be handed out, it is worth considering at what point in the meeting it would be best to do so.

If a service user feels that they have a justified complaint, you may need to provide information about independent bodies and advocates able to support the service user through any appeal over a decision.

### LOCATION FOR A GOOD INTERVIEW

The location for a social work interview is the place that is chosen – or has had to be used – to hold the interview. Since the main focus of an interview is to exchange information and views, to ask/answer questions, and to discuss personal information, the location should ideally be as suitable as possible for these activities. For the advantages and disadvantages of various locations, see Table 4.1.

Normally, a social work interview will take place in one of several typical settings. It may be held in an 'agency' location, such as an interview room in a social work office or residential home; in the service user's home; in a setting where the individual happens to be (such as a youth centre, or a day centre), or in a neutral setting (for example, a supervised access visit to children may take place in an independent house). Apart from the service user's home, all of these are 'secondary' settings (Lishman, 1994, pp142–3).

**Table 4.1** Advantages and disadvantages of locations for interviewing

| Location | Advantages | Disadvantages |
|---|---|---|
| Service user's home | More relaxed. More privacy. Information on hand. Travel for SU not a problem. Can help concentration. | Possibility of interruptions. Possibility of Health & Safety issues. Lack of admin. back-up. |
| Agency setting | More formal. More privacy. Shows SU commitment (by attending a strange venue). May be safer. | More formal. You see SU out of usual social context. |
| Activity/community based | Preferred by young people. More informal. | Fewer opportunities for confidential talk. |
| Hospital | Can see SU quickly. You are able to consult with other professionals easily. | Privacy not guaranteed. Anxiety to get home may colour the exchange. Unfamiliar location for both SU and SW. Distance from family. |

Selecting the appropriate surroundings in which to undertake the interview forms a crucial part of interview planning. A suitable setting can provide a basis for the service user to feel empowered; or it can, for instance in 'authority' situations, reinforce the message of the interview.

If possible, the first step should always be to check whether the service user has any preference about where to meet. If they can choose a setting, they are more likely to feel comfortable meeting there, so the setting will give a feeling of empowerment. This is especially important to service users with learning disabilities (SCIE, 2004, p70). Davies talks about 'detached work', where very informal settings – walking together, driving in the car – can provide spontaneously intimate surroundings for interviewing (Davies, 1981, in Trevithick, 2000, p76).

When selecting a location, it should be kept in mind that it should be easy for participants to reach. Consider the service user – if you are not seeing them at home, are they able reach the chosen setting without difficulty? Remember, there may be mobility issues, or issues of independence, that might make it difficult or even impossible for the service user to reach a particular location. (If this is so, but it is important that a particular location be used, then you may need to think in advance about transport arrangements.)

We can therefore say that an interview location should ideally be easy to reach, and preferably should also provide quiet and relaxing surroundings, especially important should service users have issues with concentration. There will obviously be times when a formal approach needs to be taken in an interview, but even so this should not undermine a need for the interview space to be as private as possible, with as calming an effect as possible (Kadushin and Kadushin, 1997, p75). If its surroundings are positive and welcoming, an interview is likely to be less stressful for all parties involved (Lishman, 1994, p17). Any lessening of anxiety should assist people in understanding and retaining information, whether this concerns the interview itself or the discussion of a decision.

If service users are to make their own way to an interview that is held away from their home, quite apart from potential transport and finance issues, such travel will usually demand an additional degree of *emotional* commitment. While such demands may be appropriate when there is a strong commitment to meet for the interview, it may well be too much to expect if there is a degree of compulsion (as in, for example, a mental health assessment).

## Choice of location

When it falls to you to select the location for an interview, there might be a surprising amount of choice. Some agencies may have expectations of home visits, or a limited choice of interview venues, but you will often have to decide where the interview is to be held. Young people, for example, may well have a preference for an activity-based location, where the shared experience can emphasise a willingness to participate and lead to better communication (SCIE, 2004, p72).

Especially if many of the issues to be discussed are likely to be of a private and personal nature, privacy will be essential for ease of interaction. An appropriate choice of location will allow you to maximise your chances of effectiveness in the interview – although even the best location cannot guarantee all will go well.

| **Practice issue** |
| --- |
| Jess, a duty social worker, was called to an incident where Tracy, a young single parent, had been badly injured. Jess had to discover from Tracy whether there were any family members able to care for her children; the interview was carried out under considerable difficulties in the hospital's emergency room. |

### Safe locations

When there is a risk of hostility, the interview location will need particularly careful thought. If a serious risk has already been identified, then, whatever the other needs may be, that interview *must* be held in a 'safe' location – for example, an interview room in the social care agency. If it has to be held, say, in a person's home, then you have to ensure support is on hand. Any interview with a serious risk of aggressive behaviour should never be held in a location where support is not immediately available.

What, though, if the risk is not extreme, and there are solid reasons for holding the interview in another setting? If there should be any suggestion of challenging behaviour, it is important to discuss the specifics with your line manager. For safety's sake, in such cases it is normally good practice to attend the interview with a colleague. Additionally, you should always make sure your office is aware that the visit is taking place, its precise location, and a time by which you will telephone in after the interview is over. Should this expected call not come, a previously nominated person should automatically be alerted, and a prepared response triggered.

If there are serious risk factors, and support will be not immediately available, it is not safe to hold an out-of-hours interview in an agency office. It is far better to hold over the interview until back-up is available. If a risky out-of-hours interview must be completed, then you should always arrange a secure location, and insist on it being used.

Such arrangements may perhaps seem elaborate, even unnecessary, but they are not. If, for example, an interviewer has not called in by a predetermined time, they could well be at real risk – without being alarmist, workers have been injured and even killed when carrying out hazardous interviews. It is emphatically better to take sensible precautions.

### Agency location

Although 'agency location' could be interpreted as an interview in a room at a Local Authority Social Services office, it is actually a broader term. An agency setting, for instance, could be a hospital in which the service user is a patient, or the Housing Department at which they have arrived and presented as in need of help; it might be a youth centre, a training centre, or the day care facility the person attends.

When considering the emotional comfort of the service user, all interview settings are likely to have different resonances. Some locations will be unknown to the service user, who may consequently feel uncomfortable and disempowered in them. Lishman points out the effect of unpleasant surroundings on service users (Lishman, 1994, p17); people always feel more relaxed in surroundings that are familiar to them. (Kadushin and Kadushin, 1997, p81). Even if the setting is familiar, though, some locations may not be ideal. For example, if people have been in hospital for a long time, they may not feel 'in control' of their environment, and want to get home. They are unlikely to act as they might do at home because of this **hidden agenda**.

> **Definition**
>
> ### Hidden agenda
>
> A part of interaction between two parties that may not be verbalised or apparent, but nevertheless has a strong impact on that interaction. The participant may be aware or unaware of the pressure, which is normally related to strong feelings ('I want to get away, so I will say everything is all right'). A hidden agenda can sometimes be a plan with an ulterior motive, or, in a group, it could be an individual's agenda, at odds with the overall group plans.

One of the advantages of agency surroundings is that they are often specifically designed to accommodate people who need to talk about private matters. This can both mean that quiet rooms are available, and that people who work there will understand the need for privacy. On the other hand, there may be people within the setting who do not value social work, which may make for difficulties (Lishman, 1994, p142).

In addition, agency interview rooms should be designed for safety, have an alarm or panic button, and be free from objects that might be thrown. Moreover, in an agency setting supporting staff should always be available, and are likely to have training in what to do should aggressive behaviour occur.

There are, however, disadvantages to an interview in an agency setting. It inevitably means that you will have to see the service user while they are divorced from their support, that is, their familiar environment, and perhaps also from members of their family. Additionally, while an agency setting may be comfortable for a practitioner, a service user might perceive it as a powerful and controlling setting (Lishman, 1994, p17).

Figure 4.2 is intended to illustrate this point. Ms Wang appears to be simply seeking validation of her decision to move away from the area; but, in the official setting of an agency interview room, she is unable to do more than make a statement; discussion is not possible.

It is clearly important for the interviewer to pick up on this feeling, and to allow Ms Wang sufficient space to fully address the various issues that would be involved in her proposed move – by setting an interview away from the agency, in what Ms Wang considers a 'secure' location.

Ms Wang's situation can be taken as a useful starting point for a discussion on the issue of when it may (or may not) be appropriate for a duty interviewer to give up.

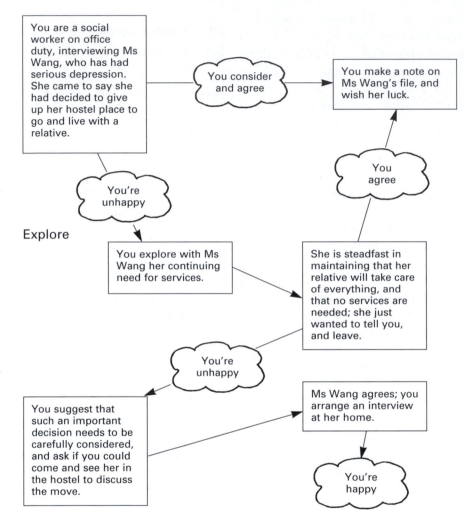

**Figure 4.2** Flowchart for interviewing Ms Wang

| **Consider this** |
|---|
| Under what circumstances might it be appropriate to 'make a note on the file', wish Ms Wang well – and say goodbye? What *disadvantages* might there be to such an action? |

What, though, if you have assessed the space where you propose the interview takes place – but it is *not* safe, relaxing, or even private? What might then be done? Clearly, if it is possible to request a change of location, or modifications to the suggested location, then this should be done. However, it is possible even for an experienced professional to feel intimidated by unfamiliar surroundings. As a consequence, if you are away from your usual 'space', you may feel much less comfortable about requesting changes that might make a better environment for the interview. However, you need to find a way through this, whether by enlisting the aid of a colleague, or by some other method.

### Planning hospital interviewing

Hospital interviews form a special case for specific forward planning. Although, in most hospitals, private rooms are available, a hospital setting can make it particularly difficult to coordinate arrangements for interview privacy.

While medical professionals should automatically understand the need for privacy, in reality they may forget, for example, that bed curtains do not block out sound. Consequently, hospital staff may sometimes be less than whole-hearted in helping find an alternative room that is away from curious ears. Additionally, general background noise can also be a problem in a hospital setting.

The hospital itself may often be a long way from service users' homes, making it hard for family or support network friends to visit – which can obviously also make their presence at interviews more difficult. Should the service user wish them to be present during your interview, this may be hard to organise.

A final, specific problem for a hospitalised service user concerns their mobility. By definition they are unwell – or they would not be in hospital; so will they be able to reach a proposed interview room unaided?

| **Consider this** | |
| --- | --- |
| Mr Mudd is recently widowed and had been in a motorbike accident, leaving him paralysed from the waist down. He is on a bay in the ward, with five other patients. You need to talk to him about plans for when he leaves hospital. The discharge will take some arranging, because of the dramatic change in his mobility. Ward staff say he is 'bed bound'. | What preparations should you make before talking to Mr Mudd? (One is noted below; but what other advance preparations may be helpful?) |

In this case we have a double problem: a service user who is unable to leave his bed, and a clear need for an interview to take place in a location offering privacy. A worker who simply turned up at his ward might therefore be forced to interview Mr Mudd at his bedside, while with an advance call to the ward you might well arrange for a (temporary) move for Mr Mudd and his bed to a private room.

## Interviewing in the service user's home

While initially it may feel uncomfortable, for many social workers knocking on strangers' doors in order to talk to them about very personal information becomes an accepted way of life. The experience of variety is part of the rewards of the profession, and it can be both a privilege and a chastening experience to share in the details of service users' lives. However, the choice of a home visit should not be automatic. As a part of the interview planning process you need to establish why you are visiting a service user at home, rather than at any other venue.

Service users normally accept practitioners into their homes; in many instances, too, they may prefer to be seen in their home environment. Such visits may well be necessary because the service user's environment forms an integral part of an assessment: for example, a service user may wish to point out hazards in their housing that have a negative effect on their health. Another reason could be that the social worker may wish to observe family interactions, or perhaps wish to talk to the main carer.

Whatever the reason for the choice of a home visit, the home setting will usually be where people feel most comfortable and relaxed, and where privacy is likely to be guaranteed. It is also the place where the situation that led to referral to the agency may well have arisen. Practically, too, people are also likely to have information to hand, should occasion call for it (checking on their benefits, perhaps); and it is obviously the location where you can best understand the service user's life. A full assessment of circumstances can hardly be accomplished without at least one visit to their home.

However, a decision by a service user to allow a stranger into their home, particularly a stranger with an official role, is likely to open up a new range of dynamics of interaction, potentially affecting their wider family, and even their relationships with friends and neighbours (Kadushin and Kadushin, 1997, p81). If it is necessary to see service users in their home surroundings, therefore, it is sensible to request explicitly about visiting them *at home*, and to give sufficient time before a planned appointment for them to prepare to receive visitors. (Obviously, if it is urgent, then other priorities take over.) It is important to keep in mind that cultures and people vary widely in how they feel about allowing newcomers into their homes. Also, as we have said, you will be visiting as a representative of what most people perceive to be 'Authority', adding to the potentially complex mix of feelings.

While most people live in separate houses or flats, a service user's home will sometimes form part of an institutional setting, such as a care home or nursing home. It can be strange to live in a place where people come in to work every day, often working in shifts. Very understandably, such an environment can give rise to feelings of disempowerment. Important issues of privacy, and even of control over who comes in through your front door, may be overlooked or forgotten in such a setting – but such issues should not be forgotten by you, and will need to be at the forefront of your planning.

We make no apology for stressing again that social work visits where there is an elevated risk of violence should *never* be made without first taking precautions. Indeed, it is sensible to take similar precautions at other times: for example, when interviewing a new service user (where the unknown nature of the situation is a potential risk) or when visiting a service user in an *area* known to be unsafe. It is also sensible not to make such visits late in the working day, and especially not late in the day on a Friday, when offices close and support will be much harder to coordinate.

Consideration of how to handle risk in interviews is dealt with in more detail in Chapter 9.

## How to arrange the venue for easiest communication

If a first interview is in a service user's home, it can be difficult to decide in advance where to sit, but thinking about this can be useful. This is because we can usually make some general assumptions: for example, people may draw emotional strength from their family, so would want to sit near them. This is especially likely if a service user is anxious, or emotionally frail, or perhaps too stressed to communicate clearly. Alternatively, if you are visiting because of family problems, tensions may be made worse by unthinking seating arrangements. Such factors will need taking into account in your interview planning.

As you will want to foster easy communication, you will need to be within a comfortable communicating distance of the service user. If you are aware of this need, and have planned for it, then there is obviously a better chance of it happening. There are also ethnic needs and customs to consider, which as we have said will need exploring beforehand. An example might be proximity – how close it is appropriate for an interviewer to sit to a service user? Appropriate proximity will also depend upon age and gender (Thompson,

2002, p101). If a male worker needs to interview a female service user, there may be ethnicity considerations as well as cultural gender issues to consider. Careful preparation is vital here, and drawing up a clear plan in advance is indispensable. Generating such a plan is likely to involve checking with service users, and confirming what feels right to them when you meet them.

### Symbolism in seating

You also need to be aware of possible wider implications inherent in seating arrangements. For example, if families are hesitant about choosing where to sit, then it is sensible to confirm directly with the service user whom they would prefer to have sitting next to them – and try and make that happen.

On other occasions, families may not be aware that where they sit in relation to others may be symbolic. Space can become uncomfortable if someone emotionally close to the service user is sitting far from them. One further example: if the parent or relative of a service user is sitting very close to them, this may not only make your communication more difficult, but could indicate the person's feelings about control.

---

### Practice issue

Pal went to see the Manni family, who had a long, thin living room, with comfortable chairs in all four corners. He had to decide which location was preferable: sitting far away from Mrs Manni, with whom he had come to talk; finding a smaller chair that he could place near Mrs Manni; or pushing all the chairs closer together. After checking with Mrs Manni, he chose to get a chair from the kitchen, but soon regretted it, as he was then sitting at a different height from her. On his next visit, after confirming Mrs Manni didn't mind furniture being moved, Pal was able to reach a more comfortable talking distance – and relaxed situation – by moving one of the armchairs.

---

If you do reorganise the seating, you should look for an arrangement that will foster the relaxation and easiness – or, in some circumstances, the authority – that you are seeking. Relaxing chairs are usually best, and chairs set at equal heights will reinforce the partnership and equality of the meeting. Even if there is no need to move them, changing the orientation of chairs is possible – for instance, seats placed at right angles rather than opposite to each other are likely to feel less confrontational. If there are only chairs of unequal height available, work out with the service user who should take which one, as symbolic power differentials may otherwise come into play (Lishman, 1994, p17).

Why did we say earlier: 'depending upon the nature of the interview'?

This is because some interviews need to be more authoritative, or business-like – for instance where formal papers need to be signed – so a natural welcoming strategy of offering comfortable and relaxing chairs may not then be appropriate. Additionally, some roles you will take on are those where it may be important to present more formally. For example, if you are acting as a representative of the justice system, arranging more formal, upright seating may well be preferable – and more effective.

### A welcoming environment

If you are thinking about arranging a peaceful atmosphere in which to discuss personal information with the service user, what else might help foster a welcoming environment? One common aid can be overlooked. The availability of refreshments – tea or coffee – can be very helpful both in generating a relaxed atmosphere and in encouraging communication.

### Distractions, external and internal

In an interview, the service user needs and deserves your undivided attention. In return, you hope for the focused attention of the service user. This means that either beforehand, or, at the very latest, before the interview has begun, you need to find out whether there are likely to be any distractions – and decide how to deal with them.

### External

Distractions come in many shapes and forms, but will be either external to the interview space, or internal, within the room. There should, of course, be the absolute minimum of *external* interruptions. If the interview is in an office, the telephone should be diverted if at all possible, and a 'do not disturb' notice clearly displayed on the door. It is sensible, too, to consider what else might have been planned, and so avoid holding an interview next door to an office party. On a home visit, if a service user's house is being redecorated, or is located next to major building works, or a neighbour's dog barks continually, it may be sensible to move the interview to a quieter location (Koprowska, 2005, p64).

### Internal

Make sure there are as few competing demands for attention as possible in the room itself. For example, if the interview is in the service user's home,

| **Box 4.1**     **Methods for asking for the television to be turned off** |
| --- |
| 'When your TV is on, I can't concentrate on what you're saying, and it's really important that I do. Would you mind turning it off?' |
| 'I can't hear what you are telling me with the television on in the background. I do really need to hear what you are saying. Could we turn it off, please?' |
| Keep speaking quietly. |
| Some self-disclosure of a hearing difficulty, if you have one, can emphasise your wish to hear effectively. |
| 'Can you hear me all right? It would be better for me if the TV were off. Do you mind?' |

you will need to negotiate with the service user before starting whether an 'on' television can be turned off. Turned off is preferable if at all possible, because just killing sound will leave flickering images, which are a surprisingly serious distraction (Kadushin and Kadushin, 1997, p83). See Box 4.1 for effective methods of request.

At home, young children can be especially demanding of attention. Strategies to try to prevent interruptions include carrying felt tip pens (and paper); and perhaps some baby Lego, so that there is always an activity for distraction. Parents are unlikely to be able to focus if the demands from their children are too great, so it often needs a visitor's encouragement to allow them to deal with their offspring's needs first. If the demands of children are likely to make an important interview particularly difficult, though, discuss together how this could be prevented, and perhaps reschedule for a better time, or even arrange childcare.

Animals are often overlooked as a source of distraction, but attempting to compete with a large dog for the attention of a service user can be tricky. Politely requesting that any animals are made safe before beginning the interview would undoubtedly be sensible.

The best plan is to identify possible distractions, and then plan with service users beforehand to fix times and dates when they think interruptions will be at a minimum.

## TIME FACTORS

Interviews should not be planned as **open-ended**. If you fail to set a clear time limit (at the very least in your own head), this will almost certainly lead to potential problems with focus, as well as making objectives harder to reach, and very possibly the interview itself a waste of time.

In more informal settings, setting time limits may sometimes be difficult. Conversations may turn into interviews (just as interviews have

> **Definition**
>
> ## Open-ended
>
> An interview that did not have an ending time defined before it began.

often more than one purpose); or interviews may have a diffuse agenda: 'How is this person today?' for example. If you have a *reason* for the meeting, and the service user understands it even in simple terms, then you can think of it as an interview.

These less formal encounters may well be more open-ended, but they are likely to be kept short by the brevity of the agenda. If the situation becomes more complex, however, then a more formal interview is likely to emerge. For example, at a skills centre you might enquire regularly about a service user with fluctuating mental health needs. If, one day, they appeared to be quite low, then this could be a trigger for a more private, and more focused, talk together.

In practice, the approach that tends to work best is to plan in advance. As soon as an interview is arranged, you will need to establish (as an essential part of your pre-interview planning) the time you consider would be reasonable to allow for you and the service user to achieve your joint aims.

If you are alert, it is at this stage that **overloading** may become clear. While the risk of excessive content is a potential danger, it can all too frequently be overlooked. Particularly when drawing up the aims and goals of an interview, you should always keep the risk of overloading in mind.

> **Definition**
>
> ## Overloading
>
> When the practitioner's expectations of what an interview may achieve exceeds what might reasonably be accomplished in the available time.

If you consider the issue of interview duration early on in the process, it will encourage the most productive use of time, and form an essential part of your overall interview skills.

### How urgent is the interview?

When deciding when to visit a service user, one obvious question to consider is how quickly you need to see this person. While easy to say, urgency may not necessarily be easy to evaluate – especially for inexperienced practitioners.

A useful tool in deciding how soon to visit is to measure the *importance* of a visit against the *urgency* of a visit (see Figure 4.3). Different parties may well interpret the degree of urgency in varying ways. Your viewpoint, as the

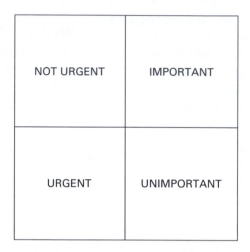

**Figure 4.3** Importance/urgency matrix

social worker, may be different from that of the service user, or even of the referrer. A useful rule of thumb here is to weigh up whether the person making the most sound is the person most deserving of urgent action. A practitioner will also be aware of other case demands, and will often have to make – sometimes very difficult – decisions about the degree of priority to be given to a particular request for involvement.

An agency normally takes the receiving of a referral as marking the beginning of the relationship with a service user. However, it is worth bearing in mind that before a referral is actually made, the service user may have been deliberating about the idea of making a referral for some time. There may also have been long-standing family complications that eventually precipitated contact with the agency (Kadushin and Kadushin, 1997, p69). It should be appreciated that even if, in terms of the agency's current priorities, contact does not appear urgent, the fact that reference to an outside agency has been made is likely in itself to have made an emotional impact on the service user:

> Social workers who are good at communication recognise the loss of dignity people experience when approaching social services for the first time – the 'cost' in this – and respond sensitively.
>
> (SCIE, 2004, p14)

Promptness is a trait understandably valued by service users, who are likely to appreciate speedy contact.

## Summary

- Plan how long an interview should be, given the needs of the service user, and what you need to accomplish together.
- Decide how urgently you need to see the service user.
- Inform the service user of any likely delays.
- Leave time *after* a meeting for recording, telephone calls, etc.

## KEEPING IN TOUCH WITH THE SERVICE USER

A good principle of communication is always to keep the service user up to date with events, even if there is actually little to report. A telephone call to give an estimate of a likely delay, or perhaps even an explanatory letter, can quell service users' apprehension. Not knowing when (or how, or even if) someone will establish contact with them can understandably raise anxieties. If a visit is not to be immediate, if at all possible offer an emergency telephone number, as well as a contact name. This will ensure that, even before a worker is formally allocated, service users will be easily able to communicate with the agency should it be necessary.

### Urgent requests

When faced with a demand for an urgent visit, it is even more important to consider whether there are investigations, file checking or communications with other agencies that ought to take place *before* the interview. A pressurised worker can easily become caught up in the perceived urgency of a situation, and want to respond to the service user's need to see someone quickly. However, it is always sensible to judge whether rushing to make an early visit will actually accomplish anything worthwhile. Would it be better contemplated after other events, for example, a doctor's call, have occurred? And what essential information will you need before you meet?

On the subject of timing, it is also worth considering whether you plan to contact other people, such as another professional, *after* you complete the interview. If so, how urgently might you need to make that contact? You will need to allow sufficient time for this part of the follow-up administration of an interview, *before* moving on to other demands. Allowing space for post-interview work is a good time management skill, and one that needs early integration with your interviewing practice (Kadushin and Kadushin, 1997, p297).

## Summary

- Critically examine issues of difference and empowerment, and adapt any plans in the light of anti-discriminatory practice.
- Carefully review information from the file.
- Contact others (if appropriate, and if permission is given).
- Read/enquire about specifics, e.g. illnesses, culture.
- Make yourself familiar with agency forms.
- Research other likely resources or agencies.
- Decide with the service user on the most appropriate location for the interview.
- Give some forethought to the practical arrangements.
- Consider how you can minimise distractions.
- Check out any time constraints.

## WHO SHOULD BE PRESENT AT THE INTERVIEW?

### How to decide

An important part of reflective planning is to decide which people to include in the interview. Perhaps the first question to be asked is: do I need to see this person alone? There are many instances – for example, when working with couples – where it may be quite difficult to see one person absolutely alone. Of course, particularly if involvement is relatively straightforward and does not involve an investigation, you are unlikely to need to see someone without their family. However, there are certainly occasions, for instance when the relationship between the carer and service user is in conflict, when it will be very important to interview people by themselves. If such a 'solo' interview is necessary, what methods can you use to make sure it is accomplished?

There are no universally applicable approaches. You will obviously have to be aware of cultural practices, especially important if gender or age differences are at issue. It can help if you make your goal clear from the start – usually best done when you arrange the interview. It may also help to explain what the agency expects you to do: for instance, your employer might expect you to see the person alone, even if only for a short while.

It is usually best to be frank about the need for an interview alone with the service user, rather than skirting around the subject, or attempting to arrange it obliquely. For example, you could say:

> Mrs Padel, as you know, I'm calling to see your son about some issues he's been having at school. I'd like to see him alone for a little while, and then perhaps you could join us.

Sometimes it may be necessary to deliberately *exclude* someone from the interview – for example if a partner were in fear of marital violence. The position will need to be carefully evaluated in advance, and special preparations made to request such exclusion appropriately. One obvious way to make it easier to see a service user alone is to negotiate an interview with them away from their home, or at a particular time or date when they will be on their own.

Why else would you need to exclude someone? As is made clear in the GSCC Code of Conduct (GSCC website), a service user has a right to privacy and confidentiality. This may, by their choice, exclude their family or friends from your interview. If it is not clear whether they would prefer to see you alone, then before the interview you should proactively seek that information.

Often, however, the reasons why you are not given space to see someone alone are more complex. A common one concerns issues of power in family relationships, where typically one person always speaks on behalf of another. In so doing, the family spokesperson is likely to dominate the conversation, so that the wishes of the service user are not heard. In other situations, ambivalent relationships may make a service user reluctant to express their true feelings. In such cases, you may understandably feel that unless you are able to see the service user alone, their wishes will go unexpressed.

Sometimes you may need to see the service user with an additional person, such as a professional colleague. There may be questions concerning joint or inter-professional interviewing (see Chapter 3) that will need additional pre-planning. Here, negotiating times and joint tasks beforehand is always good preparation, especially if the service user has not previously met the other professional.

## CONCLUSION

This chapter considered why it is important to plan interviews.

■  You need a clear understanding of why you are meeting with that service user at that particular juncture, and at that particular place. You especially need to be able to explain this in 'partnership' terms together.

- You need to understand both your and the services user's goals in advance, in order to assess whether the interaction has met them.
- Keep your aims in mind throughout the interview. Share and remind the service user of your mutual aims in a collaborative manner.
- Plan so that you do not 'overload' the interview.
- We looked at the role of information gathering before the interview, and the management of paperwork and forms.
- We looked at issues of location in terms safety, privacy and distraction.
- We addressed time factors, and the presence of other people at the interview.

## QUESTIONS

1   You have been asked to see a single parent who has requested that her school-age child be looked after. What preparations might you consider appropriate before the interview?

2   You wish to interview one partner of a couple where there have been allegations of physical violence. How might you arrange to see one partner on their own? If the other partner insists on attending the interview, how would you respond? Are there safety issues to consider?

3   A new GP referral has arrived. It concerns a man living alone, whose behaviour has been causing friction with his neighbours. It appears there may be mental health issues, as the doctor has also referred him to a psychiatrist. There is a next of kin listed on the referral, in the area. To whom should you speak, to get more details of the issues? Why?

    If you subsequently learned that the person speaks English as a second language, what might you additionally do to prepare for meeting?

## FURTHER READING

Egan, Gerard (2002) *The Skilled Helper*, Chapter 2.

Koprowska, Juliet (2005) *Communication and Interpersonal Skills in Social Work*, Chapter 4.

Thompson, Neil (2002) *People Skills,* Chapter 13.

# Chapter 5

# Questions and Interview Techniques

**NOSSC RELEVANCE**

The material discussed in this chapter relates to the following National Occupational Standards for Social Care:

- **Key Role One**, Unit 2 (2.2 to 2.4). Work with individuals, families, carers, groups and communities to help them make informed decisions.
- **Key Role Two**, Unit 5 (5.1 to 5.3). Interact with individuals, families, carers, groups and communities to achieve change and development and to provide life opportunities.
- **Key Role Six**, Unit 20 (20.1). Manage complex ethical issues, dilemmas and conflicts.

*In order to gather information during an interview, it is necessary to consider the use of appropriate questions. This chapter looks at the different types of questions that you may want to pose in the interview, and discusses suitable uses. As a contrast, we then consider the use of silence in interviews, and go on to other skills, drawn from counselling. There is also a section on non-verbal applications.*

**INTRODUCTION**

So far in this book we have talked in general terms about social care and social work interviews. We have described the settings in which interviews may occur, and have discussed in broad terms the reasons that social care interviews take place. Later, in Chapter 8, we will stress the need for 'observational distancing', so you will become aware of the process of monitoring your actions and techniques as they happen. This is all part of your skill base in communication.

As this book focuses on the practical side of interviewing, we need to examine just how you, a professional keen to improve your skills, may actually go about doing so. What should you say in an interview, and how might it best be said? What might it be sensible to *avoid* saying in an interview? These, and related issues, will be addressed in this chapter.

## AN INTERVIEWER'S SKILL BASE

An interviewer's collection of particularly effective interview skills could form what we describe as a professional 'toolkit', comprising a variety of practical techniques, practised, understood and ready for you to employ: a social skills model of interviewing. If we were able to examine it, what skills might this bag contain?

To answer this, perhaps we first need to take a step back, and consider what we mean by a 'skilled' interviewer.

It is easy to say that some practitioners have accumulated considerable interview experience, but what does this actually mean? Of what exactly is this 'experience' composed? What precisely *are* those practised skills and techniques that are likely to be of specific help to a less experienced person – or indeed to any worker keen to carry out an effective interview? And, importantly, from where do they come?

A good start would be to consider the attributes in an interviewer that are particularly valued by service users (Kadushin and Kadushin, 1997, p391):

- Being accepting
- Having emotional warmth, with empathy
- Being flexible, but with control of the interview
- Being psychologically open.

Generally, a competent interviewer will cover these points by having built up their expertise through experience and reflexive practice. They will remember the tactics that were successful for them, and which were well received by service users, and will then have refined these skills through reuse. They will also have remembered those tactics that did not work, so will avoid repeating their mistakes. While this method of empirical learning undoubtedly works, it has two major disadvantages.

First, such a learning process inevitably takes time. Gaining practical interviewing experience cannot be rushed, which is why so many capable interviewers have unavoidably spent years in painstakingly accumulating their knowledge. Although other variables may have an impact, it must follow that, in one sense, for much of the time they were only building up to their best practice.

Second, the process of 'learning by doing' must inevitably involve making mistakes. The consequences of mistakes in interviews are potentially wide reaching; we must remember that all our slip-ups in the field of social care interviewing involve service users.

A simple analogy may make this point clearer. Take the process of learning to play an instrument by ear; while this may be a lengthy process, it can certainly work. However, if, while learning, you accidentally play wrong notes, the result is value neutral – the only loss is your time. In strong contrast, mistakes made when learning social care interviewing are very seldom value neutral, and may quite easily involve considerably more than just your time.

By taking seriously the need to avoid unnecessary interviewing errors, this chapter is intended to encourage a much faster accumulation of basic interviewing techniques. Our discussion will therefore focus directly on a wide variety of potentially effective approaches and methods that may all be usefully included in an interviewer's skill base – or toolkit.

First, it always needs to be borne in mind that what are 'appropriate' methods will vary according to the type of interview. Choose what is the best and appropriate approach for each specific interview.

Nor is there one single skill. Any interview is dynamic, constantly changing – and sometimes dramatically changing. No single approach could possibly cover every interview with every possible service user. The effects of some techniques may perhaps be unfamiliar, and may need practice, while even familiar interview processes may benefit from a fresh approach. Our range of possible interview 'tools' is therefore very wide: for obvious reasons, they are mostly spoken – questions, comments, humour; but some are also unspoken – silence, respect.

## PLANNING REVISITED

In Chapter 4, we discussed the need for preliminary reflection and analysis, together with the need, before any interview, for some form of 'plan'. This will normally be a list of objectives, the targets to be aimed for during the course of the interview; and these may be practical or emotional in form.

In addition to creating this list, your planning should consider the potential feelings of powerlessness and difference that service users may experience, and may perhaps bring to the interview. You should also think about any specific methods of communication in relation to this interview.

Once all this has been accomplished, how might we actually go about achieving our goals?

## METHODS AND SKILLS

In the introductory chapter, we suggested that one way of looking at an interview was as a 'conversation with a purpose'. Let us think about how we might best accomplish this purposeful interaction.

In an ideal world, a service user would instantly and clearly provide all the details and information needed, and would always listen carefully and attentively to everything said to them in return. We must accept that such a scenario – while admittedly attractive – is unrealistic. Instead, you may well need to empower the service user by using your ability to instill confidence and trust, or to encourage them, through positive reinforcement. These are important skills; but chief among the additional skills necessary to an effective interviewer is the ability to generate and ask pertinent questions, and to ask them in a respectful and genuine manner.

## QUESTIONS

The most effective approach to the use of questions in an interview is to have thought ahead. Social work interviewing can be a complex business, so it is sensible to have thought through possible questions beforehand. Such advance work will not only allow you to prepare questions that are effective and relevant, but will reduce the likelihood of misunderstanding and confusion (Kadushin and Kadushin 1997, p77–9).

While it is obvious that you must be able to ask questions in an interview, in practice it is often far from simple. To generate suitable questions spontaneously is certainly not easy. To assist, let us break down the task, by looking at various possible *types* of question, before moving on to the practical application of these question types to specific interview situations.

## QUESTION CLASSIFICATION

The simplest and most widely known classification of questions distinguishes between two types:

■   Closed questions
■   Open questions

Kadushin and Kadushin (1997, pp235–65) also consider ambiguous questions, directive/non-directive questioning, leading questions, multiple, and open–closed questions.

Burnham (1986, pp110–25), approaching interviews from a family therapy perspective, considers (open) questions, and their importance in illuminating a hypothesis. He also talks about circular questioning, sequential, action-classification, diachronic, hypothetical, and mind-reading questions, all used in family therapy. Trevithick (2000, p86–93) also reflects on open questions, closed questions, 'what' questions and circular questions (as does Burnham, above). She also considers other questions (such as leading questions) that may best be avoided.

As we are primarily concerned with basic interviewing skills, some of the more specialised questioning techniques are not appropriate here; but it may help if we can consider questions normally used in social care interviewing as principally belonging to four main groups:

1   *Open* questions
2   *Closed, direct* and *specific* questions
3   What we describe as *intermediate* questions
4   More diverse questions.

### I   Open questions

Before the interview starts, all the information that you might need to gather from it may be far from obvious. Frequently, an initial plan may indicate merely that some aspect of a situation needs clarification, which usually means that some 'puzzling out', or asking for the information, will be necessary. Fortunately, our skill base contains a relevant tool – the 'open' question. These are questions commonly beginning with 'how', 'what', 'when', 'how much', 'where', 'who' or 'why'.

### Why do we ask 'open' questions?

In a social care interview, what actually *is* an **'open' question**? Perhaps the easiest way to explain this is by analogy. How might information be gathered on other occasions? Most people have had experience of completing a questionnaire, so think of your experiences when filling in a paper-based survey.

**Definition**

### An 'open' question

An 'open' question invites a service user to give a longer, and more informative, reply, rather than a simple 'yes/no' answer. It therefore allows the service user to interpret the question more subjectively, and so should provide more individual and possibly more 'feeling' information. Open questions usually begin 'when', 'where', 'what', 'can you tell me how', and similar phrases.

Most well-designed questionnaires consist of a series of simple questions, usually answered by ticking boxes. (Ticked boxes are analogous to the use of direct questions in an interview.)

However, the well-designed questionnaire is also likely to include space for you to provide answers that the designer of the questionnaire had not anticipated. For instance, if we were asking you to complete a questionnaire about your views on this book, we might ask 'Did you read Chapter 5?' – and the yes/no answers would certainly be helpful. However, if we also asked: 'What did you find was the best thing about Chapter 5?' your answers would give additional, relevant facts and opinions – information that would otherwise be very hard to find.

In an interview, open questions perform exactly the same role as those written 'best thing' questions, and provide a platform through which the service user can give us wider-ranging information.

Open questions, designed to create space for the service user to give their views about their situation, are probably the most important type of questions to be used in interviewing. They are particularly useful in the first stage of gathering information, when service users' viewpoints need stating and expanding. Fuller responses allow you to appreciate viewpoints, and understand situations more clearly. With this form of questioning you will hear service users' 'voices' more plainly, even if in consequence there are unanticipated responses.

A simple example of closed and open questions:

[closed question (defined below)]
Practitioner:    I understand you have been having trouble at night?
Service user:    Yes.

[open question]
Practitioner:    What exactly happens when you have trouble in the night?

### 'Why' questions

A why question – for example, 'Why do you feel that ... ?' – is an open question that can help you to understand motivations. However, service users may find a direct 'why' question uncomfortable, because it candidly asks people to analyse their motives. Not everyone can be self-aware enough to respond to this question; and directly asking 'why' may also reinforce feelings of guilt or blame. It may therefore be better to ask more oblique open questions, for example, 'What was going through your mind when … ?' (Kadushin and Kadushin, 1997, p258).

### 'What' questions

'What' questions are a very useful sub-group of questions to master, especially in the form, 'What if … ?'. They are broad and vague enough to be helpful in exploring the nature of the service user's issues, but can also play a part in the service user beginning to think through reasons ('What caused … ?') or even solutions ('What if you did … ?') (Trevithick, 2000, p89). The careful use of 'What if' questions can introduce future or parallel timelines, in which you and the service user can safely explore alternative actions and possible solutions. 'What if' questions can consequently be particularly useful to the service user in opening up the third stage of the problem resolution in Egan's framework of intervention (Egan, 2002).

### 2    Closed, direct and specific questions

The purpose of a direct question should be to establish a simple statement, of fact or belief. Ideally, a direct question should always be capable of being answered with a simple 'yes' or 'no', or a choice between alternatives. It should never require a lengthy response. A key aspect of the direct question is a need to clarify; this is because such questions are best suited to specific points. They should not, therefore, be compounded into more complex multiple questions.

For example, the question 'Would you mind if I brought a colleague on my next visit?' is a **closed question**; it can be answered 'yes' or 'no'. However, if the interviewer tried to gain additional information by adding to their direct question, 'I'd like to call next Wednesday. Or Thursday, but it may not be until Friday afternoon; is it OK if I bring a colleague?', then confusion is likely to follow. It certainly will no longer be possible for the service user to answer with 'yes' or 'no'.

**Definition**

### A 'closed' question

Closed questions are those that have a simple one- or two-word reply, usually 'yes' or 'no'. They are most often used to clarify situations, although, where there are communication issues, service users may prefer this type of question.

A direct question should therefore be both brief and clear. If you are not sure of a service user's capabilities, use of direct questions may be particularly appropriate. You should not assume that all service users are automatically able to understand complex or convoluted questions.

If there is a need for both simple questions *and* more information, you can approach a potentially complex question by breaking it down into simpler, direct sub-questions.

For example, if you are visiting an older person to find out whether or not they are receiving visits from their GP, district nurse, occupational therapist, daily meals – and perhaps also a voluntary visitor – how should you frame the questions?

SW:   Mrs Adebowale, Can you tell me – is the doctor visiting you? And the district nurse, and occupational therapist? Oh, and are you getting hot meals delivered, and what about a voluntary visitor?

You can see that service users may understandably feel bombarded and confused by this overload of interrogation. Far better for you instead to use a succession of limited direct questions:

SW:   I'd like to ask about people who may be visiting you, Mrs Adebowale. Is that all right? [pause, for agreement] Fine.
SW:   First, does the doctor call on you?
SW:   Good. Now, what about the district nurse? Do you see her?

'Specific' questions are another type of closed question. They are fairly simple to define, as they always seek detailed information on a narrowly defined topic. An example would be: 'What is your date of birth?' Specific questions are similar to direct questions, in that they require an explicit response, but cannot normally be answered with a 'yes' or 'no'.

Generally, when used in an interview, a specific question will provide an answer to an objective. For example, 'I need to find out if the Müller family are receiving any allowances' might translate into the direct question, 'Can you tell me what benefits you are getting, Mr Müller?'

Specific questions can be extremely useful, especially if time is limited. Their main disadvantage is that they may change the power relationship within the interview, and give the impression that you are not carrying out the interview in partnership, and that the service user's part in it is minimal (Nicholson and Bayne, 1984, p35). The service user may well perceive this approach negatively, particularly if a series of questions is asked without some preliminary explanation.

Clients can easily feel overwhelmed by a series of specific questions. For this reason, it is seldom sensible to ask several specific questions one after another. It is normally better to break up the series by inserting other questions, or even general comments designed simply to help the interview along.

SW: Now, you're OK with me asking you some questions, Aysa, to see whether we may be able to help you?
SU: Yes.
SW: Right. First, then, can you tell me your age?
SU: I'm twenty.
SW: And the ages of your children?
SU: Paula's four, and Mandy's three.
SW: Thank you. I should think they can be quite a handful, at that age?
SU: Yes, they certainly can!
SW: Mind you, they certainly look angelic enough now. Still, you probably could do with a break – do either of them go to a playgroup . . . ?

Here the worker deliberately broke up her questions with a comment about the children; such comments help prevent the appearance of cross-questioning, keeping the interview informal.

In summary, *closed* questions are:

■ best used to establish straightforward facts;
■ always easily understandable;
■ will, ideally, always have a simple answer.

A final use for closed questions relates not to finding out new information, but to the conduct of the interview itself. During the course of an interview, it can be useful to have reassurance that a service user is following what has been said. This also gives the opportunity to repeat points that you may not have expressed clearly. Here the direct question, 'Would you like me to go over anything?' can be a useful tool. An alternative is to ask the service user to repeat back to you what they understand of your conversation. Sometimes this may be difficult to phrase in a respectful manner – perhaps 'It's important that I know you've taken in what I have said. I'd like to hear in your own words', but the request is worth practising, as this is a very satisfactory method of ensuring that your communication is clear.

The main disadvantage of direct questions is that they tend to anticipate an answer, and are therefore less suitable in more complex situations, or where the service user may be influenced in their replies. If, for example, there is a

**Definition**

### A 'leading' question

Leading questions are those posed with a specific answer in mind; so, unlike the other questions we have discussed, they are not phrased neutrally. They close down choices and may lead service users into inexact answers. While leading questions have their place in some interviews, they should be avoided where the difference in power between service user and interviewer is great. Apart from the power issues this raises, the respondent may be led into trying to please you rather than be exact or truthful.

possibility of police involvement, **leading questions** (where a witness is led into an answer by cues in the question, rather than giving it unprompted) will need to be totally excluded.

An example of a leading question is, 'Did you sleep at your mother's house last night?' rather than using the open question, 'Where did you sleep last night?'

## 3 Intermediate questions

Before beginning an interview you will have planned your objectives, and should have a reasonably good idea about the questions you will need to ask. In reality, though, there may well be blank spaces in the scheme of questioning, because it is important always to be flexible, and capable of being responsive to where an interview may be heading. It is to fill these gaps that we may have recourse to what are called 'intermediate', or 'fishing', questions. These are designed to provide an interviewer with preliminary data; the answer to an intermediate question is not in itself important, but is intended to provide information to allow the later asking of a more consequential question. A (manufactured) example:

Stage 1, intermediate question:

SW: Do you want to get away for a break this year?
SU: Yeah, me and my boyfriend want to go for a week in Brighton.

Stage 2, specific question:

SW: If you went away, who would look after the children?

## 4 More diverse questions

Many other types of questions may be used in interviewing; some core ones are as follows:

■ Reflecting questions
■ Circular questions

- Hypothetical questions
- 'Scaling' questions
- Statements.

These are briefly discussed below.

### Reflecting questions

If you need to deflect, or buy time to think over a difficult question, a counselling approach may be helpful. An interviewer can reflect a question from the service user by echoing it back to them (Burnham, 1986, p105). Undoubtedly annoying if overused, this is the tactic of answering a question with a question. However, it can sometimes be very useful, and should become part of your skill base.

SU: Did you know that I was going to be evicted?
SW: What makes you think that I knew?

You can also use a reflecting question to better explore feelings:

SW: You ask me why you are feeling sad. What was going through your mind when you said that?

Reflecting questions should be used with caution, as they can feel awkward, and do not normally fit comfortably with the usual interactive 'flow' of an interview. However, service users do respond to such a non-natural format and the reflection of interest back to them, as long as the emotional tone of the reflection is apposite.

### Circular questions

Circular questions are another device used in family therapy (Burnham, 1986, p110). The term is used to describe questions you may ask of a third member of a family about the relationships between two other members (the dyadic relationship).

Example question:

SW: Zara, how do you think your father gets on with Dylan?

Burnham points out that this approach can provoke interest and curiosity in the family, and may lead to less stereotypical answers, and therefore to more honest communication. One essential qualification in their use, however, is that you need to be clear that you are only asking the *opinion* of the third person in this interaction. Should families appear reluctant, or do not have the skills to express emotional relationships clearly, a circular question can be particularly useful as a way to stimulate communication.

## Hypothetical questions

These are 'what if' questions (Burnham, 1986, p114). You can preface such questions with phrases such as 'Let's just suppose . . .' (see 'Statements', below). In family therapy, their purpose is to make differences of opinion clear: 'If your parents were away, which one of you would miss them most?' Or,

SU:   What would you suggest I do to stop him swearing at me?
SW:   Well, think about your family; who do you think would be most successful at stopping him swearing?

## 'Scaling' questions

Brief therapies, such as solution-focused therapy (de Schazer, 1985) may use a scale of 1 to 10 as a technique for service users to self-define priorities and feelings. The same scale is then used to define and move towards goals by incremental steps, such as:

SW:   So, you feel your level of depression is a 5. What do you think might help you to get from that 5 down to, say, 4?

This approach can be confusing or hard to grasp for some service users, or they may not see the point; and scaling questions may often be an inappropriate method for the setting and/or the interview. However, the rationale behind the use of scaling questions is to empower individuals to identify their own solutions, and then be able to move by small achievements to a position of confidence in managing their life. It may therefore be worth spending time beforehand explaining a scaling question's method of operation, and the reasoning behind it. If you are able to make conscious the methods you are using, and can engage service users, this approach can have significant effects.

## Statements

Although questions are the main method of drawing out information, information may also be gathered by use of a statement. This method may also be known as 'probing', or 'non-questioning information gathering' (Alberta Campus website). As mentioned earlier, service users may perceive an interviewer who is asking too many questions as intrusive. This can emphasise a difference in power, and negate partnership work.

Instead, by making a statement, or summarising what you think is happening, you may prompt the service user to vocalise, either in agreement or disagreement. At a simple level, using phrases such as 'Tell me . . .' or 'Describe for me . . .' can help the service user to give the same information as open questions, but with less formality. Using statements in this way is a method often employed by more experienced practitioners, and can be used to better understand motivation.

For example, instead of:

SW:    Why didn't you turn up for our meeting last week?

use of a statement might generate something similar to:

SW:    When you didn't turn up for our meeting, I thought that you were uncomfortable with talking about home. Am I wrong?

Naturally, the tone in which these statements are phrased is likely to be crucial; but undoubtedly the careful use of tentative statements in an interview can allow a more emotional and client-centred agenda to emerge.

## NON-VERBAL ASPECTS OF COMMUNICATION

While, until now, we have considered speech as the primary method of communicating between interviewer and service user, it is by no means the only way for you to establish positive communication and a helping alliance in an interview.

Non-verbal communication plays an important part in the skill base of an effective social care interviewer. In this section, too, we look at verbal *presentation* – in other words, emphasising not just the importance of what is said, but also *how* it is said.

## What is non-verbal communication?

Non-verbal communication (NVC) describes how we communicate without words, outside a language form. This type of communication may be used both consciously and unconsciously. Non-verbal expression can involve the use of many parts of the body: limbs, eyes, and head, for example, while holistic NVC derives from the total impact that individuals make, including the way they dress. Appearance can be a powerful reinforcer of speech, in either a negative or positive way.

A word of warning: *context* is important. Identical non-verbal gestures or acts will be perceived and interpreted in different ways, depending upon the emotional context in which they are being displayed. For example, sitting forward may show interest and concern, but sitting forward is also a pose of tension and anxiety.

Whether or not it is recognised, NVC is very likely to play a significant part in an interview; most researchers suggest that well over half the information conveyed in an interview is communicated in a non-verbal manner. Importantly, if there is dissonance between your verbal information and your non-verbal messages, a service user is likely to choose the non-verbal message as being the true one (Thompson, 2002, p97).

## For what do we use NVC?

Non-verbal codes and cues have a considerable range, and are not limited to just one area. So, although NVC will convey messages within the emotional arena of the interview, it may also touch on interpersonal communications, attitudes, roles and social skills.

First, NVC can be put to good use in communicating to the service user that you value them. This might be conveyed by something as general as arranging a relaxed location, but your posture and eye contact can also convey a 'positive regard' for the person, as well as indicating an interest in the subjects under discussion.

A simple instance of NVC lies in how interviewers stand – for example, if you conducted a home visit while remaining standing in a doorway, your client is unlikely to perceive you in the same way as they would an interviewer who accepted their invitation to come in and sit down.

NVC can also put across the impression that you accept people for who they are, and that you will not pass judgement on the environment in which you find yourself interviewing. This does not mean condoning inappropriate behaviour (if children are being physically chastised during the interview, for example), but it does mean that you should be very careful about demonstrating negative feelings regarding cleanliness, decoration or furnishings.

Importantly, where verbal expressions may fall short, non-verbal gestures and actions are able to reach out emotionally. A service user who is relaxed is more likely to be a proactive participant in an interview, but while someone in their home environment is likely to be more relaxed than someone interviewed in an office setting, this advantage may be quickly negated should the interviewer respond awkwardly or inappropriately.

---

### Practice issue

A field social worker (SW) once visited a service user who had been living on her own since her husband had died, some years previously. She lived in a state of confusion, and, due to physical limitations, had been unable to effectively clean her house for some time. However, a desire to be hospitable remained, and on the SW's first visit she offered tea. She normally only used one cup, she explained, producing a second cracked and very dirty cup for her visitor; although wiped on her dress, it remained smeared with grease and dirt. Anxious to avoid getting the interview off to a bad start, and aware that he should try not to turn down her offer, after rapid thinking the SW explained that, while greatly appreciating her suggestion, he never drank tea. He would have done much better to have been honest, because, on his next visit, she proudly presented him with a cup of coffee – in the same dirty teacup – which she had made by mixing 50% of liquid Camp coffee with 50% of (cold) evaporated milk.

---

At the same time, it can be important to be on the alert to *pick up* cues from service users about their state of mind, or to see if they are feeling any distress. Sometimes abrupt changes in physical behaviour, such as suddenly getting up to make tea, or fetch documents, can provide cues. Be aware of the concept of emotional 'leakage', too.

NVC, therefore, is likely to serve or reflect the quality of the interpersonal relationship between the interviewer and the service user, and will be a direct link to the emotional content of the interview. If you are to function effectively in an interview situation, you will do well to study non-verbal behaviour, and be alert and sensitive to its demonstration.

### Leakage

**Definition**

Where the usual expressions of non-verbal feelings may be held under conscious check, but show in, or leak through, another part of the body. Perhaps someone is irritated or bored, but still interacting as though they are concentrating. But their feet or fingers do a quick tap-tapping that shows there is another level of emotion behind the verbal exchanges.

### Non-verbal communication context

So far in this section we have made clear that NVC is of considerable importance both in conveying information to a service user and in helping you make sense of the complexity of information in the interview.

However, one important point to keep in mind is that NVC always occurs in a *cultural* context. This means that what may be normal and accepted non-verbal gestures in one culture might cause grave offence when used in another. Should you be planning an interview with people from different cultural backgrounds, then trying to learn what would be appropriate and relevant non-verbal behaviour in advance of the interview would undoubtedly leave you on surer ground.

| **Consider this** | |
| --- | --- |
| Different cultures have different cultural norms. A *downward* nod of the head may mean 'No'; a lively personality may be viewed as arrogant; wearing footwear in the house may be perceived as rude or unclean; prolonged eye contact can cause offence. To a Chinese person, it is seen as more respectful to present your card using both hands. | We have listed five ways in which typical UK behaviour may be perceived by other cultures as inappropriate. How many other examples of differing interpretations of non-verbal behaviour can you identify? Do you feel there are any other ways in which non-verbal behaviour may give rise to problems in an interview? If so, what might they be? |

### Faces

Importantly, on both sides, people 'read' the information gained about gender, race and age that they perceive as contained in a face, and may apply it consciously or unconsciously to their situation. 'You're too young to help me with my problems' is a reaction with which some practitioners are presented, and which they will consequently have to explore with service users.

Our faces and hands are the most expressive parts of our bodies, and the face has a wide range of expressions. Basic emotions (happiness, sadness, anger, surprise, fear, interest and disgust/contempt) can be read there. Facial expressions can also convey a strong sense of interpersonal attitudes, ranging from friendly to hostile, and superior to submissive/inferior (Cook, 1971).

Smiling, eyebrow raising and lowering can all convey messages that people will interpret emotionally and significantly. In particular, smiling can promote a positive aura, but it may not be correct in some circumstances (in Asia, a smile may be used to cover embarrassment, for example).

A factor of importance here is emotional *congruence* – keeping on the same wavelength of emotion – with the person whom you are interviewing, so working through feelings of sadness with someone should not be an occasion for high spirits. A smile at the wrong time may easily appear to be patronising or supercilious, while too many smiles may be perceived as ingratiating. Throughout the interview you will consequently need to study the impact you are making, and to be aware of non-verbal reactions.

Head nods, too, may be significant. The management of verbal exchanges relies upon cues from non-verbal sources, and may be very much linked to approval to continue given by a movement of the head (although eye contact and gestures will also contribute to this agenda).

---

### Group exercise

Create a staged interview, using two people. The rest of the group should observe from a distance – ideally, where they can see, but are unable to hear what is being said. The interview (it doesn't greatly matter what is discussed) should then carry on, while the observers attempt to learn what is happening just from studying non-verbal communication. An alternative approach is for the 'interviewer' and 'service user' not to speak at all, while nevertheless following through on agreed interview goals. What is indicated by their non-verbal interactions?

---

Gaze is included in NVC – an interviewer who gazes around the room, rather than looking at the service user, is for obvious reasons unlikely to establish a reasonable relationship. Maintaining the correct degree of eye contact is an important part of showing interest and involvement, but may be difficult to gauge. We tend to look less at people we do not like (Cook, 1971, p77); however, too much eye contact can be interpreted as dominant and threatening. In an angry situation, trying some less dominant gestures or gaze characteristics may improve the atmosphere.

A final point to remember is that, simply because human beings use their head and face in so many non-verbal ways, this is the area in which people have had the most practice in keeping their NVC under conscious control. This does mean that, if there is 'leakage', it is more likely to happen through other parts of the body.

## Appearance

While it may be difficult for the new interviewer to fully appreciate, there can be no doubt that how you appear to a service user can convey as much information as what you may say in the interview.

Both service user and practitioner are probably conscious of the impact of dress, neatness and grooming. These areas convey not just personality, but have the potential to reinforce role identity, and with it subtle messages about the relative superiority, or inferiority, of the players.

## Positioning in the interview

We have already mentioned that an interviewer who remains standing is less likely to be viewed with approval than one who accepts an invitation to sit. At the start of an interview, it is sensible to keep a few basic rules in mind, and, if you can, use your physical position to try to improve the spatial layout of an interview.

Seating positions in an interview should not be taken for granted. When interviewing in a service user's home, for example, remember that they may well have a favourite chair, and could well resent it being casually taken over by an interviewer – so asking, 'Is it all right if I sit here?' is both polite and sensible.

How close or at what angle the seating and the body is arranged (orientation) can reflect the warmth or ease of the encounter. A service user may benefit from such non-verbal reassurance that the interviewer is there not to be intimidating, but to work cooperatively. Remember, too, that distance can easily equate to aloofness (Lishman, 1994, p21).

## Posture and gesture

Posture can reveal not only something about personality traits (degree of neuroticism; openness), but also be a clue to emotional states, such as depression or agitation. Position can be important, too; sitting bolt upright, for instance, is likely to be perceived as being more intimidating than relaxing.

It is important to remember to avoid abrupt or sudden movements. Indeed, you may well consider a policy of purposely slowing down your normal actions. After speaking, you can also consider deliberately leaning back, allowing your body to reflect that you intend giving space for a service user to respond.

## Use of gesture

Although you may seldom think about the use of gesture, in an interview this form of NVC can be functional. It is a complicated area, as gestures (usually involving the upper body) are widely used for a variety of purposes. Such contexts may include: expressing emotions; helping control spoken interchanges; conveying personality or role; and, more formally, for social encounters and greetings. Gestures can even denote rank, or liking. We should not forget, of course, that gestures can additionally stand in for verbal communications.

Observation of gesture in people is commonplace and essential. However, it is in the *interpretation* of these gestures that one needs to be cautious. Many gestures used in interviews are to reinforce what is being said, rather than to convey meaning on their own. You can therefore help service users to follow your underlying meaning by keeping your words in step with the visual reinforcement provided by a gesture. An obvious example is the offering of two alternatives, with 'On the one hand . . . and then on the other', the words accompanied by moving each hand in turn.

Gestures tend to be individual, so interviewers will almost certainly build up a repertoire of gestures with which they are comfortable, and which they have used successfully. Rather than reproducing a list of possible gestures, therefore, we would simply encourage you to become more conscious of your own gestures. Try to practise and enlarge your range, and of course monitor any impact this makes on the interview situation.

## Non-verbal additions to speech

Effective speech is not monotone. It should have pauses, emphasis and stresses, speed and tone (angry, sad, high, low, loud or soft). So your tone of voice can also be a significant and sensitive method of communication. If you are rushed or anxious, that may well be reflected in your voice – although anxiety is associated more with errors in articulation or grammar (Cook, 1971, p80). Of course, the same emotional factors need to be looked for in clients' speech patterns.

## NON-VERBAL METHODS OF INTERVIEWING

Before discussing the uses of silence in an interview (covered later in this chapter), it may be appropriate to discuss the uses of *semi*-silence – or affirmative silence, or what for some time has been irreverently known as the 'nod-and-grunt' school of interviewing. Perhaps more acceptably, Kadushin and Kadushin call use of this approach 'minimal encouragements' (1997, p139).

Encouraging a person who is not naturally talkative to speak is a common difficulty. Often, inexperienced interviewers will attempt to encourage a service user into responding by asking them repeated questions. This approach will actually be counterproductive on several levels – continual questioning will not only raise a person's anxiety, but also allows them little or no time for reflection to consider a response.

So, with more experience, you may find that to help an individual talk more freely, it is inappropriate to continue asking questions. Instead, the careful use of encouraging non-verbal interjections may succeed rather better in working towards some common ground.

Comments and minimal encouragements such as 'Go on . . .' or 'And what happened then . . . ?' may be particularly helpful. A sympathetic nod, or perhaps an affirmative noise, is likely to be just as effective. Such minimal responses (together with similar reactions, such as an understanding look, or supportive 'mmm') may be of very considerable benefit. They tell the service user that you are alert and listening: 'they lubricate the interaction' (Kadushin and Kadushin, 1997, p139) – and do not interrupt the service user.

If the service user is convinced of your interest in what is being said – and, in particular, is convinced that you are clearly listening with careful attention to the details – then they will be encouraged to continue speaking. A lack of interruption from you also means that the 'flow' of client information will continue. If these verbal comments and non-verbal responses are carefully structured so that they cannot be interpreted (or misinterpreted) as condemnatory or negative, then the service user will not simply be reassured, but subtly encouraged to continue.

There are other situations when service users may be silent. In such cases, you must always consider whether there may be an issue with lack of power. Often, such a silence may stem from a perceived difference between the client's and interviewer's status. It could be that the service user has felt powerless, and so unable to refuse to meet you, and is now expressing their negativity in silence. There may also be cultural or ethnic factors that make people reluctant to speak freely outside their communities.

In practice, when you employ affirmative silence, what will often happen is that you can build a surprising degree of empathy. Because NVC works primarily on the emotional plane (Kadushin and Kadushin, 1997, p311) a service user may assume a far greater degree of empathy and support from your non-verbal responses than from your verbal statements.

We suggest that, if you have not yet done so, you try this minimalist approach in a suitable interview. Monitor its effects, and evaluate its impact on the emotional content of the responses.

## Challenging

Challenging (or confronting) is a further communication technique. When appropriately used, it can help you point up inconsistencies and gaps in presented information. Lishman (1994, p124–7) looks at five reasons to challenge:

1  Discrepancies: inconsistencies that may happen between talk and action, between verbal and non-verbal messages or between how people appear to themselves and others.
2  Distortions: when attitudes are markedly altered or extreme. There may be anti-discriminatory issues here that you need to challenge.
3  Self-defeating beliefs: a kind of distortion in self-belief that holds the service user back from change, or from a more accepting view of their worth.
4  Games: Berne's ideas (Berne, 1964) of conscious or unconscious ways of interaction that are not honest and direct.
5  Excuses: this could be to avoid or deny responsibility.

In an interview, there may be occasions when you need to ask the service user to reconsider what they say or do.

### Practice issue

A social care worker was helping at a London charity, a night shelter for homeless teenagers. Talking in the small hours with one young man, she listened patiently for some time as he smoothly explained the list of events that had led to him becoming homeless. Everything he said reflected well on him, and on the unfairness and malignancy of fate. Eventually he paused, and waited expectantly for familiar expressions of sympathy.

'What if we assume that's not true,' she said, 'what might have *really* happened to bring you here?'

He looked at her silently for a few moments, laughed, and then for the next hour or so told a rather more honest story, and one that reflected on the complex nature of his path to the night shelter.

The use of a challenge could be employed to point out inconsistent behaviours (Kadushin, 1972, p43) or perhaps to make a service user more aware of the power they have to change their own life. It is essentially a way of causing a re-think. As it can form a significant middle part of an interview, it is again important to consider *how* these challenges are issued. The words used ('challenging', 'confronting') may sound provoking, but it is the tone, possibly tentative, with respect conveyed at the same time as the challenge, that will prove whether the service user will respond negatively.

For example:

SW:    Did you notice that you've talked about 'him' all the way through? Could it be that you're not recognising the part that your mother may play in this?

Challenging is a powerful interview tool, but one that needs careful use; like any powerful tool, it can injure. Service users who have never had a powerful role in society, perhaps someone from an oppressed minority, may well feel undermined by challenges as to how they are managing their life. Challenges may be especially unwelcome from an authority figure with perceived power. You will need effective interpersonal skills to effect success here, especially to avoid presenting challenge as criticism.

## USE OF SILENCE IN AN INTERVIEW

If asked, you may well feel that an interview should normally consist of just two states: either the service user is talking while you listen, or you are talking while the service user listens. However, in practice, anyone observing an interview will see that it does not simply consist of continuous speaking, with only occasional changes of speaker. The spaces *between* what is said are of surprising importance.

When considering the skills to be used in an interview, therefore, we need not only to think about what is actually said, but to also reflect on the effective uses of silence. Deliberate silence (and not natural pauses between topics) in an ordinary conversation can give rise to social anxiety and unease (Kadushin and Kadushin, 1997, p213) and can also have this effect in an interview, too. However, in a social care interview, the deliberate use of silence has some valuable functions.

First, silence is likely to be needed to allow service users to respond in their own time. People are very individual in speech, and indeed in other methods of communication, and to respect this difference it may be necessary for an interviewer to resist speaking into the gap of silence. Filling this gap too soon may affect a service user's confidence, and additionally give the impression that you are rushing things.

Surprisingly, perhaps, silence may also often be a correct response to a straightforward statement from a service user, particularly if the information they have just provided is of importance to them. If, instead of a thoughtful silence, you instantly respond with a further question or statement, you will not only be acting without consideration, but will certainly risk appearing not to have listened to the emotional import of the statement. Rather than hastening to comment in such a situation, therefore, it is normally far better to respond by the use of an attentive silence, and back this up with any appropriate non-verbal gestures (a slow nod of agreement is particularly useful).

The planned use of silence can also be an valuable interview tool because it gives a service user thinking time – time to work out their thoughts or meditate upon them, and decide what is appropriate to say.

Let us suppose that you have asked a question, and received the awkward response, 'I don't know'. Here is some advice:

> When the client answers 'I don't know', do not nod, do not respond, do not even move. Don't do anything for 6 seconds – count them in your head. (Any acknowledgement of receiving the 'I don't know' will mean it's your turn to talk.) Something like 75% of your clients will start developing an answer within 6 seconds. The ones who don't will often repeat the I don't know, and you can then say 'It's a difficult question' and continue with 'Suppose you did know' or 'pretend you knew', or just let the 'difficult question' hang in the air . . . I have often used this technique of just waiting, and have had it work pretty well. I try not to change my facial expression (of hopeful curiosity) or body position and I wait until the client says something again. Most often they say something different. Occasionally, they say, 'nope, I just really don't know' after about 15–20 seconds and THEN I do something with it.
>
> (www.enabling.org; used with permission).

A parallel range of responses to silence, derived from Wolberg, is outlined in Kadushin and Kadushin (1997, p217).

In an interview setting, short silences also have other uses. For example, you may need to make a series of factual statements. Interspersing these with deliberate pauses will not only make each individual statement easier for a person to understand and assimilate, but will also allow additional emphasis to be placed on each point.

In practice, too, as we have said, it may well be essential for you – having made an important point – to seek confirmation that it has been fully understood. Your plea for feedback can be enhanced by the well-judged use of a brief period of silence.

For example:

SW:   . . . and those are your responsibilities under the order the Court has made.

[Pause]

SW:   Are you quite clear about what I have said?

Here, the use of a conscious pause allows time for information to sink in, while additionally, by deliberately allowing the service user a period of obvious 'thinking' space, you have emphasised the importance of what has been said. For this reason, when communicating important information in an interview, it is usually sensible to try to follow it with a brief period of silence.

Trevithick (2000, pp103–6) discusses silence in terms of 'creative' silences and 'troubled' silences. 'Creative' silences are those that appear beneficial to the service user. Productive use, in terms of thoughts and feelings, can be made of the quietness. In contrast, 'troubled' silences indicate negative emotions, such as anxiety, fear, or anger, or withholding (ibid., p104). She makes the point that the cause of a service user's silence is often unknown, and is therefore potentially much more uncomfortable and complex to handle. In such a case, it may be sensible to do some checking out, if you can, although there is the risk of further silences.

The conscious use of silence to encourage a response from a service user is sometimes known as 'drawing out', and is a powerful tool in the interviewer's toolkit. It can follow on from 'thinking time', but its drawn-out nature can become uncomfortable for you. You may have to judge how uncomfortable it is for the service user (Thompson, 2002, p125).

A brief period of silence is normal, and 'drawing out' may be employed fairly frequently, but beware of its overuse. Longer periods of silence – discussed below – may be much more complex.

## Longer periods of silence

The uses of silence that we have so far described are of those that are of fairly short duration – typically, a pause of between 5 and 30 seconds. In an interview setting, however, silence has other uses. Long silences are more likely to occur when the service user is a reluctant one, for instance a teenager being interviewed following anti-social behaviour. However, the use of longer periods of silence as a deliberate interview procedure is beyond basic core skills; in practical terms, it is essential carefully to rehearse how to handle a long silence, and discuss your use of this technique in advance with your supervisor.

Silence emerges in many situations: interviewing service users of an introverted nature, or perhaps service users who feel that privacy is not possible in the current interview setting. If possible, talk about the underlying reasons, or try to seek some common ground on which you can begin structuring connections.

Silence, in general, therefore:

- allows service users to communicate in their own time,
- gives them thinking time,
- can emphasise the gravity of statements,
- acknowledges to service users the importance of statements they make.

However, longer silences can be harmful or difficult to handle. Discuss and prepare with the supervisor. Note that talking with the service user about the reason for their silence may help move the interview forward.

## QUESTIONS *TO* AN INTERVIEWER

You may well be able, as we advise, to plan the interview and produce a list of appropriate questions in advance. This will allow you to enter an interview with confidence that you know what is needed, and how to accomplish it. However, such a rational plan does not allow for possible feelings of 'expect the unexpected', or nervousness – on either side.

In a 'real-life' interview, people are unlikely to consider themselves limited simply to the role of responder to your questions. It is far more likely that service users will themselves ask questions. Indeed, you should be mindful of power inequalities, alert to communication issues, and will normally want to encourage questioning as a way of being open and accountable to the service user. However, some questions may well feel awkward, and harder for you to answer.

## Answering difficult questions

During your interview, the precise degree of difficulty you experience when faced with a question will depend upon many variables. Generally, though, 'difficult' questions will probably fall into one of three main categories:

1 Requests for information about agency or worker actions (or actions of another agency/worker).
2 Requests for professional information that you consider to be confidential.
3 Questions seeking some kind of personal information.

## 1 Requests for information about actions

Social work operates fundamentally from a position of openness and trust (GSCC Codes of Conduct). If asked directly, therefore, you should normally give a service user whatever information they may request, in a courteous manner, providing the information directly concerns the service user, or those for whom they have responsibility.

Sometimes, though, you may not wish to provide information, perhaps for example because you may see it as likely to cause anger, and you prefer to avoid a confrontation. Rather than blocking such requests totally, it is best to *set aside time,* and then work through any potentially negative reactions. Answer fully and frankly, and then deal in a straightforward manner with any issues that the service user subsequently raises. However, given the social work tasks of 'gate-keeping' and control, occasional confrontations will unfortunately be inevitable.

Should some practical reason make it impossible to provide information or answers during the interview, the best plan is usually to undertake to provide it as soon as possible afterwards – and then remember to do so!

SW: I'm sorry, Mr Zeta, but I just don't have that information with me – it's back at the office. I can see it's important to you, though, so I'll check when I get back, and call you; or would you prefer me to write you a letter?

## 2 Requests for confidential information

In interviews, one valid reason for withholding information is that it is confidential and you are not able to disclose it. Sometimes, too, it is simply not possible to provide the information that people are seeking. In such a situation, try not to avoid the issue, or change the subject, but instead address the concerns directly, and as fully as possible.

For example:

SW:   I appreciate that you would like to know the address of your ex-wife, but I am afraid I am not able to tell you.

If at all possible, it always helps to explain exactly *why* you are unable to respond:

SW:   I appreciate that you would like to know the address of your ex-wife, but I am afraid I am not able to tell you. As you know, she has specifically said that she does not want you to get in touch with her; and I have to respect her wishes.

If you are not sure whether or not it is appropriate to give information, explain that you will need to find out; do so; and *return* – either with the information, or with an explanation.

Incidentally, while blaming management or colleagues may seem at the time an appropriate reason for not giving information, it is not professional to do so. Quite apart from other issues, you are the representative of the organisation, and are seen by the service user as the representative; you should not avoid this responsibility.

One very useful response to a service user requesting private information is to explain that, as a social care worker, you have a guiding personal and professional principle of confidentiality. So, just as you will not pass on their confidential information to other people, you are unable to give them information concerning others.

Finally, it may be important to make it clear to a service user that any information they may give you cannot be kept secret, and will always have the potential to be shared. Organisations keep records, and service users' details will quite properly be discussed with a supervisor. Should a practitioner, for some reason, be unable to continue visiting, a colleague taking over would obviously need to know what had been happening.

Additionally, there is always the risk of harm to consider. Should you be made aware of risk or injury to a child or older person, for example, this would be a prime reason for having to break confidentiality.

It is also sensible to be aware of the distinction between the sharing of information with relevant colleagues within your agency, which is totally acceptable, and sharing information with outside individuals, which is not.

## 3 Questions seeking personal information

Let us consider requests for personal information from two perspectives.

First, while an interview cannot, of course, be spent discussing your personal circumstances, there are nevertheless occasions when it may help to encourage communication or perspective by sharing. For example, 'Yes, I have some understanding of your problems – my little boy had a period when he wouldn't sleep all night either.' Although it can certainly help when people share similar experiences or feelings, it is worth remembering that situations too close to your own can lead to transference – the unconscious transferring of feelings and attitudes about significant people in your life onto others.

Occasionally, then, disclosing personal information may certainly be helpful; some service users are also genuinely interested in their social worker. However, for reasons which should be obvious, it is important to know where to set limits.

Second, it is important to consider how far it is appropriate for the interview topic to be diverted in this way. Such a total 'switching' of the focus of the interview is potentially quite complicated. Some service users may feel uneasy at having attention focused on them, so will seek to return the interview to more of a conversation. Additionally, personal questions (posed either consciously or unconsciously) may be intended to try to divert you from other areas of concern. There are also other reasons why a transfer of attention in the interview is likely to be inappropriate.

So, when faced with a request for personal information, a suitable response might be along the lines of: 'I appreciate your interest, but this is *your* time, to look at *your* situation.'

Should you learn that certain service users do not view the interview as 'their time', careful pre-interview planning can help you decide on a more formal contract together, one that should allow you and the service user to limit outside discussion.

### Positive statements

So far in this section we have considered only potentially negative and neutral questions from service user to interviewer. What, though, of statements which, rather than negative, are actually *positive*? Here, of course, we have to consider that such statements may be of two kinds: compliments concerning your professional role and work, or affirmative personal remarks.

All social workers, being human, will probably be pleased if they are, for once, on the receiving end of flattering rather than critical comments.

Unfortunately, in an interview situation it is certainly possible that positive remarks of either kind (however welcome they may be in theory) will in practice prove to be uncomfortable, and dislocating to the interview plan.

At the very least they will be disconcerting, while the motivation behind such a comment is not always clear. Why was the praise given at this time? Might this change the relationship with the service user in unforeseen ways? Did the comment have a distracting purpose? Do the remarks perhaps relate to more personal characteristics, and were therefore more unexpected? Were the remarks made at an appropriate time, such as the ending of your involvement? It is important for compliments to be balanced with all the other processes happening in the interview.

Typically, you need to be aware of the service user's feelings and of your own needs: accept the comment with thanks, but move on.

## Use of humour

It is probably unappreciated by the general public in regard to social work interviewing, but the use of humour can make the work much more manageable; it is a rare office that has never turned parts of their daily working life into a subject for laughter. An ability to view the work lightly at times does not in any way negate the importance of taking service users' lives seriously, and with respect. However, the occasional use of humour can leaven anyone's work, and show that you are keeping the stresses and strains of the job in perspective.

What, however, of your face-to-face involvement with the service user? Is there a role for humour here, too? Well, yes, there may well be. While we are certainly not advocating packing a joke book in your briefcase, we do say that it may on occasions feel right to bring a sense of humour to your interview – as well as an ability to laugh at yourself.

Kadushin and Kadushin say humour can help cement your relationship with the service user, be a vehicle for offering general and personal insights, help release feelings, make challenging easier, or assist in breaching barriers to communication (1997, p227–8). While it must obviously primarily depend upon the service user's situation, the use of humour to lighten a mood, to round off an interview positively, to shift a depressing conversational direction, or just simply to bring pleasure and enjoyment to the interview, is potentially a great strength.

Humour can sometimes be used as an 'avoidance' tactic, though – it can prevent you being serious about something. You will also need to judge the effect that your sense of humour will have on the individual situation. As long as you keep respect for the person, and the humour is monitored for any prejudicial feelings (Thompson, 2001, p23), fun or jokes may well make for both a more enjoyable, and more productive, interview session. However, when considering the use of humour, keep three points in mind: humour is hard to learn – it probably has to come from your own personality; you need to have known someone a long time before you can judge whether – and when – to use humour; and, finally, if you are not sure whether to use humour, refrain.

Service users are as likely as anyone to appreciate appropriate lightheartedness. And it can, of course, be a two-way process: humour may not just come from you. A social worker reported:

> one of my most enjoyable memories of interviewing came from visits to a man in his 80s, with a diagnosis of terminal cancer. His happy and teasing manner made every visit to him a pleasure; I always left feeling not sad, but uplifted.

To summarise: there is no doubt that if you are open to the use of gentle humour, and possess the ability to see the funny side of social work, it can transmit a feeling of optimism to the service user. Encouraging the service user to respond naturally to humour can help develop a relationship; what you say may be better remembered – while humour can certainly help lighten the bureaucratic nature of some visits.

## CONCLUSION

This chapter looked at some core skills in questioning for use in an interview.

Non-verbal communication (NVC) is a particularly significant, if not the most crucial, part of the interview. This is because it subtly conveys so much about the values and attitudes of the interviewer, and the regard in which they may hold the service user. Other NVC issues concern how to make the interview environment pleasant and relaxing, or how to set the scene for a more formal meeting, depending on the nature of the interview. This area of NVC was examined particularly in relation to how an interviewer could be conscious of, and appropriately enhance, their own NVC. Most crucially, there followed a discussion about NVC cues that practitioners need to interpret from service users themselves.

We also addressed:

- Open and closed questions, and when to use them effectively.
- More complicated questions, such as reflecting, hypothetical, or circular.
- Other ways of seeking information (such as statements or asking people to define how they feel on a scale of 1 to 10) that are more comfortable for the service user.
- Challenging in terms of what you hope to accomplish, not in a confrontational style.
- Using silence and being able to tolerate it.
- Anticipating being asked questions by the service user.

## QUESTIONS

1   You are assessing a couple from different ethnic backgrounds as potential adoptive parents. What questions would you use to get them to describe their relationship? How would you ask them about any adverse/negative aspects of the relationship?

2   A service user remarks that you look attractive today, to which you respond with a simple 'thank you'. He then goes on to admire your hair and clothes. How do you respond now? Are there gender issues here? Would you check out any cultural issues if the service user were, say, from an Eastern European background?

3   Your last meeting with a teenage boy under the Youth Offending Team has been largely silent. What different approaches could you try to make the next interview more productive?

## FURTHER READING

Brown, Helen Cosis (2002), 'Counselling' in Adams et al. (2002).
Kadushin, A. and Kadushin, G. (1997) *The Social Work Interview*, 4th edn. Chapters 6, 8 and 9 all deal with questioning skills.
Lishman, Joyce (1994) *Communication in Social Work*.
Trevithick, P. (2000) *Social Work Skills*.

# Chapter 6

# General and Specific Communication Skills

## NOSSC RELEVANCE

The material in this chapter relates to the following National Occupational Standards for Social Care. However, communication skills are an essential attribute of all your work.

- **Key Role One**, Unit 2. Work with individuals, families, carers, groups and communities to help them make informed decisions.
- **Key Role One**, Unit 3. Assess needs and options to recommend a course of action.
- **Key Role Two**, Unit 5. Interact with individuals, families, carers, groups and communities to achieve change and development and to improve life opportunities.

*This chapter examines in detail the ways in which an interviewer and service user may communicate during an interview. After outlining the importance of the relationship and some general communication skills, it describes some more detailed communication skills for working with people with special communication needs.*

## BEGINNING COMMUNICATION: ESTABLISHING A RELATIONSHIP

Interviews have many layers. One particularly significant layer is the *emotional* content of interviewing: the part of the process whereby you show that you are listening to service users, are attentive to and respect what they are saying, and have a genuine desire to work cooperatively with them, forging a working alliance.

Certainly, when a service user feels comfortable, and has confidence in you, interviews can be easier for both participants. Such an understanding is particularly beneficial when you are working with the same service user over a period of time. There can be little doubt that establishing a helping, or working alliance potentially makes an interview more relaxed, and more effective. This 'communication bridge' (Kadushin and Kadushin, 1997, p100) is likely to be of great support to both of you in reaching the intervention goals.

What makes an appropriate relationship necessarily depend upon the assessment, and the planned objectives. You may build very different *kinds* of relationship; for example, an offender who needs regular statutory interviews will need a different type of relationship to that needed for supporting a single- parent family experiencing life stresses. In the former situation, the relationship will need to be both more formal and more official, reflecting your role. In such a circumstance, any social conversation would tend to come after, rather than before, the business of the interview.

For illustrative purposes these two examples have been extreme; in reality, it is likely that at times most interviews will contain varying elements of both approaches. What should be a constant, though, is your awareness of the importance of striving to form a professional and positive relationship with the service user.

## COMMUNICATION SKILLS

In Chapter 4 we described the many stages – and ensuing efforts – involved in planning and setting up an interview. Ultimately, however, your real work will begin when the interview finally starts. Knowing what you have planned to cover, and having a clear

### Communication skills

**Definition**

Communication skills (in social work) are the combination of verbal and non-verbal skills and methods, based on psychological precepts, that help you relate to people. These skills enable you to convey information powerfully (using methods appropriate to the individual) so that information is received and clearly understood. There is also a reciprocal range of listening skills: listening attentively and giving feedback, to make sure you have heard and understood the service user's viewpoint and situation.

Communication skills often mean setting aside personal feelings in order to convey a professional positive regard for the individuals you meet.

understanding of what the interview is intended to achieve, are of course beneficial starting points. Now, you will be at the stage of the interview when communicating clearly becomes a key factor, so people will hear, take in the messages – and respond. Your communication abilities therefore form an essential part of your skills as an interviewer.

When considering improving your communication skills, a useful start is to think about the following list, compiled by the SCIE, on qualities that service users value.

---

**What Service Users Want: Key messages from service users and carers**

Social Workers who are good at communication, and

- Are courteous.
- Turn up on time.
- Speak directly to service users, not carers or personal assistants.
- Don't use jargon.
- 'Open their ears' and 'think before they talk'.
- Listen and 'really hear' and accept what carers are saying.
- Explain what is happening and why.
- Do what they say they are going to do and don't over-promise.
- Say honestly when they can't help.
- Are patient and make enough time to communicate with disabled service users.
- Recognise the loss of dignity people experience when approaching social services for the first time – the 'cost' in this – and respond sensitively.
- Don't assume anything about a user's abilities simply because of a disability.
- Understand the importance of privacy, peace and quiet and users' and carers' choice of meeting place.
- Know that closed questions can be easier for service users with communication difficulties to answer.
- Check out that they've been understood.
- Find a mode of communication that works.
- Remember that young people may prefer to talk while doing something else.
- Build trust, empathy and warmth.
- Work in organisations that help them to do all these things.

(SCIE, 2004, pp13–14)

---

Communication can use all five senses (seeing, hearing, touch, taste and smell). Perhaps the first and most obvious sense that we use within an interview framework is that of hearing – much of our interview communication depends on this, although, as we have discussed, non-verbal communication also plays an essential part.

## ACCESSIBLE LANGUAGE

Social work interviews normally have at their heart an exchange of verbal and non-verbal information. For this reason, a central issue in interviewing concerns the use of **accessible language**. When you are planning an interview, build in this consideration. Then take time to consider if there is any specific vocabulary that you will need, perhaps to discuss key areas. To emphasise: unless the person you are working with understands clearly what is being said, your chances of successfully working in collaboration are low.

> **Definition**
>
> **Accessible language**
>
> A manner of communicating adopted flexibly by an interviewer. It considers the needs, and, specifically, the verbal understanding of a service user.

In common with other professions, social work gives rise to communication between colleagues that employs specialist language and 'jargon'. We may use specialist jargon easily and unthinkingly when talking to colleagues. However, to make yourself clearly understood in an interview setting, avoid such specialist language. As an example, consider a person's compulsory detention in hospital through the use of mental health legislation. The phrase 'admitted under a section', used naturally by a social worker, understandably sounds puzzling to a layperson. Even 'assessment' may be an unknown and foreign word to many people, and so may need 'translating' into more everyday language. Words, and especially the use of specialised vocabulary in service user/worker relationships, can all too easily be distancing. Unless the worker is careful, their unthinking choice of words may easily become an issue of power, and highlight difference; while a correct choice can reinforce partnership working.

As you become more experienced, practice and reflection will ease most exchanges. With more practice, you will find that you consciously (or even unconsciously) adopt a wider but more focused range of language and expressions. What you feel to be suitable language and expressions may well change from interview to interview, reflecting the differing needs of different service users. As Kadushin and Kadushin put it: 'workers need a vocabulary rich enough to convey the meaning of their thoughts, and varied enough to adapt to the vocabulary of different clients' (Kadushin and Kadushin, 1997, p31).

## ANTI-DISCRIMINATORY LANGUAGE

You should be careful to select and monitor both vocabulary and phrasing in an interview. However, you may then be using a vocabulary that is unnatural to you, and which may sound stilted. In these circumstances, it is important to be sensitive to the issue of 'talking down' to a service user. Values of courtesy and respect should always inform your relationship with service users, so it is worth examining your non-verbal gestures and actions if you have to considerably modify your usual mode of speech, to ensure they match the verbal content of the interview.

Natural speech is also full of expressions and concepts that arise from one's own cultural experience. English, in particular, is not a straightforward language to make gender-neutral (for example, we still talk about 'manpower', and most people refer to a doctor as 'he'). Such language-related gender bias reinforces the 'invisible' nature of the female experience (Thompson, 2002, p91). Women can feel patronised by being called 'duck' or 'love'; so you will need to first check with them if you seriously intend to use these, or similar, expressions.

In the same way, oppressions felt because of class, ethnic background and other differentiations are often reinforced as a result of language used to or about individuals – and people vary a great deal in what they consider offensive. You should always bear in mind that 'words do not simply describe things, they *do* things, and thus have social and political implications' (Parton, 2002, p241).

Vocabulary is not the only aspect of verbal communication with which you should be concerned, because although you may be communicating in English, it may not necessarily be the other person's first language. You therefore need to be aware of the cultural frame of grammar, social pleasantries and subtleties.

---

### Practice issue

When meeting an Asian client for the first time, Andreas always tried to remind himself that he might think Asian speech abrupt. He knew this was because of different structures in the grammar, so abrupt speech did not necessarily carry other messages. He therefore made a conscious decision to put such speech into a cultural context.

An emphasis on clear communication will normally help the interview to flow freely, although an important secondary reason is to help the service user feel relaxed and comfortable. In some circumstances, you may want to practise speaking out loud before the interview. This helps if your phraseology is likely to be unfamiliar to the service user, or if you have to use words that lie outside their normal vocabulary. Attention needs to be given to ensure that communication in the interview will be a two-way process.

## OTHER COMMUNICATION SKILLS AND TECHNIQUES

### Paraphrasing

This attending skill is drawn from counselling, and has application beyond the interview situation. Paraphrasing (para = near, similar) is a method of repeating back to a person the gist of what they have been saying, but using different vocabulary. It is a fairly powerful tool, as the service user should hear very clearly that you have not only been listening to them, but also that they have been understood. Paraphrasing in an interview is quite different from ordinary conversation, and can therefore feel strange to practise, particularly as it requires concentration. The paraphrasing may have a cognitive aspect, but can also have a feeling or affective element (Nicholson and Bayne, 1984, p37).

For example:

> SW: What I'm picking up is that you feel you did the right thing in moving out when Nathan became violent . . .
>
> (Reflecting back on the service user's decision/intentions)
>
> However:
>
> SW: It seems that you felt alone and scared when Nathan became violent . . .
>
> (Focuses on feelings, and a far more emotional level of attending behaviour)

### Reflection

Reflection is a means of showing service users that we are connected with their experience and emotions, by reflecting back what they have said. It is a form of paraphrasing, but concentrates more on mirroring the actual words that clients use. It also needs to pay due respect to service users in terms of tone, questioning and confidence (Lishman, 1994, p26). It can be simply phrased, such as 'Tell me more about . . .', but should be used only where you have a genuine aim to know more (Nicholson and Bayne, 1986, p36).

It can be even simpler: 'He was out with a gang till one a.m.?' – or: 'A gang?', maybe 'One a.m.?'. As you can see, it gives scope for changes in emphasis or direction.

### Summarising the interview

Summarising is a useful technique to practise and learn early, since it is used so frequently in interviewing. As we have said, it is always sensible periodically to paraphrase what has been discussed during an interview – especially at turning points in the encounter – to ensure that a service user is not being confused, and does understand. (These can be called 'staging-post' summaries.) Periodic summarising is obviously more important when the interview is lengthy. However, it is also important at the end of a session to bring together the achievements, problems and unresolved issues. Summarising is the way to do this. Egan (2002, pp131–4) suggests other times when summarising can be useful:

> **Summarising**
>
> Summarising is a technique of reviewing the themes, or what has happened in an interview, so that the essence of the interview is encapsulated. It clarifies that a service user has understood the situation in the same way as the interviewer. Although a summary may occur within an interview, especially at transitions, it occurs frequently towards the end of an interview, when all the strands are being brought together.
>
> **Definition**

- At the beginning of sessions – to help things move on at a reasonable pace.
- When a client does not seem to know where to go with actions or words. Helping them to a summary can clear the thinking.
- When a person needs a new insight into issues.
- If a session is going nowhere.

While the initial interview plan will naturally have appeared realistic when you made it, it is not at all unusual for some new issues to arise. You may also have to transfer unresolved issues to a new agenda, for a future session. As will be discussed in Chapter 7, formally summarising to bring the interview to a natural close is not its only function. Additionally, a verbal summary

makes it possible to clarify the understanding of both parties: their understanding of what has been achieved, and what remains to be accomplished.

Jotting down these points at the time can be helpful. However, if informal
recording in this way is not practicable, summarising should be part of the
end of every interview.

A good interview summary should:

- be in client-centred language,
- show that an interviewer has listened,
- give time for feedback, to reassure the service user that they have been
  clearly understood,
- come towards the end of the interview, so that outcomes can be agreed.

## Encouraging specificity

Helping service users to be more specific about their issues can be a useful
technique, and is also a great help in your assessment of risk. People may be
vague about their concerns, or have a generalised worry (Nicholson and
Bayne, 1986, p39). Attaching these feelings to concrete examples in their experience helps service users to define for themselves where their priorities lie, as
well as helping you look for patterns in the behaviours presented to you.

## Paralinguistics

Paralinguistic cues are the baggage attached to speech – the tone you use, the
stresses you put on words:

- Volume
- Articulation
- Inflection
- Intensity

- Stress
- Speed
- Pitch
- Intonation

An example of this may occur when someone possessing a strong regional
accent attempts to communicate with a service user whose own accent is very
different: the cues can be very different for different communities. There is a
clear need for you to respect the cultural identity of the service user, so in these
circumstances it becomes especially important to build in checks and feedback
on whether the service user is understanding what is being communicated.

Miscommunication may also occur when a *service user* makes use of
different inflections. In this case, you can take a similar approach to ensure

understanding – summarise progress at regular intervals by paraphrasing what the service user is saying. As we have said, this will ensure increased accuracy in the interview, while at the same time reassure the service user that what they are saying is being taken in and understood.

As well as attempting to avoid language that might prove hard for service users to understand, you should also consider speaking more slowly, and pausing at regular intervals to check the service user's understanding.

You should never assume that either your own or a service user's understanding of an interview is total.

## Meta-communication

We all use meta-communication. It is a way of diversifying the message of the verbal communication, sometimes even contradicting it. 'I'm sure you're right' is a typical sample phrase that, depending on the way it is said, and the emphasis given to individual words, can give very different messages. Non-verbal actions may also negate or alter the spoken message. Service users may give complex or mixed messages, which you may then have to puzzle out, by using clues in the messages, to interpret what is *actually* being expressed and felt.

Meta-communication essentially suggests that you should educate yourself not to take everything that is said to you at face value. While the words may appear to indicate one thing, careful assessment may reveal their real, very different meaning.

## SPECIAL COMMUNICATION NEEDS

We now come to a varied group of service users: those individuals who have **communication impairments**. This issue needs to be approached with structural aspects of discrimination clearly in mind. How much is the preferred manner of communication a matter of the service user's decision – or do they have to 'make do' because the organisation hasn't taken on board their needs? Are services adaptable enough not to cause, or reinforce, oppression? As a representative of your agency, what might you be able to do to improve the way the agency communicates with its public?

People may have communication impairment from birth, or it may emerge later in life, following illness

> **Definition**
>
> **Communication impairment**
>
> 'Although people may have language, and understanding, they may use it in ways that are difficult for other people to understand; or they do not use speech at all' (SCOPE, 2002, p1).

or accident – for example, after a stroke. There are also service users who have a sensory loss, such as a visual impairment, which may affect their communication. Communication issues also include those individuals who are in need of support services, such as interpreters, in order to optimise their communication with English-speaking people.

## Language impairment

First, let us consider a service user who can speak, but has difficulty in verbalising their thoughts so that others can understand them plainly. To help their communication, it may be possible for someone who knows them well to assist in the interview. Such help can certainly be invaluable, although there are two potential problems. First, the dependence may detract from a person's confidence, and your direct communication with them. Second, it should not be automatically assumed that a person who knows them well necessarily has a beneficial emotional relationship with them. You may therefore need to reinforce the individual's sense of independence by encouraging them to communicate without assistance whenever possible, but listening if they, indeed, do want a friend or helper to be present.

When you are working with a service user who may have slow thought processes, or who is slow in speech, you should be prepared for your communications to take as long as is necessary. The service user needs their say, combined perhaps with some non-verbal interaction. You should certainly not attempt to move the interview forward by briskly contributing what you believe are the word or words for which a service user is searching. An ability to wait patiently for a response, and, especially, to avoid distracting contributions, is important in any interviewing; but it is particularly relevant for supporting service users who experience expressive communication impairments.

A service user's lack of ability to interact verbally does not mean we can't carry out an interview. In such circumstances, the use of gestures can be invaluable. You can also use a note pad and pencil, allowing written language to substitute for speech. Drawing can help. We remember one occasion when a service user with throat cancer was reduced to helpless laughter by attempts to help him communicate by drawing pictograms. (In case you are tempted to try: draw a series of representational pictograms (or cartoons) covering the points you feel the service user may wish to make, and ask them to select the appropriate one – or to draw one themselves, of course!)

Learning one or two words in any special gesture language, such as Makaton (used to communicate with children with learning disabilities), may be particularly useful. Such gestures – especially those of greeting, or of significance to the service user – can make the rapport stage of an interview far easier.

A wide range of devices and aids that have been specifically designed to assist individuals in communicating is available – examples include the artificial larynx, speech amplifiers and similar devices. Should you not already be familiar with such aids, it is well worth taking the time to become aware of them.

## Visual impairment

When speaking with a person who has a visual impairment, keep in mind that 'the voice should convey the expression'. While always important, the paralinguistics of speech (tone, volume and so on) will assume paramount importance here. When communicating with a service user having a visual impairment you should speak in your normal voice. Be aware of paralinguistics, and be particularly careful not to speak too rapidly.

A useful learning experience for anyone concerned in working with people having a visual impairment is to practise carrying out an interview with your eyes bandaged. You will rapidly appreciate being unable to evaluate the meaning of a conversation by studying appearance and other non-verbal cues. It can be especially hard to depend solely upon tone of voice in an interview in order to judge emotional reactions.

Even though touch is now a sensitive and culturally laden area in interviews, you should be prepared for a service user with a visual impairment to wish to use *tactile* communication. While it may be unusual, you should appreciate that anyone with a visual impairment is often able to obtain valuable additional information through touch – for example, by feeling the outline of your face. Be prepared not to display shock, or indeed to react in any way that could be perceived as rejection. Some people suggest that you should be proactive, and ask whether the service user would like to feel your face.

Generally, an adult will always be likely to ask permission before making this sort of approach; but children with visual impairment may understandably be less aware of the social norms that make feeling a face unusual.

---

### Practice issue

One worker reported: 'I can remember one child with a serious visual impairment assessing me at an early meeting by touching my face, and then saying, "Oh! You've got a beard! I didn't think of you as having a beard . . ." However, I'm still not sure exactly what that meant!'

---

**Interviewing a person with a learning disability**

Talking with service users who have a learning disability can certainly be one of the most complex areas of social care interviewing. This section deals directly with some special approaches needed, and we gratefully acknowledge the help of Mencap, UK, who wrote guidelines especially for this book.

First of all, an 'interview' suggests a formal process that may be linked to some form of assessment. Formality can be intimidating, so it is important to make the process as relaxed and non-threatening as possible.

## How to make the interviewing process more relaxed

- As far as possible, hold the interview at a time and in a place that the person has chosen, or is known to be comfortable with.
- Explain clearly who you are, why you are here, and what will happen next. Make sure you tell people how the information they give you will be used.
- Interviews near mealtimes or other important activities for the individual should be avoided.
- Make sure the environment is well lit, calm, and without distractions.
- Make any information that you send the person prior to the interview clear and easy to understand. Use Plain English and appropriate symbols and pictures to support the written word. Use a clear font, like Arial or **Comic Sans**, and make the font size at least 14 point, and bigger if you can.
- Be on time, and make sure that you have allowed enough time to do the interview.
- Be prepared to terminate the interview and re-organise for another time. A person may become tired, lose concentration or just have had enough, particularly if there are lots of questions to deal with.
- At the end, remind the person about what will happen to the information they have given you. Explain what happens next, and, if appropriate, leave behind a reminder of the next actions. This is particularly helpful if the interview is part of a process.

## People with a learning disability will have difficulties with communication and comprehension

Acknowledging this fact is not patronising, but recognition of the worth of the individual, and your responsibility to treat them equally.

Try not to make assumptions about what someone is understanding from or communicating to you. A person may not have clear speech, but this doesn't mean they don't understand what you are asking. Equally, a person may have good verbal skills that mask the fact they would find extra support helpful. Focus on each individual, and adapt your questions and style to them.

## Tips for effective communication

- If you are asking something long or complicated, break it down into smaller steps.
- Use pictures, symbols and photographs to support communication, both to ask questions and for giving answers. Talking Mats™ are an excellent tool for asking questions and finding out people's opinions and choices (see resources).
- Find out if the person you are interviewing uses a particular communication method or system, and be prepared to use it too.
- Find out if a person has particular needs or likes and dislikes when being talked to, and respect them. For example, a person may like you to sit on their left, or not make eye contact, or to sit on the floor. They may need quite a lot of time to think about their answer, or to find the words they want. Be patient and relaxed about this.
- If you are using pictures, symbols or photographs, choose ones that are clear, do not have too much unnecessary detail, and are unambiguous.
- Ask open questions, ones that do not need a simple yes or no answer.
- Check with the person that you have understood what they have told you.
- Some people will respond to the first or last thing you have asked them.

  For example:

  SW:  Would you like to live in a flat, a house or a bungalow?
  SU:  A bungalow.
  SW:  OK, let me check that. Would you like to live in a house, a bungalow or a flat?
  SU:  A flat.

- Pictures may really help, as they can be spread out, moved around and talked about. Using a picture as a starting point, you can give more information, or tease out what a person really wants to tell you. In the example above, for some people, visiting the different types of home may be the best way to understand the choices on offer.

■ Thinking in the abstract, projecting into the future, or about things of which you have no experience can be really hard. It can help if the interviewer relates questions to things the person, or people they know well, have experienced.

■ If a question is proving really confusing, leave it and move on. If it is essential to the interview that the person answers the question, think of other ways to ask it.

■ Don't be scared to try drawing to support your questions! Even simple stick figures can really help understanding.

Remember, *everyone* can communicate.

**UK Resources for people with learning disability**

**(1)   Mencap**
Mencap's Accessibility Unit can help you make documents easy to understand. They can give you advice on layout and choice of words and images. The Unit can also make documents accessible for you.

   The Unit also delivers training on communication awareness, use of symbols and pictures and making things easy to understand. The Unit will also develop training to meet particular requests.

**Contact**
Accessibility@Mencap.org.uk
www.Mencap.org.uk

**(2)   Clear Consultants**
Clear provide a wide range of training, including making things easy to understand, communication, and how to use symbols and pictures.

**Contact**
Jill.eddlestone@clearforall.co.uk

**(3)   Talking Mats**[TM]
Talking Mats were developed at the University of Stirling and are an excellent tool for finding out an individual's choices, likes and dislikes. If you are new to Talking Mats and using symbols and pictures it is strongly recommended that you buy the training video and booklet.

**Contact**
aacscotland@stir.ac.uk
<www.psychology.stir.ac.uk/old/AAC/about>

**(4) Worth A Thousand Words**
A huge bank of photosymbols that are tailored to the needs of people with a learning disability. All the models in the photos are people with a learning disability.

**Contact**
Pete@photosymbols.com
<www.photosymbols.com>

**(5) Change Picture Bank**
Black and white illustrations that are widely used by adults with a learning disability

**Contact**
changepeople@btconnect.com
www.changepeople.co.uk

**(6) Widgit**
Widgit produce a range of packages that allow you to write using symbols and words. You may find that children and younger adults in particular use symbols to support communication.

It's important to remember that just putting a document into symbols will not automatically make it easy to understand. Mencap, Clear and Widget can all give advice on using symbols.

**Contact**
info@widgit.com
www.widgit.com

**(7) Useful websites**
See Bibliography for these.

### Interviewing through an interpreter

We hope, after reading the previous sections, that when you are interviewing you will be keen to ensure that a service user clearly understands you. However, one of the most difficult situations you will face occurs when you must move beyond communication aids. Consider a situation where there is no shared language at all between you and service user. A third party will then need to become involved, someone with sufficient language skills to act as a 'bridge', allowing communication to take place that would otherwise be impossible.

In such circumstances you will need to seek the assistance of a bilingual interpreter, whether of spoken or sign language. With their help you can ensure that the purpose of the interview is fulfilled, and that you are able to establish a working alliance with the service user.

Sometimes a young person may be put forward to act as an unofficial interpreter, perhaps for a parent or grandparent lacking spoken English. However, while certainly convenient, this is rarely appropriate. Quite apart from privacy and confidentiality issues, it can lead to serious confusion in family roles. If offered such an unofficial interpreter, try to devise an alternative strategy.

If the service user and you speak a common language, but understanding is less than perfect, there can be a real possibility of mutual misunderstandings. While a complete lack of a common language presents an obvious need for assistance, you and the service user need not be *totally* uncomprehending of each other's language before the involvement of an interpreter becomes appropriate. Should the reason for an interview be sufficiently serious, it will be essential for you to convey any information clearly. If the information provided by the service user could be ambiguous, then the services of a translator may become indispensable.

A couple of useful indicators may help identify a service user in need of a translator. You should ask a question that the person needs to answer in a sentence. Avoid closed questions that can be answered with 'yes' or 'no', or a very familiar question such as 'Where do you live?' Listening closely to the answer should give a fair idea about the service user's comprehension. Kadushin and Kadushin point out that communicating in a second language often uses mental concentration in the translation, and emotional vocabulary may be restricted in the second language (1997, p348).

A second method of judging a service user's command of reasoning in spoken English is to ask them to repeat back in his or her own words some information that you have just given them.

## Arranging for an interpreter

First, make sure to arrange the interpreter's appointment with as much notice as possible. There can often be a wait for an interpreter to be free, and, if so, this will need acknowledging.

Remember, the interpreter is there to enable *everyone* to do their jobs completely, not just one person. The interpreter should primarily be used for the purpose of conveying information from you and to you, in a language that the service user can understand. The interpreter is not supposed to analyse what is said, or decide what information should or should not be conveyed. She or he is also bound to maintain confidentiality.

When requesting an interpreter, find out which language and dialect is appropriate. For example, Taiwanese people sometimes become confused by terms used by an interpreter from China, Hong Kong or Malaysia.

The ethnicity of the interpreter is also important. Some service users may not wish to have interpreters from specific communities, perhaps for political reasons, or because of confidentiality fears in small communities. For example, it may be inappropriate to provide a Serbian interpreter for a Bosnian Muslim.

When deciding if an interpreter is needed, try to explain to the service user their right to an interpreter – and the interpreter's role, if they are not already aware of this. Also explain the interpreter's professional obligation to preserve confidentiality. It may well be helpful, if forms or paperwork need completing with the service user, to send them to the interpreter in advance of the interview. You may need to ask them to translate a letter for you, giving details of the interview time.

Do not expect the interpreter to be a cultural expert, to counsel the service user, or to calm the person down. They are simply there to repeat what you and the service user say to each other, in a language that you both can understand.

---

### How to conduct an interview with an interpreter present

This information is based, with permission, on a *Working With Diversity* (Northern Ireland) publication. See website.

**Before an interview**
Arrange a place where the interview can be conducted in private.
    Allow for extra time.
    Arrange the seating to allow for easy communication: in a circle or triangle or place the interpreter to the side and just behind you.
    Brief the interpreter prior to the interview, wherever possible.
    Ask the interpreter for any cultural factors that may affect the interview – but remember that interpreters do not consider themselves to be cultural experts.

**Introduction and set-up**
Introduce yourself and the interpreter.
    Explain both your and the interpreter's role.
    Stress that both you and the interpreter are bound by a code of ethics to maintain the confidentiality of the interview.
    Explain the purpose of the interview and how it will proceed.

**During the interview**
Sit facing the service user.
    Look at the person and maintain awareness of body language. Avoid looking at the interpreter, unless you are directly addressing him/her.

Speak directly to the service user, as you would with an English speaker.

Always use the first person, e.g. 'How are you feeling?' (to the interpreter). Not, 'Ask her how she is feeling?'

Do not try to save time by asking the interpreter to summarise.

Be aware that it may take more words than you have spoken to convey your meaning.

Do not let the interpreter's presence change your role in the interview. It is not the interpreter's role to conduct the interview.

### Interview style

Speak a little more slowly than usual, in your normal speaking tone. Speaking more loudly *does not help.*

Use plain English wherever possible. Try to avoid specialist terms.

Pause after 2 or 3 sentences, to allow the interpreter to relay what you have said.

Stop speaking when the interpreter signals by raising a hand, or is starting to interpret.

Summarise periodically, especially when complex issues are involved.

If the person does not understand, it is your responsibility (not the interpreter's) to explain more simply.

Seek the service user's permission if you need to obtain cultural information from the interpreter.

Avoid long discussions with the interpreter. If you need to talk to the interpreter directly, then the interpreter should explain to the service user the nature of the conversation.

### Ending the interview

Check that the service user has understood the key messages in your interview. Ask for any questions.

Thank both the service user and the interpreter. Say goodbye formally.

Debrief the interpreter, especially if the interview was emotionally taxing. Clarify any questions you have arising from the interview.

(Debriefing may need to happen later, as it may make the service user uncomfortable if you are seen to be in a detailed conversation with the interpreter.)

For most people, it is important to engage an interpreter of the same gender as the service user. If this is not possible, ask the service user if they are willing to accept the opposite gender *before* engaging an interpreter.

## Effects of the involvement of an interpreter on the interview

First, it should always be remembered that the interpreter is *not* the person carrying out the interview. They are primarily the means by which your words are conveyed to the service user, and the channel by which the service user's responses are returned.

In practice, though, a three-way interview becomes more complex, and may take off in unexpected directions. It is even possible for the service user and the interpreter to gradually engage in a direct conversation, leading to an interchange from which you are effectively excluded.

It is good practice, therefore, before the interview begins, to discuss the planned interview with the interpreter, before you meet the service user. You should specifically make clear your perceptions of the interpreter role, and agree some general rules. It should be arranged that, if unexpected problems develop, the interview should be placed on 'hold', to allow time for a further discussion between interpreter and interviewer. Any issues on the interpreter's role need to be ironed out *before* you meet the service user. This can be especially important if you have to use an informal interpreter.

Payment to interpreters is sometimes difficult. A few employers, working within tight budget parameters, for instance, may well be reluctant to authorise the use of expensive translators. Nevertheless, it needs to be understood that many problems can be avoided if a capable interpreter enables efficient worker/client communications. LASSDs, however, are increasingly conscious of the need to make their services available to all members of the community, reinforced by the provisions of the Disability Discrimination Act, 2005, and usually have access to resources such as a group of approved translators, or even a formal translating service, such as Language Line (<http://www.languageline.co.uk/>).

Finally, although you will be concentrating on verbal language as the main communications method with an interpreter, this should not lead you to overlook wider aspects of ethnicity and cultural expectations. It is not sufficient for words to be accurately translated if they are then perceived by the service user as damaging, or insulting.

### Techniques for interviewing through an interpreter

Supplementing the advice from *Working With Diversity*, this subsection offers some further suggestions on using an interpreter in a social care interview.

Body language has already been noted elsewhere as playing a significant role in interviews, and the relationship of body language to success in interpreter interviews is of equal, or probably greater, importance. Even though you, in these circumstances, may not be directly interacting with the service user, remember to behave (and appear) as though you *are*.

Especially at the beginning, in order to establish the nature of the interview dynamic, use a series of short statements or questions, even if, at a later stage, more lengthy interactions are necessary. Short exchanges have the advantage of involving the service user and you in a more dynamic and interactive situation, while also providing the opportunity for rapid feedback. Periodically ask whether the service user has understood, and still understands, what the interpreter is saying to them. Asking for the service user to feed back their understanding of the situation (always good practice in an ordinary interview) is even more important when there is the additional danger that translation may distort the meanings of questions and answers.

**Other interpreters**

The same guidelines apply if you are meeting someone with a hearing disability, who uses sign language as their first language. As the structure and grammar of sign language are different to those of English, it is not easy to understand.

It should be remembered, too, that people tend to develop hearing problems as a result of ageing. While they may have a similar hearing disability, older people are unlikely to be familiar with signing, or other specialist communication methods, so you will need to consider different approaches, some of which are discussed below.

**Speaking with someone who is deaf, or hard of hearing**

Given that many service users need assistance with communication before an interpreter is employed, what special measures can you take? The Royal National Institute for the Deaf (RNID) lists some important points you should consider when meeting a deaf or hard-of-hearing person:

- Find a suitable place to talk, with good lighting, away from noise and distractions.
- Remember not to turn your face away from a deaf person. Always turn towards your listener, so they can see your face.
- Even if someone is wearing a hearing aid, it doesn't mean that they can hear you. Ask if they need to lipread you.
- If you're talking to a deaf person and a hearing person, don't just focus on the hearing person.
- Make sure you have the listener's attention *before* you start speaking.

■ Speak clearly but not too slowly, and don't exaggerate your lip movements. Use natural facial expressions and gestures.

■ Don't shout. It's uncomfortable for a hearing aid user, and it looks aggressive.

■ If someone doesn't understand what you've said, don't just keep repeating it. Try saying it in a different way.

■ Check that the person you're talking to can follow you. Be patient and take the time to communicate properly.

■ Use plain language, and don't waffle. Avoid jargon and unfamiliar abbreviations.

(Information based, with permission, on RNID material)

In this kind of case, too, there is a greater need to consciously incorporate attention to the monitoring of body language.

## Communicating with young people

The subject of communicating with children is wide, and can be a complex, specialist one. Many situations with children are complex because of the harm that may have been caused to them, or because there are severe difficulties in communicating. Handling interviews in these situations needs specialist experience, and more advanced interviewing skills.

What follows are some basic guidelines about interviews with older children or young people (taken to be the teenage years). The reader is referred to more specialist texts for a closer look at interviewing younger children.

Remember that interviews with young people do have major differences from interviews with adults. You must consider how mature the person may be. Children develop at different rates, which can mean one child – of say, 11 years – may be operating at a very different level of cognitive ability and maturity to another person of the same chronological age. In order to be aware of any complexities in functioning it is helpful to develop some understanding of human growth and development (Inhelder and Piaget, 1958; Coleman and Hendry, 1999).

There are also differences between earlier and later adolescence. Younger teenagers are usually more shy, and their cognitive abilities not as developed (less reliable memories, able to give less details, may embellish stories more). In particular, they are more suggestible, and are more aware of power invested in adults (Rosado, 2000, p19). In an interview, all of these points will have implications for you.

## Need for an adult?

In these circumstances, you should consider whether the interview needs to be in the presence of another person, as children or young people should not usually be interviewed on their own.

This means that when a young person is the service user, you should not interview them alone without evaluating whether this is the right course of action. Some social work interviews will be in the child protection arena, and additional precautions must be taken. (Many agencies will have specific rules about this.) Particularly if further and official action may follow, a responsible, adult advocate must also attend the interview. They are not simply there to monitor proceedings – should it become necessary during the interview, this advocate will be in a position to act on the child's behalf.

While most people might be reluctant to accept that their interviewing techniques could ever be anything less than well thought out and appropriate, we all need to appreciate that the perceptions of an independent third party on the conduct of our interviews might well be different from our own. For this reason alone, the involvement of an adult with a brief to safeguard the interests of the person being interviewed should be viewed as a welcome safeguard, rather than a stressful intrusion.

---

### Practice issue

Ganesh, a duty social worker, was asked to act as an independent adult when the police were interviewing a young person of 14. Once the interview got under way, however, it rapidly became clear that Ganesh's view of his role differed considerably from the perception of the police officer carrying out the interview. The police officer confidently expected that the 'independent third party' would sit quietly in the background, and make no comments at all, clearly feeling Ganesh was there to merely make sure the letter, not the spirit, of 'the book' was being followed. However, Ganesh interpreted his role in a rather more proactive way, so did not hesitate to interrupt when he felt the child was being inappropriately questioned. He became unpopular, but the child's interests were protected.

---

We have considered here a situation of protection. Other interviews will, however, involve young people with special needs. In these circumstances, you may have to make particular efforts to learn how to communicate effectively with them. This is essential, because their full involvement is necessary not simply to seek their opinions, but to work in partnership in planning for their future, and to involve them in decisions likely to affect them.

**Points for interviews with young people**

## 1 Observation can work as well as talk

When a young person is in the presence of an adult, you can observe the interactions between them. This can be of great assistance in identifying the quality of their relationship, especially if you can observe them working on a task together. This will allow you to see the cooperative nature of the relationship, or its absence, as well as the concentration levels as they work on the task.

## 2 You need time to get to know the individual person

Preparation is essential, especially for working with young people who may have difficulty in directly expressing their choices and feelings. Your preparation may well take more time than it might with adults, because there may be other significant people in their lives: a teacher, for example, whose ideas about how to communicate best with the child may need to be explored. The important message here is that, however severe the communication issues might be, with time and patience necessary information can be discovered and used to aid communication.

A common complaint made by children with special needs is that adults do not 'listen' to them, and do not use a variety of methods to try to communicate with them. It is crucial to allow a suitable period for the rapport stage of the interview (defined in Chapter 7) before moving on to more formal or more structured questioning. Finding some common ground at the beginning of the conversation can be a direct way of working towards a trusting relationship. The time-honoured question, 'Can you whistle?' may now be outmoded, but with preparation you can work out a similarly suitable opening remark. Rapport time allows both sides to evaluate the other in an informal way, and can also help you refine your communication methods.

You may have to recognise and resist an understandable temptation to rush straight in to the 'real' business of the interview. Instead, a careful 'lead-in' should make your interview easier for any young person to handle – and more likely to be effective.

## 3 Young people often prefer to do something while talking

A formal interview can understandably seem an unnatural atmosphere to someone younger, and their powers of concentration are also likely to be substantially shorter than an adult's. Having something on hand as a diversion, such as pen and paper that they can use, can make the interview less intense for them.

Young people in particular may prefer to be engaged in something, such as a physical activity, if it is possible to talk privately at the same time.

### 4   Young people may need reassurance that the subject of the discussion together is not necessarily their fault

Although their emotional maturity is obviously developing, young people are likely to be still very much focused on their own place in the world. It is consequently easy for them to accept a disproportionate responsibility for being the cause of events. It is therefore a part of both the preliminary work and of interview discussions to state (and, if necessary, restate) a neutral view of their family situation, and the reason for the interview.

### 5   Pay extra attention when young people may perceive a situation of divided loyalty

Do not put young people into a position where they are likely to be confronted with conflicting loyalties – unless, of course, this is absolutely essential, and has been discussed and planned in advance. Issues concerning loyalty to parents or caregivers are very relevant here. Any prior assumptions will need checking out with the young person.

### 6   Look for someone the person trusts to act as an advocate; or consider an independent advocate

Young people are likely to have close relationships with their peer group, and, because a close friend can give confidence and assist communication, a young person may like to have someone from such a group present at the interview. If there should be severe difficulties in communicating, it is all the more important to find someone who is trusted, and who can help interpret answers and facilitate expression of their feelings. If it does not compromise confidentiality, involving such a supportive friend can be a positive act.

### 7   Be very aware of language. Keep to simple and honest communication

Adults may not remember that young people very frequently have special vocabularies or individual words to describe objects, emotions and people they experience in their day-to-day lives. It is all right to be honest if you find that you are ignorant about the language used, and seek to work out a common understanding together. If there is some communication issue, you may be able to find out in advance any special relevant terms that the person may use.

It is almost always preferable in these circumstances for you to deliberately avoid complex questions in favour of simple and direct interaction. It is particularly important that in the interview you give room for expression of feelings, rather than a tick list of questions.

SW:   Hi, Jakob. My name is Paul. [*pause*] I work for the council's special needs services for young people [*pause*] and I'd like to talk to you about you having a break away from home [*pause for confirmation*].

Here the interviewer has clearly stated who they are, whom they represent, and what they wanted to talk about. Importantly, they also made sure the service user had space to respond. Note also the frequent pauses, designed to allow time for at least minimal (and quite possibly non-verbal) feedback. Deliberately allowing space for feedback is particularly important, as it helps ensure that the young person understands what is being said.

## 8   Interview length

Interview duration should be carefully considered when you arrange interviews with young people. Lengthy interviews are very likely to be counterproductive, as tiredness sets in. As mentioned earlier, concentration levels also vary between adolescents, or even in one person, at different times of the day. Finding out when they are likely to be fresh is therefore a sensible start.

## 9   Communication aids

In order to communicate as clearly as possible, some young people may need the help of specialist aids. If this is the case, find out if these aids are available at the location where you plan to hold the interview. A practical tip – you will need to be quite sure you know how they operate.

## CONCLUSION

In this chapter we discussed the nature of the relationship between service user and interviewer. We concluded that:

■   The interviewer and service user need to establish communication with apt and accessible language, so that they form a working alliance.

- Skills such as paraphrasing and summarising will help within the interview.
- Special guidelines are needed for people with communication impairments. We considered the need to involve an interpreter.
- Older children and adolescents need special treatment, although the communication principles are the same as for adults.

## QUESTIONS

1 What would you take into account in communicating with a young person with cerebral palsy?

2 When might you use written communications with service users?

3 You are making a visit with an interpreter for the deaf. What do you need to clarify with them beforehand?

## FURTHER READING

Kadushin, A. and Kadushin, G., *The Social Work Interview*, Chapter 2.
Lishman, Joyce, *Communication in Social Work*.
Thompson, Neil, *People Skills*.

# Chapter 7

# The Stages of the Interview

**NOSSC RELEVANCE**

The material discussed in this chapter relates to the following National Occupational Standards in Social Care:

- **Key Role One**, Unit 2. Work with individuals, families, carers, groups and communities to help them make informed decisions.
- **Key Role One**, Unit 3. Assess needs and options to recommend a course of action.
- **Key Role Two**, Unit 4. (Respond to crisis situations).
- **Key Role Two**, Unit 5. Interact with individuals, families, carers, groups and communities to achieve change and development and to improve life opportunities.

*This chapter examines the actual interaction between the service user and the interviewer. This is the interview aspect that usually causes most anxiety to practitioners – but is also potentially the most interesting. It is here that all your planning comes together, and you are able to put into practice the sum of your learning: knowledge, values, planning and communication skills. The areas covered in this chapter include:*

■ *An overview of processes in the interview*
■ *The 'small-talk' or rapport stage/beginnings/middle stages/ending – of interview and involvement*

- *More challenging scenarios*
- *The special needs of duty interviews.*

## INTERVIEW PROCESSES

Even the simplest and shortest of interviews may, nevertheless, be a complex entity. Apart from the overt verbal interactions, there are also emotional, non-verbal and interpersonal messages – and thinking – going on. Often, such unspoken processes can assume as much importance as what is actually said. You will need a grasp of communication and interpersonal skills to fully participate in these processes, which are likely to play an essential part throughout the interview.

---

**Practice issue**

Mikey's mother said he did not appreciate his social worker. When she visited him, she sometimes stood there, jangling her car keys, while he tried to tell her how stressed his week had been. She always seemed to be looking at her watch when they were talking together, and although she sometimes asked how he had been, she never sounded particularly interested.

---

In an interview, the element that is specifically concerned with tangible exchanges is often named the **content** of the interview. As well as the setting down of any verbal interaction, interview content is also a way of describing what in practical terms actually happened: 'He came in, took a chair, shook hands', and so on.

The **processes** of an interview are the sum of those parts of the interview that relate strongly to the interaction between the 'players' and the emotions of both parties. For this reason, Kadushin (1972) likens an interview to an orchestra playing a symphony, where some parts will be to the foreground at one point, only to be background at other times; but all are progressing simultaneously. As with the parts of a symphony, it is the

**Definition**

### Content/processes

The *content* of an interview is what happens during the interview. The *processes* of the interview are the other elements of the interaction: what is happening on a non-verbal level and on a feeling level. We talk of *dynamic processes* because the interactive development between service user and interviewer can change, for better or worse, throughout the interview.

whole that matters. It is artificial to separate out the different processes of an interview, but inevitably a degree of division is needed in order to better analyse and understand them.

As well as being able to communicate in a clear and understandable way, an effective interviewer needs to demonstrate that they respect service users, are actively listening to them, and hope to work together in a partnership, or a 'helping alliance' (GSCC Code of Conduct, 1.4). Such an approach is often described as 'making a relationship' or 'working collaboratively' with a service user, or perhaps 'engaging' someone in the process of work together. This relationship is described more fully in Chapter 1.

## INTERVIEW OVERVIEW

Most social work interviews begin with introductions, usually followed by either a recap of a previous interview, or, if this is an initial interview, an explanation of why the interview is taking place. In a first interview, the outline is likely to be simply a review of the details of the referral, while a later interview will begin with a synopsis of the previous interview, and a description of what has happened since.

This 'opening' stage usually leads on to an introductory and exploratory stage, followed by a 'middle' stage, when the focus is on the work the service user and you have jointly identified as important for that day. Finally, the interview will wind down with an 'ending' period. Here, clarifications, contracts and future plans become the important features. This model of describing the course of an interview is based upon Egan's Skilled Helper model (Egan, 2002, pp26–39):

- What is going on? (Exploration)
- What solutions make sense for me? (Understanding)
- How do I get what I need or want? (Action)

Also relevant here is Nicholson and Baynes's model of the interview (Nicholson and Baynes, 1984, pp31–48), together with an interpersonal skills interview model (Hargie and Tourish, 2000, pp71–87), which were discussed in Chapter 2.

While an understanding of the stages of the interview is important, you should appreciate that at times any stage might be considerably shortened, or drawn out, or even require repetition. As an obvious example, clarification or reflection may frequently be needed several times. Repetition may also be necessary because stages of an interview should always reflect the individual needs of the service user. If the service user's needs will not be met by the original plans, for instance, an initial decision about when to wind down and finish an interview may need modification.

It is also possible that in certain instances the interview may be interrupted, or forced to end abruptly. Additionally, interviews are dynamic, and may well change focus as they proceed; this is to be expected, so for an interviewer flexibility is an asset. After all, until they have experienced a particular interview, even knowledgeable practitioners cannot be certain of all the information and relationships that may develop during it. Inevitably, therefore, such a dynamic makes even an apparently straightforward interview into a potentially complex item. This means that, as in other 'people work' – for instance teaching or nursing – an

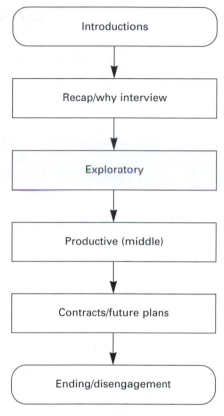

**Figure 7.1**   Simple interview process

essential part of the learning experience will involve other people and their reactions. Because of this, there will not necessarily be a straightforward progression from novice interviewer to skilled worker – too many variables are involved.

In practice, a degree of resilience is crucial. Should an interview not proceed as you had anticipated, especially if it is your first interview, it can be very disconcerting. Quite frequently there *will* be unexpected components to the interview. Each person will bring something individual to a social interaction, and, while the main issues in an interview may appear to be identical, there are so many variables (gender, ethnicity, setting, time available, emotional state, character, to name just a few) that the interview dynamic will be on a broad spectrum. (Hargie and Tourish, 2000, p79).

| **Consider this** | |
|---|---|
| You are to meet Wesley, who has just been diagnosed as HIV positive, together with his partner. | What differences might need to be made in your thinking or your approach:<br><br>■ If the partner were male – or female?<br>■ If you had to meet them in a hospital setting?<br>■ If either Wesley or his partner were from a culturally different background?<br>■ If you only had an hour in which to talk to them? |

Perhaps some of these issues relate to you being thrown off guard by your own expectations, or by having theorised too rigidly in advance. Typically, you may have been led to make incorrect assumptions about the social situation, or perhaps something unexpected may have happened since the referral, or since your previous interview.

Being asked difficult questions unexpectedly can be another problem. One exceptionally hard opening question that springs to mind is: 'Did you know I've got cancer?' In such a case, responding to a question with a question can be a useful tactic, which at the worst should provide a little thinking time – 'What makes you think I might know that?', for example.

As interviewing is inevitably a dynamic process, an interviewer must develop flexibility, and if necessary always be prepared to depart from their pre-arranged plans.

However, for obvious reasons such flexibility cannot be total; you *must* always keep in mind the goals and agenda that you have set with the service user, or that have been set by your agency. So, despite flexibility, it should always be possible for the conversation to be guided back – or 'directed' – to the reason the service user wants (or needs) involvement with the agency (Thompson, 2002, p123).

## BRINGING IN A CONTRIBUTION FROM A THIRD PARTY

Given an interview has many possible variations, there are certain to be occasions when there is more than one person present. Typically, a relative or friend may be there, their presence giving reassurance to the service user. You may yourself have asked for others to be included, often because members of a family have a perspective on the service user's situation that may be helpful to everyone – issues to do with memory are an obvious example. Should there be genuine family issues that have an impact on the total situation, then if possible these issues should be brought into the open, and discussed.

While you will have gained advance agreement from the service user to include others in the interview, sometimes you may arrive only to find that other parties are present, by chance or by arrangement. You will then need to make a judgement about whether to continue the interview, modify it, or abandon it.

On the positive side, such chance meetings are often an opportunity to explore wider social relationships with the service user. However, confidentiality is an important issue, and always requires consideration. When you are confronted unexpectedly with a changed interview situation, there is unlikely to be sufficient time for careful deliberation. Finding out what the service user feels, alone in private, before deciding to begin a shared interview is therefore normally good practice.

## CONTACTING PEOPLE

The beginning of an interview is when – either consciously or unconsciously – many decisions are made that will set the mood for the whole meeting. As was discussed in previous chapters, you will already have:

- decided where the interview is to be conducted,
- determined the physical layout of the interview environment (if possible),
- considered any likely distractions,
- thought about whom to include in the interview – and whom to exclude,
- checked on communication issues, and resolved any needs, such as interpreters.

All such prior preparation aims to assist good communication with the individual service user, with the specific purpose of ensuring that the interview has the best possible chance of a positive outcome.

A decision should already have been made about whether this is a pre-arranged appointment. If it is, how should it be organised? Possibilities include telephone or letter, fax (written communications may be essential for people with a hearing impairment) or, increasingly, the use of email and text messages.

### First contact: telephone

Rather than the more traditional method of sending a typed appointment letter, many social workers today prefer to use the telephone to make contact for a first visit. Are there advantages in using a telephone to arrange an interview? A voice at the end of the phone is likely to appear less bureaucratic than a formal printed letter on headed paper, and should immediately personalise the service the agency is offering. For a teenager, verbal communication may be the norm, and informal enough for him or her to respond easily; a phone call can certainly be an informal first contact.

A telephone call may also give an early indication of whether there are likely to be any communication difficulties. Any advance indication will give you time to consider how to deal with communication in the live situation, rather than being faced with a potential communication complication on first meeting. For service users with communication impairment, such as visual impairment, a verbal approach may be essential. Indeed, even when a written letter is preferred, it may be necessary to consider putting your letters into audio format, to ensure that communication is directly with the person concerned, and not through their carer or personal assistant (SCIE, 2004, p71).

Another important point in favour of telephoning is that the personal communication of a telephone call encourages the beginning of a two-way relationship. A person on the other end of the line can ask questions, can indicate how urgently they need to see you, and may essentially start to make the working alliance with you. In return, you can tell the service user how soon you intend to see them, and discover if delay is acceptable.

Finally, if the time you have in mind for the interview proves to be inconvenient for the service user, using the telephone will allow you to negotiate an alternative immediately.

### Telephone disadvantages

The assumption that every service user has the use of a telephone is almost certainly incorrect. Even if a telephone was once available, debt issues may have forced people to give up their telephone; and there may well be more complex reasons. And, as we have said, communication impairments may exist that would make written information the service user's choice. Hearing impairment and profound deafness are major barriers to easy telephone use. (Issues of communication were considered more closely in Chapter 6.)

A further disadvantage of arranging an interview by telephone is that it is all too easy for people to believe they will remember times or names, especially if they do not write them down. For this reason, even if a visit is for the same day, it is sensible to provide your name and a contact telephone number, and to allow time during the telephone conversation for this information to be recorded. If the visit is not immediate, the problem of fallible memory may be offset, of course; appointments made by telephone can always be confirmed in writing.

When using the telephone, privacy can also be an issue. You cannot be sure that the service user answering the telephone is able to speak freely (Koprowska, 2005, p58), so it might be appropriate for you to check this out.

### First contact: letter

A typewritten letter with a printed heading will clearly make a different statement about the intention and purpose of an interview. It inevitably carries a certain formality, and will represent 'officialdom'. Why then might you choose to write to set an appointment, rather than using the telephone?

The main functions of letters are likely to involve one or both of the following scenarios – empowerment and clarification.

## Empowerment

Sending an appointment letter may be appropriate when it is necessary for you not to disempower the service user. In a letter it is possible to clearly explain and emphasise the purpose of the visit. When written, this can be done in a controlled manner, with consideration of appropriate vocabulary for a particular individual. A letter may therefore be actively phrased in language the service user will find easy to read – and if necessary reread – and understand. This means that important information can be deliberately given in a way that is easily accessible to the service user. For instance, there may be reasons that an appointment time and date should be strictly kept: perhaps another professional's commitments need to be considered, or enough time is needed to write a detailed report.

It is possible, too, that the service user has memory impairment, so a clearly written record of the interview time would be of help to them.

## Clarification

It may be that specific information must be available during the interview, perhaps documents that you must see. A detailed letter can identify those papers in advance, allowing you to make best use of time. In a letter, too, some advance mapping of the anticipated interview topics is possible, which, particularly if there are difficult areas to cover, can give service users time to prepare practically and emotionally for the interview.

If there has been some trouble about telephoning (perhaps the service user's line is out of order), then a letter will be a visible reminder that the worker has tried to get in touch informally and quickly. If you have the person's consent, the use of a letter also allows for a duplicate copy to be sent to a third party, perhaps a concerned relative.

Sometimes, setting a date well in advance by letter can be a useful technique. There are always individuals whose needs do not clamour for attention; perhaps some psycho-dynamic 'avoidance' is taking place on your part, or for some other reason it may be hard for you to follow up an individual's needs. How might such people be easily given more attention? One way is by making an appointment some weeks into the future, and ensuring that it is confirmed in writing to the service user. However, if there is any doubt about the level of reading skills in the person that you intend to see, a letter might be inappropriate.

---

### Practice issue

- When would you choose to write a letter to a service user as a first point of contact?
- How much notice of an interview do you need to give? Should age, or ethnic background, make any difference to this?
- What can help you decide how to address a service user? Does age or ethnic background – or any other factors – affect this?

---

### First contact: no prior notice

Writing a letter or making a phone call gives a service user advance warning of an interview, but there may be times when this is not possible, and may even be inappropriate. When might you consider seeing someone without any warning?

There may be occasions – perhaps in an informal day-care setting, or in a youth club – when it is possible, and even usual, to sit down with a service user and just get on with the interview. If the goals of the interview can be accomplished this way, and there are no issues of anti-discriminatory practice or confidentiality to consider (such as preferred communication methods, or privacy), then this is perfectly acceptable.

In some situations, such as those relating to protection, there may be issues of risk or uncertainty that need a more investigatory approach. In such a case, you may contemplate an unannounced visit.

Such **doorstep visits**, where you may be unsure of your welcome, may help if a positive relationship can be made at the door. The lack of prior notice can prevent anxieties and barriers being built up beforehand, but it may also have an acute effect on the emotions and behaviour of the service user. People may find it disempowering to try to refuse entry to an agency official. They may need time to tidy up. A crucial supporter, such as a partner or a mother, may not be present; consequently levels of anxiety can run high. You may therefore not get as true a picture of the situation as may be necessary. Doorstep interviews are a course of action needing to be discussed with your supervisor, and carefully planned beforehand.

> **Definition**
>
> ### A 'doorstep' visit
>
> A 'doorstep' visit is one in which the practitioner will arrive on the doorstep of a service user with no warning, unannounced – and possibly unwanted – by them.

In practice, an excuse often given for seeing someone with no prior notice is that there was 'insufficient time' to contact the service user. However, an assumption of insufficient time should never be accepted unquestioningly. It is usually possible to make an effort to alert a service user about a proposed visit, perhaps by detouring earlier in the day (or asking a colleague to detour), in order to deliver a note saying that you plan to call later.

If the unannounced visit is a duty call, or to somewhere unknown, it is important to remember the basics of security. In such circumstances, consider a joint interview with a colleague.

## HOME VISITS

For new service users, it is likely to be an unfamiliar and disempowering experience to have a social worker visiting their home. Feelings of nervousness are therefore very likely to be present, reinforced by the presence of an 'official stranger'. This may also be a reminder that the issues to be discussed have become too great to be contained within informal support (Lishman, 1994, p8).

However, visiting someone in their own home is also likely to be an anxiety-inducing experience for an *interviewer*, even if they are prepared for the challenge. Such anxiety is more likely when the interview is not being carried out in a familiar space, such as an interview room in the agency. Recognising that these feelings of anxiety are normal, and to be expected, should help a little in coping with them.

A first consideration when seeing someone in a domestic setting is to begin thinking about the situation from the service user's point of view. What are the possible emotions involved? (Trevithick, 2000, pp73–4).

It is essential to arrive on time. As you might expect, interviewer punctuality is one of the attributes most highly rated by service users (SCIE, 2004, p13). Arriving late starts the interview poorly, and may also understandably be perceived as a lack of respect.

Once you have arrived – on time – think where to stand when ringing the bell, or knocking on the door. If there is not a convenient lower step on which you may wait, it is better to move away from the threshold. This is because if you are standing too close to the door, you may give an unintended physical impression of dominance, reinforcing negative preconceptions. The power in the social exchange between professionals and their clients can be perceived by service users to be quite unequal (Mullally, 1993, p149), and for this reason non-verbal cues that acknowledge inequality, and address it from the beginning, can significantly help gain the respect and confidence of the service user.

## No answer

Sometimes there might not be a reply to a knock on the door; or the person inside (whether deliberately or not) may ignore your knock, and not answer.

We will deal first with situations where there is no reply when you arrive for an *arranged* interview. Here, mobile phones can be really useful; telephoning a service user from their own doorstep may prove effective. It is surprising how often people who may not hear a doorbell are able to hear their phone.

However, if telephoning produces no results – or the service user has no phone – is it possible for you to try another door? Many people may expect visitors to automatically go 'round the back', rather than knocking on the front door – one service user told us 'My front door's only for weddings – and the rent man.' While some service users may regard it as an intrusion, if you are expected for an arranged meeting it is nevertheless sensible to try an alternative entrance.

If there is still no response, and you are concerned that the person inside might have fallen, or be ill, you should assess the property for signs of life. Observe whether curtains are drawn back, or closed; and check for full (but uncollected) milk bottles, or papers stuffed in the letterbox. It is surprising how soon you can get a 'feel' about this, and work out for yourself if you believe there is someone in the house.

If you genuinely suspect an emergency, what should be done?

A judgement may be needed here about whether to seek information from neighbours; but this may not be straightforward. All service users have a need for privacy, and a right to it; so, unless there is recorded information on a positive relationship with next-door neighbours, contact with them may upset either party. (The service user may be perceived as becoming a 'nuisance' to the neighbour, so any call relating to the 'nuisance' might arouse negative feelings; on the other hand, the service user may see the neighbours themselves as 'nosey'.)

Before making contact, then, be sure that you can justify including or consulting a neighbour with a good explanation – to the service user and to the neighbour.

If you are unsure, it is always worth contacting someone in the office, perhaps a duty officer or a supervisor, to help in making the decision.

Finally, if there are no signs of life and the service user is indeed supposed to be at home, there will be a need to check with the usual persons. ('Usual persons' is likely to include the next of kin, the GP and hospitals; but this list is not exhaustive, and you will need to think about an individual's normal patterns and routines before deciding whom to contact.)

### No reply: checklist of people useful to contact

1  Family and friends
2  GP/district nurse/health visitor
3  Any social activities attended (e.g. day centre)
4  Neighbours – but with discretion
5  Hospital: Accident and Emergency, or Outpatients
6  Any other known social contacts/visits
7  The police.

If an emergency is suspected, you may need to call the police. It is very common for a worker to feel unsure about doing this, and to feel uncertain about when might be the right time to do it. However, the police are prepared to be called in these circumstances, and are professionally used to 'reading' houses. A police officer will undoubtedly be able to provide helpful information and assessment – which in itself can be a learning experience for you, and prove useful in other situations.

The police will usually first ask what you have observed, and what actions have already been taken, and then, if necessary, force an entry. We must emphasise that it is *not* up to you to force an entry; this should be left to the police.

---

### Practice issue

Mrs Storey was housebound, and lived alone. Her visiting social worker was concerned when there was no answer to his knock, and, after a series of checks, called the police. A police officer discovered that Mrs Storey had fallen, and her body was blocking the front door. Eventually two policemen lifted a third policeman headfirst through a very narrow window; the heavily secured door was unlocked, and Mrs Storey taken to hospital – where happily she made a full recovery.

---

It may be obvious to say that when an emergency is suspected, the safest course of action should always be chosen – but it should!

**No answer: anyone there . . .**

Quite apart from illness or injury, there may be other situations when the worker is aware that someone is in the house, but they are not answering the door. As was said earlier, this *could* be because they have not heard your knock; but there may be other reasons.

Certain roles that social workers fulfil contain an element of authority. This might be because the legislation that underpins the involvement has a coercive aspect, or simply that the service user *perceives* the involvement as carrying authority (Lishman, 1994, pp11–12). There are also circumstances where the service user may not be convinced of the benefits of social work involvement, or where involvement raises too many anxieties. A perceived lack of power may then lead the person to opt out of contact with you, as this negative response may appear to be the only way of expressing their independence.

'Opting out' of contact may take the form of not answering the door to you, or failing to arrive for a planned interview appointment. The behaviour may well provoke a whole range of reactions in you, perhaps ranging from indifference to 'Why is this happening to *me*?' However, it is important to remember that you will be seeking to establish contact not as an individual, but as the representative of an agency. Motives underlying the rejection of your visit are consequently likely to be reflecting the service user's feelings about your agency, rather than you as an individual. In such circumstances, once communication has been established, one way forward is to attempt to bring the feelings behind rejection of contact into discussion; but this may not always be successful.

A final consideration, if you find no answer, is whether the person's health problems may be interfering with their usual social interaction. Depression, or other mental health issues, for example, may well influence people's functioning. If it seems that the service user's health is affecting their responses, then a decision needs to be made (if necessary in consultation with a supervisor) about whether to register concerns with health colleagues.

**If there was no answer . . .**

Even if there was no answer to a planned interview visit, it is always sensible to leave a card, which will show in a concrete form that you did actually visit. Sometimes writing the time of the visit on the card, perhaps with a brief note, can be helpful – and this will, of course, demonstrate that the arranged visit was made at the planned time.

An 'abortive' visit such as this will mean that it is necessary to go back to the interview planning stage, because, unless you change your plans, another failed visit is possible. After revision, setting up a new session with different variables (such as where the interview is to be held, or who it is planned to include) may be the way forward.

| **Practice issue** |
| --- |
| Ms Dee Kwala was a single parent whose health was unstable, often resulting in crisis admissions to hospital. Her social worker called round late one afternoon, but could get no reply. The house did not seem uninhabited (curtains drawn back, washing on the line), so as well as checking with the GP, she phoned Dee's mother. Mrs Kwala came straight round with her key, discovered her daughter ill in bed, and was able to call for medical help. |

Of course, not receiving an answer to a planned call is in practice likely to be infrequent. Most visits will be met with a greeting, and invitation to enter.

## FIRST MEETINGS

The start of the interview is the time when people's names are exchanged. Although an appointment may have been made, and people will be expecting to talk to an official visitor, it is still helpful to repeat your name, and work title. Why should this be done? The main reason is that social workers should always be striving for good communication. Making a statement about who you are will clarify your role, and implicitly announce why the visit is being made. It also tells the person that they haven't answered the door to the wrong individual!

The issue of your identification is worth emphasising. Particularly if this is the first time that the service user is meeting you, at the very beginning of the appointment it is very important to make quite clear your name, title, and the agency you represent. Agencies provide ID cards, which should always be kept to hand, in case confirmation of your identity is needed. (Students, if on placement, should ensure that they have their college card, together with an identifying letter from their placement agency.) Being asked for proof of identity by a service user should always be seen as totally acceptable; production of your ID card should never be made to appear to be a nuisance, but a totally normal activity.

Normally, greetings often involve touch or gesture. However, think in advance about shaking hands, rather than expecting to do so automatically. Handshaking can be appropriate for some situations, as it allows a formal introduction, and a respectful acknowledgement of people's names (Trevithick, 2000, p79). However, touch can be a complex area. Different generations may well vary in their attitudes to shaking hands, and, most importantly, you need also to be aware of cultural messages and ethnic differences about the perceived invasion of body space. There may be gender issues, too. For these reasons – especially if this is a male-to-female interaction – it will be worth checking out in advance with the service user what method of greeting feels correct for them.

Names are usually and understandably of symbolic importance to an individual. For example, Chinese names are often a reflection of the aspirations of the family for that individual. Greeting the service user in the way they feel is correct reinforces the respect you accord that person. Although you may not manage to get the pronunciation right, it is important to find out by what name the person wishes to be called, and then to use it. Use of surnames can seem a little formal nowadays, but it is always worth reviewing exactly how service users prefer to be addressed. This is especially important for service users whose ethnic or cultural background may be different from yours.

---

### Practice issue

Sally felt a little foolish when it was pointed out to her that, by addressing 'Mrs Begum' in that phrase, she was actually calling her 'Mrs Madam' in Urdu (*begum saahiba*). Although Mrs 'Begum' had politely accepted this title, Sally went a little further, and discussed with her how names were given in her culture, before revising agency records to reflect the service user's wishes on how she preferred to be addressed.

---

### Preliminaries

In most interview situations there will usually be a time at the beginning for putting people at their ease, by making some form of 'small talk'. Trevithick discusses this ice-breaking approach, calling it a 'social chat', but links it to the importance of relaxing people and making a welcoming first impression (Trevithick, 2000, pp80–81). This preliminary period may also be known as the **rapport phase** of an interview. Allowing such time may form an important part of interview structure, because it helps to reduce the service user's anxiety and allows them to get to know you a little, before the interview moves on to discussion of more serious subjects. The rapport phase also forms an essential part of more complex interviewing, such as joint interviewing with police over serious offences (Brown et al., 1996, p51).

There is a reciprocal benefit, too. A casual period before the interview begins allows you to judge more accurately the service user's level of communication ability and vocabulary, before engaging with them in the main phase of the interview. The rapport phase will also give you thinking time in which to adjust your approach, allowing better and more effective communication with the service user.

Finally, the small talk at the beginning of an interview may also be functional. Just asking how long someone has lived in their house, for example, can provide a little information about their circumstances, and their ability to recall events.

> **Definition**
>
> ## Rapport phase
>
> A rapport phase comes at the start of the interview, before the interview proper begins. It usually consists of small talk on topics that are unrelated to the interview, but that help settle a person, and reduce their anxiety. It also allows both sides to size each other up, as well as providing a check on communication, understanding and reasoning before the interview actually starts.

How long should the preliminary rapport phase continue? Generally, casual chat is likely to seem uncomfortably long after five minutes or so (Trevithick, 2000, p80). Alternatively, of course, relaxed chat with an interviewer may well form an excellent avoidance technique, so if the rapport stage continues for too long you may need to remind the service user why you are meeting together.

Unless the interview is highly structured, the opening stage will often be the time when you may say something about yourself, in the course of conversation. Sometimes, self-disclosure (where the interviewer reveals some personal information about their own circumstances) may create issues for you; look back at the discussion on self-disclosure in Chapter 5.

Normally, of course, the service user is encouraged to disclose a great deal, whilst the practitioner makes few disclosures – and such a balance needs to be accepted (Kadushin and Kadushin, 1997, pp4–11).

It is certainly true that sharing personal information may also depend on the interview location. If your base is a day care or residential setting, where service users are seen every day, then involvement in daily happenings is likely to be quantitively and qualitatively different from less frequent contact. More frequent contact in such a setting may also give scope for **modelling behaviour**, allowing users to observe ways of handling social situations (Lishman, 1994, p139).

> **Definition**
>
> ## Modelling behaviour
>
> 'Modelling' behaviour is behaviour observed in others that people can imitate, or model, in their own lives. It is normally a component of behaviour modification programmes.

### Tea or coffee?

The offering of refreshments is a symbolic act in our society, as, indeed, can be a refusal to offer refreshments. An offer of refreshment can also be especially important in many other cultures, so you need to be sensitive to any impact on a relationship of accepting or declining food and drink. (The benefits of offering refreshment can, of course, also work for an interviewer – buying a coffee for a teenager may help cement a relationship.)

In an office setting, you can, if appropriate, arrange refreshments. Should the interview take place in the service user's home, however, the circumstances are clearly different. The service user may ask if you want a drink (unless you have the audacity not to wait, but ask 'Where's the bloody tea, then?', as one long-serving social worker allegedly asked his client). Accepting or declining the offer may be perceived by the service user as symbolic. Accepting a drink may also have the effect of moving the relationship onto a more equal footing, so taking tea or coffee can help establish a more relaxed atmosphere.

However, a decision to accept the invitation will also depend on your view of the interview situation. In some circumstances it can feel uncomfortable to receive hospitality, if, for example, you will have to deny resources, or enforce an authority role.

Some individuals may have gone to a great deal of trouble to get refreshments ready. If you then feel you must decline their offer, *how* you decline it matters. Rather than a straight 'No', an assertive but positive stroke, such as 'That's really kind of you, but . . .' is likely to be more appreciated.

## BEGINNINGS

As you move from the initial introductions to the main focus of the interview, there may be some changes to agree with the service user; if this is so, you will need to explain why the changes would be useful.

You might want to move physically nearer to someone, so that they are better able to hear or see you. There may also be an opportunity to adjust the type of seating, perhaps to give a more equal height balance – or to change any number of minor details to the interview environment that may improve the prospects of working in partnership and in collaboration with the service user.

It is not a bad idea to experiment in advance, and practise feeling comfortable when asking for such changes. Then, should you experience a more complex and potentially fraught situation, you will have already found a polite and respectful vocabulary for requesting changes.

---

### Group exercise

Create a staged interview using four people. Identify the care worker, and three members of a family (for example, parents and a child). Initially, the family are sitting close together, with the worker some distance away. What might the worker say to change this set-up? How might the possible *tasks* of the interview affect the need for changes? Experiment, by attempting different approaches – and change roles from time to time, to allow everyone to participate fully.

---

The beginning of the interview proper is also a time to make clear if there are any time constraints on the interview ('I know it's important to you that we've met today, but you do remember I said I only have 30 minutes before I have to be at . . .'). You can make clear to service users how long an interview is expected to last – particularly at a first interview; this element of good practice always makes for a more comfortable time frame. Reminding participants of the remaining time towards the end of the interview can also be a useful skill, particularly as mentioning time constraints *only* at the close of an interview is likely to cause problems.

Not all interviews go to plan. By keeping too rigidly to a pre-arranged timetable, you may upset the creation of a more positive relationship with the service user. For this reason, it is usually sensible to try to build some (unannounced) leeway into your planned time schedule.

**Reason for meeting**

At or very near the beginning of an interview, you need to make clear why you are meeting the service user. Most usefully, this can be accomplished as a question: 'You do know why we are here together, don't you?'

This seeking of confirmation will also be a first chance to personally clarify the needs and expectations of other people who may be present. An important part of interview interaction and communication is to be alert to the possibility of what may called hidden agendas (defined in Chapter 4). Working in partnership with people will call for you to be as honest and open as possible, and not to seek any hidden motivations. Occasionally people may have an unspecified interview goal, or a misapprehension about the social work role, and what can be achieved. Consequently, from the start you need to be frank with the service user about the basis of the interview, and clear about its intentions. Your use of suitable language can be crucial here. For instance, defining the issues as 'problems' or 'services' may well sound too negative for people in the initial stages of the interview (Kadushin and Kadushin, 1997, p92).

This early stage of the interview is also an opportunity for you to give a brief overview of areas you feel need to be covered. Take particular care about mentioning areas that may be perceived as sensitive, and always carefully explain *why* these sensitive areas must be covered.

The interviewer's need for information, and consequent questioning, can give rise to a common complaint:

> Why do you have to ask so many questions? All I want from you is a daily hot meal/letter to Housing/small piece of equipment . . .'
>
> (Lishman, 1994, p71)

You may have to think about your rationale for asking some questions. Some answers might include:

- My employer expects me to make a thorough assessment.
- I will try to keep my questions to only relevant things.
- There may be areas in which we could help that you don't know about, so if I don't ask about them . . .

What the service user may actually be seeking, of course, could be a *negative*. It may be that the participants have agreed to be involved in the interview because they hope that as a result, something will *not* happen – for example, an admission to hospital, or further involvement with the courts.

Clearly, initially, the actual areas needing to be discussed will vary to reflect the individual needs of the service user. This will depend on whether the interview involves assessment and inquiry, therapeutic intervention, or is investigatory.

For a follow-up interview, it can be helpful to begin by:

- summarising the situation as it was left at the last interview,
- clarifying what been accomplished in the period since then,
- asking the service user to review any plan or contract with you, to identify the issues for the current interview, and consider how much progress is being made on long-term objectives.

You may need to think of ways to ensure that the service user is empowered to put his or her point of view about the purpose of the interview. In addition to clarifying your own objectives, this beginning part of an interview should always give people time to include other topics for discussion that are important to *them*.

Finally, the beginning of the interview is about making expectations clear. It gives both parties the opportunity to incorporate newly proposed topics into the interview plan, or, if necessary, to say why an initial plan may not be appropriate (Egan, 2002, p284).

---

### Practice issue

Harry was referred to the Youth Offenders Team, but as he did not know what to expect, he was very nervous about meeting his new social worker. They went for a quiet coffee together, where Harry could talk. Alison, the social worker, began by asking Harry what he hoped to gain from their meetings before telling Harry about her role, and what goals she hoped they would set together. She expected they both wanted to prevent Harry going back to Court.

---

It can be helpful to the working alliance to give the service user priority in their choices. For example, you may want to begin by discussing family relationships, but the service user may have another concern. Being flexible and following people's priorities in this way will make them feel heard. Of course, the planned areas that *need* discussion must not be abandoned, so sometimes it may be necessary to explain why such areas must be given priority. If you make the discussion of their interview goals important, the service user's role becomes more active and collaborative.

Finally, if you state in advance the areas you intend to cover in the interview, you can observe the reactions of the service user to these topics. This also allows you thinking time, giving space in which you can reflect on the implications for managing the interview process.

### Introducing sensitive topics

As we have said, the early period of an interview is the time to put forward the planned subject areas to be covered. Most interviews will have areas of difficulty – often sensitive issues that are likely to raise emotional responses in the service user.

What might be an example of such a sensitive topic?

'Sensitive' is a flexible description, and may change depending on the perceptions of all participants in the interview. Generally, for the service user, a sensitive subject is usually one that relates to their more private, or intimate,

## Self-assessment: basic interviewing skills

*This self-assessment test is designed to help you identify those parts of the interviewing process about which you feel confident and competent, together with those parts in which you would like to improve. It is based on an original self-assessment form by Rosalind G. Hargreaves, of the former School of Social Work at the University of Kent, Canterbury.*

Rate each skill on a 5-point scale, where

1 means  I am never good at that skill
2 means  I am occasionally good at that skill
3 means  I am sometimes good at that skill
4 means  I am usually good at that skill
5 means  I am always good at that skill

| | | | | | |
|---|---|---|---|---|---|
| 1. Introducing yourself | 1 | 2 | 3 | 4 | 5 |
| 2. Explaining your role/purpose | 1 | 2 | 3 | 4 | 5 |
| 3. Listening: taking in what people say | 1 | 2 | 3 | 4 | 5 |
| 4. Listening: giving attention, showing interest | 1 | 2 | 3 | 4 | 5 |
| 5. Paraphrasing to check you've understood | 1 | 2 | 3 | 4 | 5 |
| 6. Giving information | 1 | 2 | 3 | 4 | 5 |
| 7. Getting required factual information | 1 | 2 | 3 | 4 | 5 |
| 8. Asking open questions | 1 | 2 | 3 | 4 | 5 |
| 9. Waiting for replies | 1 | 2 | 3 | 4 | 5 |
| 10. Not interrupting people | 1 | 2 | 3 | 4 | 5 |
| 11. Coping with lengthy silences | 1 | 2 | 3 | 4 | 5 |
| 12. Helping people to be specific/concrete | 1 | 2 | 3 | 4 | 5 |
| 13. Recognising the feelings of others | 1 | 2 | 3 | 4 | 5 |
| 14. Recognising your own feelings | 1 | 2 | 3 | 4 | 5 |
| 15. Helping people put feelings into words | 1 | 2 | 3 | 4 | 5 |
| 16. Expressing empathy/support | 1 | 2 | 3 | 4 | 5 |
| 17. Responding to anxiety/distress | 1 | 2 | 3 | 4 | 5 |
| 18. Responding to anger | 1 | 2 | 3 | 4 | 5 |
| 19. Responding to apathy/lack of interest | 1 | 2 | 3 | 4 | 5 |
| 20. Interrupting long accounts when necessary | 1 | 2 | 3 | 4 | 5 |
| 21. Re-focusing an interview | 1 | 2 | 3 | 4 | 5 |
| 22. Challenging what someone has said | 1 | 2 | 3 | 4 | 5 |
| 23. Summarising | 1 | 2 | 3 | 4 | 5 |
| 24. Ending session in a positive way | 1 | 2 | 3 | 4 | 5 |
| 25. Recording session in an effective manner | 1 | 2 | 3 | 4 | 5 |

areas of concern – essentially subjects that have an immediate emotional resonance. Thinking about this, and being able to identify such areas in advance of an interview, will obviously be of help to you.

Any issues where there may be differences and discrimination, real or perceived, have the potential to raise the emotional content of an interview. People living under oppression may understandably be extremely sensitive to the possibility of further discrimination. Black service users, or survivors of the mental health system (French and Swain, 2002, p394) may illustrate this point, while the social stigma attached to a physical health diagnosis, such as HIV, can be equally potent.

Unsurprisingly, people may wish to protect themselves emotionally from discussion of sensitive issues, at least until they have more confidence in you, and have built more trust in your involvement. On the other hand, your questions are likely to be very relevant to your involvement with the service user.

For many people, discussion of finances can be an emotionally sensitive subject. In addition to obvious privacy issues, this area may have complex feelings attached to it. Even if you are not directly involved in financial counselling, welfare rights will involve questions about income, while statutory authorities have charging policies for some services. Thus there is always a possibility you will need to discuss finances.

---

### Practice issue

Des, a student social worker, received an angry response from a single parent when he asked why her marriage had broken down. Later, he learnt that the grounds cited in the divorce were 'unreasonable behaviour' on her part. He resolved in future to be clearer about what information was relevant, and to try out a different way of asking for it.

---

You should always try to identify areas of sensitivity, and, once you have done so, to begin discussions with an explanation of why you are seeking the information. Remember, too, that different ethnic groups may have varying cultural expectations, of which you may be unaware. Having information about possible cultural differences and sensitivities of particular communities beforehand is important. (An example might be to be aware of death and bereavement practices if you are supporting someone at a time of bereavement.)

**Practitioner issues**

It is important to appreciate that you personally will also have 'sensitive' areas. One such uncomfortable area is likely to be when you are faced with a change in your role. For example, you may receive information that means you have to revisit a service user, but with a very different agenda.

---

### Practice issue

Joshi had been visiting Mr and Mrs Peebles: Mr Peebles had been supporting his wife, who had mental health issues. A concerned neighbour had telephoned the office to tell Joshi that she had seen bruises on Mrs Peebles's arm, said to have been caused by her husband. Joshi felt she needed to go through in advance questions she would need to ask, and to rehearse some of them with a colleague. Factors to take into consideration in the enquiry would be how to talk to the couple separately, and might well need to take into account the neighbour's motives. This event generated for Joshi an anxiety-provoking change in what had until then been a support relationship between her and the couple.

---

This particular example shows how, when allegations of harm arise, you may be forced to change from a supportive approach to an investigative role. This new interview 'focus', and the very different questions that in conse-quence you will have to ask, will clearly be at variance with your preceding 'focus'. In such circumstances, it might be useful to check that you are the appropriate person to do the new interview.

Social workers are no different from the rest of the population in perceiv-ing questioning about certain areas of personal functioning as 'intrusive'. The key to these questions should always be: is it possible to justify asking for the information? If it is, and the job demands it, then you will have to find a way through your feelings in order to ask those awkward questions. As always, rehearsal and planning will help.

**Pace of the interview**

Although there will be times when it is not possible, starting an interview in an unhurried way is almost always beneficial, even when you face pressure to go on to another visit. While the current interview is in progress your attention should be given to the service user as completely as possible. If, instead, your mind is on other things, the interview will inevitably suffer. Unconscious pressure to leave is likely to become obvious through non-verbal cues, such as clock watching, or perhaps in rushed speech. Once you observe yourself doing this, there is a need to deliberately slow down.

Since, first and foremost, the interview is the service user's time, it is important to conduct it at a pace that is comfortable for them. While you may have been involved in many previous interviews, a service user is likely to be less experienced, and may therefore need time to follow what is happening. People also vary widely in mental capacity or understanding, so you need to look for feedback in this area.

You should therefore develop the ability to vary your pace during different interviews, together with building a capacity for patience and empathy.

## TRANSITION TO THE MIDDLE PHASE

It can be unclear exactly when an interview moves into the middle stages, or as Kadushin and Kadushin call it, 'the developmental phase'. At the beginning of the interview, you will have started to explore with the service user the background, history and intensity of the issues in their current situation. In that context, you will be using open-ended questions (Chapter 5) in order to come to some understanding about the service user's world, and their views about their circumstances. In a therapeutic interview, you may well have started by explaining the methods the service user and you will be following together, or by recapping on what changes there have been since you last met.

It is at the interview's middle point that you should begin to use your paraphrasing and summarising skills to feed back to the individual, in different vocabulary, how you perceive their situation. This is an important stage, as it not only gives you an opportunity to ensure that your active listening and processing of the given information have been on track, but should also reassure the service user that you have been hearing and understanding them.

If there are misconceptions, then, if your summarising means you discover them by the middle stage of the interview, it is still early enough in the session to resolve them. This experience should help the service user to build confidence in your willingness to try and understand their point of view.

The middle part of the interview proceeds from this point, frequently into a further but more detailed exploration of the important areas of a person's life, and the issues that have led to your involvement. This more precise definition of the situation is usually intended to confirm whether the preliminary views you have been formulating are valid, or whether they need modification.

---

### Practice issue

Moran (social worker) spent about 30 minutes exploring with Gemma the events that led to her first breakdown. He wondered whether the miscarriage she had had so close to her father's death was a significant factor in precipitating her mental stresses. With her agreement, he talked with her about other times when she had experienced loss, and her coping mechanisms at those times.

---

## Completing documentation

To help in completing a form, try giving it to the person to read through before starting to talk about it, not just after it has been completed (or perhaps keep a spare copy handy, so the service user can follow as you complete it together). Remember empowerment issues, and – for example – make quite sure that the form you are using is available for a service user in a style appropriate for them (perhaps in large print, or in their first language).

Where there are communication or literacy issues, it will be particularly important to spend more time in talking things through. It is always sensible to confirm what type of communication is most comfortable for the sharing of information; for example, reading back a completed assessment form aloud may be preferable to simply handing the form over to be read. Vocalising the content of a form can highlight whether the phraseology you have used accurately reflects the service user's vocabulary and understanding.

The 'history' of a person's life may be part of your assessment (Bögels, 2000, p4), but how much you ask will depend upon your agency, the person, and your individual style. Some evidence suggests that a life history approach helps the understanding of older people, and assists the choices they may make. If it helps you understand the person to know a little of their background and life experiences, then you can preface any questions in this area with, say, 'It would help me understand you a little better if . . .'

## Meeting goals

This middle part of the interview is when you hope to meet planned objectives. The precise subjects, or agenda items that need addressing will obviously vary from interview to interview, and may also depend upon whether your visit is for assessment, or a further visit for ongoing work. Finally, priorities or feelings may cause a change in the original aims of the interview.

As we have said, it is preferable to have prepared a list of headings or general areas that you plan to discuss, but it is also good to be flexible, and able to take your lead from the client. This means that if the service user mentions a subject area you had planned to deal with towards the end of the interview, you should quickly consider following their initiative, and discuss that subject there and then. While to a less experienced interviewer it can feel unsafe to abandon the plan of intervention, taking the opportunity to explore a relevant area is usually sensible, especially if it appears that the service user may have this issue at the forefront of their mind. If the chance is not taken, the service user may feel you are ignoring topics that are important to them.

Lengthy discussions are often a part of assessment interviews; but not all interviews are for assessment. For follow-up interviews, interventions, or review meetings, this may mean you need to re-explore the changes the support has made, or the work that either of you may have undertaken in the interval since you met. Such 'regrouping' of objectives may mean that open questions will need to be reused frequently.

---

### Practice issue

Azzi had been in trouble with truanting from school, triggered by the discrimination she experienced in a largely white school population. She had worked out with Meri, her social worker, a plan of how to combat and cope with the discrimination. When Meri next saw Azzi, he needed to ask 'open' questions first, to find out how well the strategies they had developed had worked, and how they had affected Azzi's confidence.

---

## ENDINGS

The transition to ending the interview can be the most difficult section. During the interview, you may have created a powerful and emotional atmosphere, in which people have been encouraged to discuss significant events in their life, and their own functioning. Service users may understandably be reluctant to break that intimacy, and consequently slow to do so (Trevithick, 2000, p108). Summing up and finishing an interview may take longer than you expect.

### Summarising

Summarising, sometimes called 'recapitulating' (Kadushin and Kadushin, 1997, p150) is a technique of reviewing both the themes and events of an interview, so that the essence of the section of the interview is clearly encapsulated (discussed in Chapter 6). It essentially confirms that both service user and interviewer have understood the situation in the same way. You can use it especially at transitional points, to help the interview move forward. However, a more comprehensive summary should be made towards an interview's end, when all the strands that have been discussed can be brought together.

The closing stage of the interview is therefore the natural time to summarise, and to restate and confirm the plans that you have made jointly. Your summary should state the situation, as you understand it, and clarify any plans for change or support. You should then ask for feedback from the service user.

It might seem fairly straightforward at the end of an interview to spell out what needs to be done by you and the service user. However, ensuring who has the responsibilities and deadlines for plans to be completed may not be so clear-cut. To help, you could use informal or formal contracts – simple communication aids that can help maintain clear communication with the service user.

## Contract – plan

Part of the process of concluding an interview is to decide with the service user 'What route do we take from here?' There will often be a verbal agreement about what needs to be accomplished, and by whom. In many instances, though, you need to consider whether to set this agreement down in writing, as a type of formal contract. Doing so admittedly involves power issues: the freedom of choice implicit in the notion of a contract does not necessarily combine well with the complexities of the service user/practitioner relationship (Lishman, 1994, p91). However, there are considerable practical advantages to the use of contracts in social care.

One primary benefit is that a written note should ensure that all parties involved are quite clear about what is expected to happen, who will be helping to bring it about, and how they will be doing so. As well as these major points, such a written agreement could also include anticipated time scales, the breaking down of long-term objectives into shorter goals, and perhaps even identifying factors that might suggest when planned intervention will become unproductive.

Even if your organisation does not have any relevant documentation for you and the service user to complete together, it is advisable to consider writing down formally what has been agreed. You may at first find this procedure awkward and bureaucratic, but sharing agreed decisions in written form is a skill well worth acquiring. This can improve communication with many service users, and, apart from other advantages, writing something down will leave an agreed record with the service user.

You will need to consider the type of language you use. For whom is the agreement made? If it is for the service user, then that must be reflected in the vocabulary chosen – but, in any event, service users should be given a copy of the agreement. Where there are communication issues, such as a visual impairment, then the words may have to be typed in large format, or another and more suitable method chosen to record the plan.

Essentially, a written summary should reduce the possibility of any misunderstandings, and will certainly reduce the risk of confusion and problems later on – it might also act as a prompt to your memory. It gives both sides – the service user and you – a valuable reminder of what is expected of them.

## Timekeeping – when to end the interview

Whatever the purpose of the interview, you should always, if at all practicable, leave sufficient time to end your involvement without haste. The ending of the interview is also not a sensible time to introduce any new subject, especially one that is emotionally charged (Kadushin and Kadushin, 1997, p272).

For some interviews, the ending time may already have been determined by the way the agency functions, perhaps with a policy of time-limited appointments. Individual techniques are possible, too. For an adolescent, perhaps subtly timing an interview so that it happens just before a football session will allow a natural ending. In these and similar cases, an expectation has already been created that the session will end at a certain time.

However, you will normally be responsible for judging when it is timely to bring the interview to a close, and then to do so appropriately. (Of course, this responsibility does not also prevent service users themselves from deciding, too.) Even when you have agreed an ending time in advance, a reminder may be necessary. People differ a good deal, and may be understandably wrapped up in their own thinking – so an interviewer cannot always be certain that advice on timekeeping given at the start of the interview will always be heeded at the end (Kadushin and Kadushin, 1997, pp271–2).

Several techniques may be useful here. Making sure there is a clock in the room that you can observe (without making it obvious) may help with timekeeping, both by keeping track of the progress of time, and identifying a point at which you should start to pull things together, and begin the concluding phase of the involvement. Don't forget, too, that a deliberate look at a watch or clock, while breaking eye contact, may serve as a non-verbal reminder to the other person that the interview is drawing near a close.

Another helpful practice worth considering is to advise the service user *deliberately early* that the interview is coming to an end. This is because, in many situations, emotional revelations tend to come at the end of interviews, frequently even after goodbyes have been said. Trevithick calls these 'door-knob revelations' (2000, p108). Somehow the arrival of an ending time can unlock a psychological process, opening the way for more personal or intimate information to be shared, frequently in a less formal way. Such sharing may often happen even without planning, but it may be a good idea to specifically trigger the process through the suggestion of an earlier end to the interview.

A similar development can occur at the end of a home visit. Here, a carer or third party may use the opportunity given by goodbyes to engage you in a discussion on their views of the service user's predicament. While such a chat may potentially enlarge your understanding of this carer's role, it can create a dilemma. Should you participate in the discussion? The service user may perceive you to be 'talking behind their back', perhaps colluding with the third party. To avoid such misunderstandings, you will need to monitor carefully the length of time spent and the subjects under discussion, balanced with issues of confidentiality and trust.

Finally, it is not unknown to arrive back at the office only to discover some information has been missed. If it is a fairly straightforward piece of information that has been accidentally overlooked, simply telephoning the person involved may be practical. Otherwise, in the final resort, it should always be possible to arrange for a follow-up visit, this time replanning the intervention to cover this area.

## Disengagement

So far under 'Endings' we have looked at how to depart from a single inter-view, but the term 'disengagement' refers more specifically to the process of drawing the *relationship* with a service user to a close. This relationship may have lasted some time, and there may perhaps have been clashes, but it must end. It may not always conclude in mutual consent.

One key factor to affect disengagement will be the intensity of the rela-tionship, but other variables are likely too, for example the independence of the people involved, their personalities, and of course the outcomes of the particular stresses that originally led to involvement with the agency. All will individually combine in forming the ongoing interaction between service user and social worker, and will ensure it closes on an individual note (Trevithick, 2000, p107). There are, however, some general rules and guide-lines that can be applied.

The first principle is that the longer and deeper the relationship, the more notice is owed to the service user for disengagement. Some practitioners will find it difficult to say to service users that they are leaving, or are transferring case responsibility to another worker. This may be a reflection of the emotional impact they feel disengagement may cause service users. Of course, not everybody enjoys goodbyes; but if you feel you are deliberately delaying breaking news of your departure to the service user, you may need to examine this reaction.

Sometimes, the knowledge of disengagement can be built into your professional practice from the start: 'As a duty worker, I deal with things just until you have an allocated social worker . . .'. 'As an intake social worker, I work with families for a maximum of three months . . .', and so on. A reminder to the service user toward the end of this limited period can then help to assist courteous disengagement.

However, if involvement has not been time-limited, how best to prepare the ground for withdrawal? This must obviously depend upon individual circumstances and your knowledge of the person, but if it is possible to give some notice by telephone or letter before an actual visit, this can be beneficial. On the other hand, remember that a personal visit will help in sharing and addressing feelings, and is certainly owed in a closer professional relationship.

Ideally, there should be some warning, rather than a sudden ending.

Version A: 'Oh, by the way, Pat, I won't be seeing you any more . . .'

Version B: 'You've been getting along so well, Pat, that I may soon have to stop coming to see you . . .'

*Interview* endings are a time to:

- summarise decisions and plans,
- consider a written contract/plan.

*Involvement* endings are a time to:

- restate optimism about the future,
- decide how to say goodbye.

## DUTY INTERVIEWS

Duty visits or interviews are normally carried out

- when a situation is referred urgently,
- when the usual social worker is not available, and there is an element of crisis or urgency.

A duty visit can be one of the most stressful interviews for social workers to undertake, so we are including here some specific points on the issues involved.

1   People are likely to be in distress, or in crisis, so there may be a high emotional element to the interaction. If it is their first contact with the agency, a service user may additionally be confused about what to expect.
2   In particular, the amount of available information about an individual and why they wish to see a duty worker may well be very sparse. Because of emotional factors, the information available to you may be jumbled or unclear (Koprowska, 2005, p60).
3   Duty interviews are almost always made at short notice, and in consequence preparation time may be virtually non-existent.
4   The inevitable element of the unknown or unpredictable about the situation may often provoke anxiety.

Duty interviews undertaken in an office environment, rather than at a person's home, are slightly different; but they still retain some elements of the above.

The range of reasons why a service user feels they need to see someone can be wide, from a straightforward request for information about services to a disclosure about severe abuse. More usually, the reason will lie somewhere in between, but will include a perception of urgency.

The pre-planning sections of this book are particularly relevant to a duty interviewer. Clarifying whether any forward planning or telephoning could be done to help towards the actual interviewing, as discussed in Chapter 4, should be particularly helpful.

We examine below some specific duty interview strategies that may also be worth considering.

## Support strategies

One helpful method can be for you to consciously acknowledge your own particular anxieties in advance, while in a secure environment. Are there any particular scenarios that you feel will cause you stress? If so, then discussion with a supervisor in advance may help; and colleagues could be made aware of the scenario, so they can offer support. Such support might range from participating in the visit to being around afterwards, in order to help you unwind from the experience.

It helps, too, to try to speak to anybody who has seen or spoken that day to the service user who is to be interviewed. This is primarily to discover if there is any other available information that may not have originally been given to you. Sometimes information does get missed, or may be misinterpreted in the referral process. Of course, it is not always appropriate to try to obtain further information from, say, reception staff; but even so, they may be able to offer you some help, perhaps by giving an idea about how distressed the person seemed to them.

One tactic well known to intake workers is – to finish that cup of tea! This may involve checking that the person concerned can wait five minutes, but such thinking space can be invaluable. The reason for deliberately delaying the interview slightly – rather than rushing to it – is because panic and anxiety adversely affect your thought processes. By deliberately trying to calm down for a few minutes, not only is more rational and analytic thinking likely to predominate but you will also be in a better and more relaxed state to undertake the interview.

If you are able, run through ideas with a colleague in advance, as this can aid your plans, too. Just talking about the situation will often help you get a perspective. The colleague with whom you share ideas will be able to provide a check on whether the options you are contemplating are realistic, or if perhaps a different approach could be more appropriate.

It can also help to appreciate that the 'horrendous' situation described in a referral may, in reality, present very differently.

Finally, in duty work, keeping a client-centred focus on the emotional distress that the situation may be causing, and keeping an open mind about what you will find, will always be a support to you.

## CONCLUSION

This chapter dealt with the interview itself, essentially by considering the interview content, and the structure of beginnings, middle and endings.

In the interview:

- Remember that several processes will happen simultaneously – besides the verbal exchanges, there is the development of the two-way relationship, the non-verbal encounters, and the emotional agenda.
- Consider whom to include, and whom not to include, especially if confidentiality and privacy are issues.
- Don't forget or hurry the interview's preliminary stage: it helps both parties get the measure of the situation.
- The beginning is a particularly crucial time, giving you the opportunity to establish easy and relaxed communication, and time for you to clarify

any limits on time or content, making the anticipated course of the interview clear to all.

- Consider the work necessary in the middle stage of the interview. This
is where the main work with service users happens.
- Remember staging-post summaries and check out frequently, especially
at transitions, throughout the course of the interview.
- Carefully summarise at the end of the interview; consider the use of a
written contract, formal or informal.
- Think how to 'disengage' from the interview, and from your involvement. Ensure respect for the feelings involved.
- Duty interviews may be particularly stressful. Always try to carve out
some 'thinking' time before a duty interview, and before duty visits
discuss your approaches/plans with someone else.

## QUESTIONS

1   A GP asks you to visit a couple urgently. The wife is seriously ill, and is
going to hospital as soon as the ambulance gets there; her husband has
dementia. What areas of questioning would you jot down to discuss with
the wife?

2   What phrases could you use to start the ending process of an interview?

3   You are starting some sessions of brief therapy with a service user. How
would you structure the introductory time to the sessions?

## FURTHER READING

Egan, Gerard, *The Skilled Helper,* Chapter 14.
Koprowska, Juliet, *Communication and Interpersonal Skills in Social Work,*
Chapter 4.
Trevithick, Pamela: *Social Work Skills.*

*Chapter 8*

# Thinking and Interview Handling

## NOSSC RELEVANCE

The material discussed in this chapter relates to the following National Occupational Standards for Social Care:

- **Key Role One**, Unit 2. Work with individuals, families, carers, groups and communities to help them make informed decisions.
- **Key Role Five**, Unit 14. Manage and be accountable for your own work.
- **Key Role Six**, Unit 18. Research, analyse, evaluate and use current knowledge of best social work practice.

*In this chapter we discuss some different types of thinking involved in handling an interview, and consider the use of interview plans, together with their need for dynamic modifications.*

For a new practitioner, keen to do well, a decision to learn at least some of the skills and interviewing techniques used in social care interviews is obviously sensible. However, while a successful interview may well depend upon such knowledge, no methods are foolproof; even the best communication techniques can fail if used in the wrong circumstances.

For this reason it is not possible to choose a standard approach for interviews. Before selecting any interviewing method, you need to be sure your preferred approach will actually accomplish its purpose in that specific interview. (A Rogerian approach may not be successful in a court enquiry interview, and so on.) As was said earlier, in order to choose effective methods for a particular interview you will need to first consider the setting of the interview, the needs of the service user, and of course your own individual skills and abilities.

However, no interview is static; so selecting interview methods in advance is no guarantee of satisfaction. Depending on changing circumstances and the needs of the service user, it may well be necessary *during the interview itself* to review whatever you are doing, and perhaps make changes in your methods or decisions. In order to observe the effectiveness of what you are currently doing, you will need to monitor yourself and your performance constantly. Essentially, you need to become aware of what is actually a vital underpinning of any interview – the ability to dynamically analyse the events of the interview as they are happening, and use the results of this analysis to modify your actions. Koprowska calls these 'second-order' skills, ones that are not direct communication (first-order), but 'skills in thinking about skills' (2005, p8).

## 'THINKING' ASPECTS OF INTERVIEWING

Without a doubt, an interviewer is not machine-like, programmed to carry out an interview by slavishly following a pre-planned course of action. Preparation is certainly necessary, but as the needs of the interview change, you may have to change your approach. As well as discussing specific practical communication skills, it is therefore necessary for us to spend a little time dealing with the *thinking* aspects of interviewing.

'Interview thinking' may at first seem peripheral to the interviewing task, but it is not. A careful approach here is analogous to an artist, before starting to paint, carefully choosing the correct brush. It is unlikely that any work of art will be best completed using only a single brush; when change becomes necessary during the course of a painting, a skilled artist will be prepared to change their first choice of brush for a more suitable one. In exactly the same way, the methods – both verbal and interpersonal – used in a social work interview need to be constantly monitored and reviewed by the interviewer, and changed for more appropriate ones should this be necessary.

Interviewers will build up knowledge and experience throughout their careers. This accumulating knowledge will enable them to draw upon an increasing range of interview approaches, and so be better able in advance of an interview to select, or instinctively choose, appropriate methods. What might happen after the interview has begun, however, is likely to be less predictable. However good your interviewing performance might be in theory, in practice you will always need to think carefully about the best way to *dynamically* use your communication skills and techniques. How to do this is discussed below; the interview techniques themselves are described in Chapters 5 and 6.

## WHO ARE YOU?

While methods and aids may be essential to skill, there is an old saying that unsuccessful workers will 'always blame their tools' rather than themselves. In a situation such as interviewing, it is hard to disentangle the tools from the person. So, while it seems straightforward to discuss a range of methods of carrying out interviews well, before we do so we need to consider a central factor in the success of any social work interview; this is not the interviewer's techniques – but you, as the interviewer.

For most of us, one of the most rewarding aspects of social care is that it provides many day-to-day involvements with people. However, as we have stressed before, practitioners are likely to deal not only with a huge range of individuals, but also an enormous variety of issues. This means that the job may well involve constantly facing different people, in different circumstances. Therefore you must be prepared for considerable variations in the demands your interviews may make upon you.

This point is important to appreciate, because clearly not everyone will be able to deal well with every interview situation. Inevitably, even the most skilled interviewers have individual strengths, together with individual 'attention points'. For example, while some people may be particularly comfortable and skilled in certain types of social work interview – interactions with children, for example – they may well find other kinds of interview far more challenging and demanding. In reality, however much a person studies, they will always be more effective in some types of interview simply by virtue of their *personality* and their *life experiences*.

To be clear: we emphatically do not mean to suggest that some interviews should or should not always be undertaken by particular people. However, we do believe that every social care worker should grow to understand where their strengths – and gaps – in interview skills may lie. Once you have established this knowledge, skills may naturally be improved. Training, rehearsal, experience – and, of course, reading – can go a long way to improve interview practice, and bolster confidence.

Throughout a professional career it remains important for a practitioner to continually identify and understand their current personal strengths and weaker points. For you as an interviewer it will usually make sense to play to your strengths, but knowledge of your limitations is valuable, too, in avoiding possible problems. For a trained and experienced interviewer this means that an analysis of your personal strong points, and learning areas, should form an essential first step in interviewing.

So, what if, after careful consideration, you decide that – in your opinion – you are less efficient and perhaps dislike some aspect of interviewing, and are good at, and really enjoy, others?

| **Practice issue** |
|---|
| Erika, a social worker we knew, was a really quiet person who found even loud voices upsetting. Once, outside an interview room, and faced with a complex family therapy interview, she was physically shaking; but she loved working with children, and was outstanding at getting them to 'open up' in interviews. |

Should Erika have continued to attempt the family therapy work she found difficult and stressful? Or should she instead concentrate on working with children, a job she loved and at which she was successful? Put like that, the answer may seem obvious, but to Erika herself it was not so clear, until her supervisor encouraged her to think through the issues involved.

A supervisor can also gain considerable assistance from knowledge of an individual worker's strengths and weaknesses. For example, ideally, cases should not be allocated on a first come first served basis, but in a way that accurately reflects the knowledge and abilities of individual social workers.

What, though, if you are working in a setting you find uncomfortable, where you need to constantly employ interview practices you personally find stressful? Clearly, this is not a recipe for successful interviewing. However, unless you have spent time working out exactly where your talents lie – and are best used – you are at risk of a similar situation arising.

If only for this reason, it is an excellent plan to periodically spend time thinking through your interviewing skills. You can do this by reflecting on past interviews, revisiting comments and feedback you may have received, or perhaps looking again at the responses of service users you have interviewed in the past. The purpose of this exercise is to identify those aspects of inter-viewing where you feel confident, or less confident; and, it is hoped, also to recognise those areas where, with more training and experience, you would *become* more confident.

The process of analysing individual skills is an important stage in the devel-opment of a professional worker. While the techniques described in Chapters 5 and 6 are all potentially useful, to be fully effective you will need to employ them as a worker well aware of your own strengths and weaknesses. If, as a result of this reflection, you build an accurate understanding of your own abilities, you will be able to consciously select interview approaches that are best suited to bringing out your strengths – and minimising your weaknesses.

## THINKING BEFORE ACTING

The previous section encouraged you to think about your personal strengths and learning points. We need next to consider, for a moment, a different type of thinking – the actual process of dynamic analysis involved during the course of an interview.

As we have said, you should consider the needs of each interview in advance. Planning the timing and location of an interview, for example, is key, but it is equally relevant at this early stage to consider how the interview itself might progress.

We will assume that you have identified your personal strengths and learning points, considered any anti-discriminatory issues, the needs of the service user, the influences of your employer, and the special requirements of your role within the organisation.

The next stage in planning the handling of an interview is to build on this 'basic' reflection by taking into account the *current* needs of the interview, and of the service user. The questions that need to be asked, and answered, are, 'How should I work with, or address, the service user's needs?' and 'In the particular circumstances of this specific interview, what skills or approaches are likely to work best?' Even though you may have already identified the *practical* points to be covered in this interview, to optimise your chances of an effective outcome it is important to appreciate that you may need to consider a more detailed 'interview handling' script. This evaluative process need not take too long.

---

### Practice issue

Ed had communication issues to do with severe hearing deficit. Interviewing him for his views about his further education, Bea, his social worker, had originally tried a mixture of written and non-verbal methods to communicate. She eventually found that Ed was most at ease with British Sign language (BSL). Bea involved an interpreter, and found that this gave Ed more power.

---

Normally, of course, if there is more than one approach that seems to fit a specific interview, it will be best for you to select whichever method you personally feel is the most effective – and comfortable.

## MODIFYING PLANNED APPROACHES

Your initial choice of an approach will probably not be final. Once discussions are under way, emerging needs may be different from those you had previously assumed; perhaps the situation might prove to be more complicated, too. Many variations are possible; you may need to reconsider initial choices and interpersonal approaches fairly frequently.

Interviews are, by their nature, dynamic; so such changes would not be needed because your initial choice of approach was wrong, but because the interview circumstances had demonstrated that the requirements were changing – and you had observed this. However skilled your initial thinking may have been, however accurate your initial plan, what actually happens during an interview is unlikely to be *exactly* what you had anticipated before the interview began. This Likelihood of Changing Needs (the 'LCN' of an interview) means that you should keep your thinking about the interaction with the service user under constant review throughout the interview. What is *currently* appropriate may – and probably will – change during the course of the interview, even if it had not changed before.

High LCN during an interview is unfortunately particularly unkind to new interviewers. This is because if you have less experience you will – reasonably – have attempted to prepare carefully for your task. An untried interviewer, particularly if they are feeling insecure, may wish to stick to such plans. However, while to plan is always an excellent policy, it is never sensible to insist on clinging to a predetermined agenda in an interview, especially when you are confronted with drastically changed circumstances. Reactions from service users may be especially difficult to estimate; but you need to listen to them, and to respond to the emotional content.

---

**Practice issue**

Kaddi had gone to review services with her client, Leanne, who had learning difficulties. Leanne disclosed that she had received some unwelcome sexual advances from a voluntary helper. Kaddi abandoned her original plans about what was to be discussed in the interview and how she had thought it was going to progress, and, as well as trying to detail the exact events, focused on Leanne's distress.

---

To summarise: before an interview you will have made choices about skills and methods that are appropriate. Yet, however accurate this initial choice may have been when first made, it should never be fixed – because the needs of both service user and interview may change. To monitor these possible changes, you will need frequently to study the dynamic process of the interview itself. Always be ready to listen to and observe the service user's feelings and reactions, and be prepared to modify your chosen approach and methods of interaction.

## HOW MAY CHANGED NEEDS BE IDENTIFIED?

The conclusions of the previous section naturally lead on to an obvious problem: exactly *how* can you discover potentially changed needs? In practical terms, how might an interviewer realise – *during* an interview – if a change in their approach and interaction is warranted?

The answer obviously calls for some form of objective examination and analysis of the interview process. However, while it might theoretically be useful to involve external observers in social work interviews, such a plan is clearly unrealistic. (With necessary permissions, of course, observers, or even the videoing of interviews, may be possible; but this is far from usual practice.) Usually, if the interview process is to be observed, you must make the observations *yourself*.

## INTERVIEWER AS OBSERVER

How might you respond to this challenge?

First, although an experienced practitioner will undoubtedly have planned their approach, they will not follow a rigid strategy. Second, they will respond flexibly to what is called the *interview dynamic,* which means they can recognise the LCN. Third, they can effectively change their initial plans (and consequent interview approach) during the actual interview.

As we proposed in the previous section, such modifications will normally be triggered by a continuing dynamic analysis, both of the interview processes (verbal, non-verbal and interactive) and of the interviewer's personal role.

'Continuing dynamic analysis' means that the interviewer constantly monitors what is going on in the interview. They simultaneously observe the *effects* of what (as the interviewer) they are doing, and (very importantly) study how the service user participating in the interview is responding. While this process may be straightforward to describe, it probably does not sound particularly easy to achieve. What might help you to accomplish it?

A recommended approach, which can prove of considerable benefit in most social care interviewing, is for you to act both as participant and as observer. The technique is to try taking a metaphorical step back, in order to deliberately view yourself, and your actions in the interview, objectively, as if from a distance.

To quote from Hargie and Tourish:

> Thus, skilled interviewers are not constantly and consciously aware of the goal which is guiding each of their verbal and non-verbal responses. However, the distinction made by Brody (1987) between 'being aware' of what is happening, 'and being aware of being aware' of what is happening is important.
>
> (Hargie and Tourish, 2000, p76)

In social work student training, there are several methods to encourage such observational distancing. We mention elsewhere videotaped interviews and process recording (where a student is requested to write a complete transcript of the processes of an interview).

Some reality television programmes employ a team of experts to advise a participant from a distance, by viewing their actions on a monitor, and communicating feedback to them through a radio link. Building on this example, probably the most straightforward way to accomplish observation of the interview dynamic is to think of the operation of your voice and body from within a central control room in your brain. Then, instead of 'you' participating directly in an interview, your 'controller' instead makes decisions regarding the appropriate way to act and interact. The 'controller' will then issue instructions that your body should carry out – 'smile', 'look thoughtful', or perhaps 'quietly disagree'.

Service users will best relate to you, if you have genuineness and naturalness of manner, and a relaxed approach – which may sometimes sit uncomfortably with the need to be aware of personal reactions, and modify them for the needs of the service user.

What the self-monitoring technique effectively achieves is to interpose an extra 'thinking' stage between 'plan' and 'action'. When you first try it, it will almost certainly slow down your responses – but, that can often prove beneficial in its own right, as signifying more thoughtful responses. The potential advantages of this technique are considerable. Once you have in place a confident method of reflecting on your performance, the process of continuing observation should effectively help to head off many potential interview problems before they become too entrenched, or even before they occur.

As an example, should your 'control room' scanning show that a service user is not responding to one approach, your internal 'controller' could be instructing you to modify that approach. Simultaneously, you could be observing the service user's reactions to changes, and thinking of appropriate ways to alter what is being said.

By this illustration we aim to encourage you to think about the separation of your *interviewer* role from your *observer* role.

However, if you find the 'control room' concept too complicated, there are several other approaches you could use. You could attempt to distance the interview by viewing it as if through a closed circuit television, or by means of a one-way mirror, or as if you were an actor playing a role. The exact manner in which a distancing technique is carried out is relatively unimportant – the important point is for you to develop the ability to practise using the distancing process.

Once it has been mastered, observational distancing should allow you, when participating in an interview, to observe the interview process as objectively as possible, and, very importantly, to be able to observe the dynamic effects of what is happening to service users. Such observation and analysis should be performed during the course of the interview. Once the technique is mastered, you can use the results of the analysis to dynamically change your behaviour. This will mean, in effect, that you should always be capable of appropriately handling the shifting needs of even a complex interview.

While complicated interview situations need some form of observational perspective on the interview dynamic, the technique will be useful in any interview.

## CONCLUSIONS

This chapter examined the thinking process behind an interviewer's task in handling interviews. It looked at the further thinking needed within the time and space of the interview.

- For interviewing in general, you may need to examine your personal strengths with regard to communication skills.
- Interviews are not static but dynamic, so are unlikely to always follow their anticipated, planned path. This means you will need to build up flexibility in your skills.
- One way of being flexible is to develop 'observational distancing'. This is a method of looking from outside at your performance, perhaps by imagining yourself as director and actor, so that you can monitor, decide to alter and then change your methods of interaction with service users.

■ The interview dynamic can sometimes be difficult to handle, as you will need to 'think on your feet', to meet the changing needs of the service user within the interview frame. At the same time you will be trying to understand what is happening – and of course working out further lines of enquiry.

## QUESTIONS

1 What grounds can you think of for planning an interview in detail? What are the strengths and weaknesses of this approach?

2 List *three* reasons why an interview may not go according to plan.

3 What method/s do you think you might employ to make sure you were able to practise observational distancing? Can you think of any methods that were *not* mentioned in this chapter?

## FURTHER READING

Koprowska, Juliet. *Communication and Interpersonal Skills in Social Work*, Chapter 1.
Thompson, Neil. *People Skills*, Chapter 1.

# Chapter 9

# Potential Pitfalls

## NOSSC

The material discussed in this chapter has particular relevance to the following National Occupational Standards for Social Care:

- **Key Role Four,** Unit 13. Assess, minimise and manage risk to self and colleagues.
- **Key Role Five,** Unit 14. Manage and be accountable for your own work.
- **Key Role Six,** Unit 19. Work within agreed standards of social work practice and ensure own professional development.

*In dealing with the reality of social care interviewing, it is important to acknowledge that everything may not always go according to plan. This chapter directly studies difficult issues that crop up from time to time for even the most skilled of interviewers, and discusses practical recovery strategies.*

## CATEGORISE PROBLEMS

To assist with discussion, it may be helpful to first divide the issues you may face into four broad categories:

1 Issues with *planning*: aspects of the interview related to pre-interview arrangements and preparations.
2 Issues during the course of the interview itself that result in not reaching planned *goals*.
3 Other potential difficulties, including time, lack of information, concluding an interview early.
4 Issues of perceived and actual *physical risk* to the interviewer.

## I Issues with planning

This category of difficulties relates both to a conscious lack of planning, and to a feeling that may arise during the interaction. The feeling is that, despite excellent advance preparations, you realise you have planned for the wrong type of interview.

### Pre-interview planning issues

As we discussed in Chapter 4, an interview is more effective if you have thought through the aims and objectives in advance. Specifically, you should have identified why you think the interview needs to be carried out, as well as tentatively identifying what the service user might wish to accomplish with you.

Unfortunately, in practice there may be many reasons why this process may not be achieved. Typical causes can include forgetfulness, unexpected work demands, or simply lack of time. Additionally, in an emergency you may be faced with needing to plan an interview at very short notice – and sometimes with no time at all.

### If possible, prepare

Before discussing what can be done to improve such a situation, it is well worth stressing that prevention, rather than recovery, is preferable. For this reason, even minimal preparation for an interview will be considerably better than no preparation at all. So, when faced with the need to carry out an immediate interview, it is sensible to see if you can delay even a crisis interview for a few minutes, in order to speed-read files, talk to a supervisor, or quickly research useful information.

---

### Practice issue

Brenda was a duty social worker. She was called out following admission of Mr Taupe to hospital. He had been caring for his wife, who had a severe mobility difficulty, and was now alone in the house. The couple's social worker was away on a course, and their GP, who was waiting with Mrs Taupe, requested the duty officer to come at once, interview the wife at home, complete necessary forms, and arrange an emergency admission to residential care. It would have been natural for Brenda to respond immediately to what was presented as an obvious emergency, but she first took time to bring herself up to date by checking the file. She discovered two of the couple's daughters were actually available, but at a distance. Once Brenda had alerted them, the family rapidly arranged for support themselves, and residential admission was averted.

In this case, what was initially presented as a need for an emergency interview and action turned into two very different interviews – with Mr and Mrs Taupe's daughters – and, while these telephone interviews were necessarily lacking in detailed preparation, their narrower focus on the provision of family support meant that the objective was clearly defined.

If you have scheduled an interview, but have not carried out the necessary planning, one option you should *always* consider is to cancel or postpone the interview. Although cancelling a planned interview is not best practice, concluding early an interview that is already running is equally poor practice, and far harder to accomplish. In either case, you will need to carefully negotiate changed plans with the service user. If, though, a lack of forethought only becomes clear when you are already with the service user, you will understandably need to spend time dealing with the individual's feelings of frustration and expectation.

The hope that, by carrying on the interview regardless, everything may turn out all right is understandable. However, if you are unprepared, then the chances are much higher that the interview will not be of much benefit to the service user. While this situation will, it is hoped, be unusual, we should emphasise that, quite apart from a waste of time and resources, carrying through an 'empty' interview may well make a future, productive interview far more difficult.

## Errors in planning

What happens, though, if you have carefully planned your interview, but on arrival discover you have made your well-thought-out plans in ignorance of a vital piece of information? In this case, you may again need to cancel or postpone the interview. This is because plans that have been based on incorrect information are as likely to be a barrier to an effective interview as a total lack of planning.

---

**Practice issue**

Mr and Mrs Llewellyn were an older couple in poor health who, through their district nurse (DN), were requesting Social Services support to remain at home. The worker asked to visit had done their homework; had checked with the DN and couple's GP, had made sure they were carrying copies of all relevant forms, and so on. However, on arrival they discovered that the Llewellyns were not in fact Welsh, as had been understandably assumed, but were instead ethnic Vietnamese, and spoke no English at all. (The referrers knew this, and had assumed the social worker did, too.)

---

When previous preparations, however thorough, are so clearly inadequate, the best thing for a prospective interviewer to do is, almost always, to apologise, and leave. Return as soon as you have made the correct preparations.

## Interview process planning

While a lack of preparation may sometimes become crystal clear to you before the interview starts, sometimes the need for further preparation becomes unmistakable only after an interview has actually begun.

Let us assume an interview is already under way when you become aware of the need to obtain further, external, information, either from colleagues or from paperwork. Without this information, you cannot carry out an effective interview. What should you do?

Although cancelling the interview could perhaps be justified, it may still be possible to save the situation.

One tactic that often works well is to ask the service user if you may have a quick break. Once away from the interview setting, and in a quiet location, it should be possible to make urgent use of a mobile phone to seek help and advice. Of course, if the interview is being held in offices, a quick consultation will be somewhat easier. Nevertheless, even if the interview is taking place elsewhere, support should still be available with the aid of a telephone.

Your request to the service user should always be as honest as possible:

SW:    I hope you'll excuse me for a moment – I need to consult with my office/a file/a colleague.

If this approach feels too awkward, or not possible in the circumstances of that specific interview, think of another reason for taking a break.

When seeking urgent support from the office in this way, it is very important to ask specific questions, in a structured manner. Remember, the purpose of the call is to ask for focused information that will enable you to rapidly plan and proceed with the interview.

SW:    Please can you check the C family file? I need to know how many children are living at home, their ages, and when exactly Mrs C first approached us . . .

However, if it is not going to be possible to carry out the interview without further information that is not immediately available, you should be prepared to explain the position honestly, and negotiate other arrangements with the service user. Continuing with an interview, just because it has started, is a natural reaction, but, apart from the fact that it will be lacking, the service user's feelings and expectations should be your central focus.

### Urgent advice needed?

You may need external help if something serious or urgent arises unexpectedly during the interview. It may then become essential to seek specific advice (authorisation – or perhaps a ruling) from a manager in order to continue effectively with the interview.

SW: Let me see if I've understood, Mrs Hope: your daughter's 14, but you're telling me you're sure she's got to leave unless she is offered immediate support at the family centre? You realise this isn't a decision I am able to make alone, don't you?

What is best for you to do in these circumstances will obviously depend upon the nature of your involvement, and the degree of urgency involved. Generally and understandably, managers prefer to be asked for advice in person, and then to be given a well-thought-out summary of the position – together with a fully written-up file. It is only reasonable, therefore, that if an unexpected need for authorisation does crop up during an interview, it may be better to postpone it.

To summarise this section: should more information be necessary in order to complete an interview, there are two major responses:

- Take time out to obtain the essential information, whether in person or over the telephone.
- Postpone the interview until the information is available.

Which of these choices is preferable will depend upon your assessment of the particular interview.

### 2 Not reaching goals

What if the goals for an interview are clear, but nevertheless during the course of the interview it becomes obvious that they are no longer appropriate, or cannot be achieved at that time?

If the objectives are crucial, the meeting should quickly be wound up, and rearranged at a time and in a manner allowing for greater cooperation between the service user and you.

However, a natural response is to modify the goals. For example, if the service user has unexpected and overwhelming priorities to discuss – maybe an eviction notice has been served – then they might clearly prefer to discuss possible respite care at a later time.

Changing priorities during an interview will trigger a need for some rapid thinking, but it can often be straightforward to modify your agenda. If a list exists – even a mental list – of interview objectives, there may have been more items on it than could reasonably have been achieved anyway. In such a case, you can alter your priorities by moving items upward that were lower on the list.

For example:

### List for Wednesday's interview with the Roberts family

1   Talk to Craig Roberts about how the opportunities club is going.
2   Discuss Craig's school attendance with Mrs Roberts.
3   Does Mrs Roberts need any further help?
4   If time, talk to Mrs R. about her finances.

Should Craig Roberts not turn up for the arranged interview, item 1 on the list will clearly not be achievable, but that is no reason to abandon the other items.

Altering objectives may not always be practicable, as goals could be collaborative and service user directed. In that case, you should plan with the service user to change the focus of the interview, and to bring in new but achievable topics instead.

SW:   We were going to talk together about ways to help your son's independence when he goes to the Independent Living Unit without you. As he's now not going away, are there any other issues that you'd like to discuss today?

In summary:

■   Modify your goals if necessary – be flexible.
■   Have some ideas in reserve, in case there is a change of emphasis.

### 3   Other potential difficulties

### Personally offensive remarks

Unless there are compelling reasons why you feel you should take it – and these really should be *compelling* – verbal abuse from a service user or client should not be considered acceptable. In social work, you may be dealing with people in frightening or anxious situations, but if emotional control looks as though it has been lost, there are limitations to what they will hear you say. You can, with respect, see if the emotions will calm down:

SW:     Mrs Johns, while of course I want to support you, I'm afraid I do not find those comments helpful. Should they continue, I'm afraid I shall have to leave. I will come back when we can discuss things again.

Note that this response makes the interviewer's position clear, expresses a positive view – 'I want to support you' – depersonalises the comment, and does not actually accuse any specific person of the act. The main purpose of this indirect approach is to reduce the risk of creating an argument. You can consider some non-verbal reinforcement, too: putting up your hand in a blocking gesture, or shaking your head may both work well.

The intention of giving a 'behaviour alert' is emphatically not to get into a dispute, but simply to make the interviewer's position clear. It is particularly important not to enter an argument about who said what, or whether a remark was a derogatatory comment. Whatever the reason for the interview, its progress will not be helped by fuelling disagreement.

If the behaviour persists after you have given clear guidelines, decisive action should always follow:

SW:     Mrs Johns, I did say I found those comments unacceptable. I am going to have to leave now.

It is important, once you have announced that you have concluded the interview, that it *is* quickly ended, and *remains* ended – even if the service user tries to modify the decision. By all means reassure the service user that you can rearrange the interview for a later date, but working out your threshold for acceptable behaviour will help you in your future work.

## Time

Probably the most common problem faced by any interviewer – even a skilled one – is lack of *time*. (Time management in relation to interviewing is also discussed under 'pre-planning', in Chapter 4.) In this situation you may gradually begin to realise during the interview that you have allowed insufficient time. You then try to speed up the interview process, and in consequence it becomes rushed. If you are rushed, there is a good chance that you will communicate your anxiety to the service user. The service user may then respond negatively to these non-verbal messages, which can dramatically change the mood of an interview. This means the interview might take even longer, or could even negate what you are trying to accomplish together. Running completely out of time will force the interview to be brought to an abrupt and unprofessional conclusion (Kadushin and Kadushin, 1997, p273).

To prevent this problem arising, you need to ensure that you allow adequate time for the interview. With caseload pressures, this is probably more easily said than done; nevertheless scheduling sufficient time is *always* worth attempting. Remember, too, that assessment interviews – where more information giving on both sides is called for – will often take longer than subsequent interviews. It is always sensible to allow additional time at the beginning of involvement.

More commonly, though, time pressures occur because new topics are raised in an interview. If *time permits* it is usually best to tackle such issues when they are mentioned, but it may not always be possible to deal with important issues there and then. This is especially likely if there is little time available to handle them sensitively.

SW:    I hear you, Mr Vidal, and that clearly is something we do really need to discuss. While of course I understand it's important to you, as I mentioned when I arrived, I'm afraid I'll have to leave in about 15 minutes. I really don't think it is fair to spend so little time on something that is clearly so important to you. Could we arrange for me to come back on . . .

Starting to discuss a new topic of importance to a service user when there is insufficient time to deal with it adequately is not recommended – although some acknowledgement of its priority will be needed. It is preferable to discuss with the service user how soon it will be possible to return for a reasonable length of time, when there will be sufficient space for a proper discussion of the newly introduced issue.

In summary, therefore:

- Time allocation is a common problem. You may need to allow more time in initial assessment stages, or for unexpected situations.
- Allow adequate time for the interview, and make available time clear at the beginning of the meeting, if you can.
- If the service user can accept it, be prepared to postpone important new topics to an occasion when you both have sufficient time.

## Concluding an interview early

Every interviewer should be able to round off and bring an interview to a conclusion effectively (for methods of ending interviews, see Chapter 7). However, here we need to address the unusual situation of a premature ending to an interview.

Bringing the interview to a close before you planned to do so may appear to be an extreme decision, but there are several situations in which you may well need to consider it. These can be divided into two areas: practical and emotionally-related issues.

### Practical issues

First, let us consider two *practical* issues. Sometimes it will become clear that – for whatever reason – an interview is simply not going to achieve its hoped-for goals. However much you might have tried to work in partnership with the service user, no progress is being made. Perhaps the service user is not communicating, and, even after giving them time, you can see response is minimal. Or perhaps the service user is trying to work with you, but the intended interview goal is still looking less and less achievable.

---

| **Practice issue** |
| --- |
| Donna had been to see Lucky for a mental health assessment. Although they had talked together about him going to hospital for an informal assessment, his moods were so liable to change that his ability to give informed consent to a hospital assessment was severely compromised. |

---

If the interview still appears to be stalling despite your best efforts, you must decide whether continuing to work in partnership will eventually be productive, and decide how long it is reasonable to try.

Should lack of progress be due to unproductive communication, responsibly challenging the service user with the fact should come first, rather than just abruptly stopping the interview.

SW:    Jack, as you know, we're meeting today to talk about your issues in school. So far, though, I don't see that you've responded to my efforts. Unless you feel able to talk to me a little, I don't think there's going to be any point in our meeting. Where do you think this is going?

It is hoped that an honest but polite challenge such as this will bring about a response, but, if it does not, then drawing the interview to an early close is appropriate.

SW:   Jack, we still appear to be going nowhere . . . However much I want to support you, I can't do so without your help; so I'm going to be leaving now. Let me know if you change your mind.

Where relationship difficulties bring about the likelihood of a premature ending to an interview, one important point should always be kept in mind. Behaviour may well alter if you renegotiate opportunities for a change in your working alliance with the service user, but you might first need to explore the consequences of their *not* changing. An alternative might be to go into the next interview aiming for a 'rapport' phase, to allow more time to make connections before you approach more serious objectives.

There are many other circumstances where bringing an interview to an early conclusion may be sensible. Perhaps the service user is feeling unwell, or becomes tired (something you may have to monitor throughout the interview), or grows unable to concentrate. It may be that an unexpected disruption effectively ends the interview (one abrupt ending we remember was when a family member, released early from a custodial sentence, turned up unexpectedly, to be greeted with considerable – and interview-disrupting – enthusiasm). There are numerous other possibilities.

*Emotion-related issues*

Second, we consider the emotional impact of your visit, and the issues it raises. If your visit intensifies too many anxieties, or the service user begins to feel emotionally under threat, perhaps because the needs of the main carer are receiving prominence, then the interview becomes counterproductive. You should consider retreating if the issues under discussion are not urgent.

---

### Practice issue

Wyn had been diagnosed with a serious mental health disorder in adolescence, and, in his mid-20s was still living at home with his parents. They needed a break, and had asked Fallon, the day centre worker, to discuss ways for this to happen. However, when Fallon saw Wyn in the centre, he was against any discussion of the merits of respite and became distressed. She suggested he talk it over with his family again, and arranged to see him the next week.

In Wyn's situation, there would have been little point in continuing to discuss the possible provision of support that was being so clearly declined. The fact that his parents felt such support was necessary might have originally triggered the meeting, but could not justify it continuing in the face of Wyn's opposition. Fallon's decision to try to reconvene the interview after Wyn had time to discuss things with his family would allow for a different interview, with different strategies for his support in it.

## 4   Perception of physical risk to the interviewer

It is acknowledged that social work is a high-risk occupation with the potential for aggressive acts and threats to staff (Koprowska, 2005, p139). Because consequences can be severe, you should be alert for threatening behaviour, able to recognise risk factors, and understand how to respond – and, of course, be clear how *not* to respond.

All responsible employers should have policies in place to support you; they also have the primary responsibility to combat violence toward their staff. However, you must take responsibility in following the policies, and doing what you can to promote safer practice for you and your colleagues.

It can be difficult to recognise threatening behaviour, especially when in the middle of an interview. At first, a perception of risk usually only relates to a feeling of discomfort. Perhaps the individual is using language that you subconsciously identify as intimidating; perhaps the subject you are discussing is increasing the emotional charge of the reaction; perhaps the service user her/himself may have fragile mental health, and so cannot sustain a calm emotional response. An awareness of body language, and its effects, is likely to provide you with clues.

### Aggressive behaviour and risk of violence

The Department of Health (DoH) has a useful checklist for social care personnel. The DoH defines violence to workers as:

> Incidents where persons are abused, threatened or assaulted in circumstances relating to their work, involving an explicit or implicit challenge to their safety, well-being or health. This definition is taken to include verbal abuse or threat, threatening behaviour, any assault (and any apprehension of unlawful violence), and serious or persistent harassment, including racial or sexual harassment, and extends from what may

seem to be minor incidents to serious assault and murder, and threats against the worker's family.

(Combating Violence Against Social Care Staff: DOH website)

---

### Consider this

Sue was seeing a family whose daughter had been born prematurely. The father talked for his partner, and began to make Sue aware that he controlled all the partner's movements, and indeed the whole household. He then suggested that he would be very rigid over Sue's involvement, making her feel uncomfortable and dominated. Sue brought the interview to a close as quickly as possible.

How would you explain this incident to a colleague back at the office?

What kind of body language might you observe?

How might you consider moving the situation forward?

---

Although you should always make threatening incidents known to your office automatically, there are reasons why this may not happen:

- Social care staff fear blame for incidents.
- Formal reporting may take time.
- Staff feel that reporting is insignificant.

So we stress that incidents involving threatening behaviour or harm to you should *always* be properly recorded, and *always* reported. Quite apart from anything else, even if you felt confident you would be able to handle a potentially violent situation, a future interviewer may not be able to do so – especially if lack of any prior warning had left them unprepared. (Once reported, many agency record systems can set a records flag, warning of potentially violent behaviour.) You should appreciate that nothing is likely to be put in place unless you *do* note the behaviour.

### Situational risks

Social care staff are often called upon to communicate negative or difficult decisions to service users. Having to say 'no' about services, or conveying a decision restricting an individual's freedom, are undoubtedly powerful acts. Experiencing such authority roles may invoke strong feelings in service users, such as anxiety, anger, frustration, or distress.

This is a situation where maintaining a partnership approach, and being as honest and open as possible throughout your relationship with the client, is beneficial. Listening to what service users say, and clearly giving it consideration, are hallmarks of good communication. There is no doubt that good communication can help prevent some threatening atmospheres. You should try to be up-front about the risks that you perceive, and engage service users and colleagues in planning safe practice.

When there is increased possibility of violence, the interview location needs to be carefully considered. If there is a serious risk, the interview should always be held in a 'safe' location – for example, an interview room in your agency – and never held where support is not immediately available. The location should, however, still be private, and welcoming to service users. An interview room should have a clear escape route, an alarm or panic button, and ideally should be free from objects that could be thrown. Additionally, supporting staff should always be available, and alerted in advance that they might be needed.

If the interview is not to be held in the agency, it can often be helpful to visit the proposed location jointly with a colleague. Including another worker in this way should be discussed in advance with your line manager. This is because, although it can provide safety, meeting two 'authority figures' can also heighten service users' anxieties.

Safety precautions can and should be worked out beforehand. Indeed, it may often be sensible to take similar precautions at other times, for example when you interview a new service user, where the unknown nature of a location is a potential risk, or when you visit a service user in an area known to be unsafe. It is also sensible not to make such visits late in the working day, and especially not late in the day on a Friday, when offices close, and support is likely to be much harder to find.

Should a situation appear to be becoming unpredictable, even if something is being achieved, then it is sensible to make plans to leave. Remember that inexperience may make people feel they must soldier on, continuing in situations that practised social workers would quickly try to exit. Rather than delaying until risk is very obvious, your decision to depart should always include a safety margin.

## Traits associated with violent behaviour

Knowledge is important in assessing the degree of risk you may be facing, and one part of such knowledge is having an awareness of risk factors in violent behaviour. Here are some major ones:

- A previous history of violent acts.
- Gender: men are slightly more likely to be violent. (Women's violence is directed more at family, and happens in the home.)
- Dependence on or abuse of alcohol, and other substances.
- Alcohol intoxication.
- Psychotic symptoms.
- Violent thoughts and angry feelings.
- Childhood experience of physical abuse.

It should be stressed that the list is intended purely as an *indicator* of probability of risk. Every risk situation should be assessed individually, and specific scenarios weighed up.

### Signs of emotion

If violent behaviour is imminent, there may be warning signs. While individual reactions will vary, the following is a list of the main indicators of an increased probability of physical action:

- Pacing about
- Pointing
- Flushed complexion
- Opening and closing fists
- Name calling or swearing
- Verbal outbursts
- Signs of hostility
- Impulsive behaviour.

### How to reduce the risk

Violence can sometimes appear to come from nowhere, but this is rare (DoH website). However, if you are concerned, you may want to monitor any rise in risk that might be due to your own performance and behaviour. Remembering the acronym **ABC** may be helpful here: **A**ntecedent (or behaviour before the challenge); the **B**ehaviour itself, and the **C**onsequences of the behaviour (what the behaviour led to). Studying your own behaviour in this way is *not* the same as suggesting that you are causing the situation. Instead, it is intended to confirm that you are not subconsciously making the situation more tense. This situation is one where 'observational distancing' can be particularly important. You can consciously use this method to monitor and alter elements in the interaction.

In some situations, you will already be aware that the risk exists. Before such an interview begins, you should ensure that you are sitting near the door. (This is different from the usual principles, where you would make sure that a service user does not feel trapped in the room.)

Once seated, you should try to keep your eye level below that of the service user (which will be perceived as less threatening). Also, if you project a confident, calm and professional approach that will help communicate respect and understanding, you will be doing all you can to aid calm. It is also sensible to avoid sudden movements, and deliberately to speak with your voice in a lower register, in a slow, relaxed manner – even if you are not feeling particularly relaxed. It is also sensible deliberately to use non-verbal actions that reinforce a calming atmosphere, such as leaning back a little, and keeping the upper body 'open'.

It may also be wise not to turn away. Service users could interpret this movement as lacking in respect, and you will not be able to monitor expressions and actions. Can you keep a physical distance? It is always better to ensure that you do not accidentally invade 'personal space', as this can increase nervousness.

Should a situation appear unpredictable, even if something is being achieved, then again it is sensible to make plans to leave – well within a safety margin. It is *always* better to adjourn the interview to a later date, when things will, it is hoped, be calmer. By then, you will also have had time to think about and discuss ways of reducing tension for your service users.

Before beginning the process of leaving, think about your location in the room. Are you next to the door? You might want to move there *before* speaking about going. Finally, it is best to use a simple phrase, such as 'I'm sorry, but I need to leave now', and repeat it, rather than getting drawn back into the conversation.

You can also alert your office to the situation by using a previously agreed 'alarm phrase'. As well as telling colleagues, such a telephone call can also give a chance for you to break the mood and therefore make it easier for you to leave immediately.

SW:   Mr Redhill, I need to check with my office . . .
[*speed dials – making sure your office number is on speed dial is sensible*] Hello? I'm visiting Mr Redhill, and I need the YELLOW FILE. I look like being delayed . . . What? Oh, I see. [*Hangs up phone*] I'm sorry Mr. Redhill, something that's cropped up means that I have to get back to the office now.

You should be reassured that feeling you need help does not necessarily imply failure or poor practice on your part. If you are feeling threatened, leaving a difficult situation is *always* appropriate.

### Reflection

Should you end an interview early through risk or behaviour, how should you follow it up?

It is helpful to have a 'debriefing' session immediately after an episode, whether or not it involved actual physical contact. This debriefing should be in a known safe area, and in relaxed surroundings. There are two objectives for such a session: it will allow you to externalise your feelings; and it allows people to understand exactly what happened, so that someone can make a decision about whether it should be reported.

Finally, it is sensible to reassess the degree of risk with your supervisor or manager, in the safe surroundings of the office.

#### Other pitfalls, and ideas for handling them

Although it is clearly impossible to cover all the issues, we can look at some representative examples, particularly of those behaviours that are more common.

### Responding to racist or sexist statements/questions

These issues are dealt with in Chapter 1, in the section on anti-discriminatory behaviour.

### Service users who keep silent

As discussed earlier, if you are meeting with someone who has chosen not to communicate with you, it may well be best to reduce the interview time. Some silences can emerge from feelings of resistance, self-protection, or anger, and can be controlling – '*You* do something'. They may also be due to acute anxiety (Lishman, 1994, p69). The principal difficulty in deciding how to respond is that the silence results in lack of information to take suppositions and theories forward.

However, there are some approaches that may encourage the service user to engage in dialogue and seek collaboration with you. First, when faced with a person who is uncommunicative, try to refrain from blunt statements.

These have the effect of throwing a lack of response into relief: 'You're not talking to me – why not?' being a sample.

Generally, *you* may perceive direct questions to a silent client as a good way of finding out their true feelings. In reality, however, such questions have only two possible outcomes. They can elicit a response, or (more probably) they will actually reinforce the lack of a response. If a service user is not responding, any use of questions, even open ones, may often make them feel interrogated or pressurised.

In practice, it may work better to talk *obliquely*, as if giving – rather than seeking – information. In this approach you are trying to engage the person on of common ground, and thus establish communication. There may be pauses for a moment to seek tacit approval, but you will not actually ask for a verbal response. You can use the first few pauses to obtain confirmation of low-level, uncontentious matters; then gradually move on to more challenging areas.

SW:   Well, as you know, Mayanne, I've recently taken over from Claire DeSousa, who was your previous worker? [*slight pause for confirmation*] She told me that you've been having more than your fair share of hassles [*slight pause for confirmation*] but she felt, considering this, you were doing really well. One thing she did mention, though, was to do with weekends. I understand you have differences with your parents over the time you're out until . . . [*longer pause*]

and so on. In reality, the monologue would be more extended, with pauses for the service user to acknowledge agreement situated rather further apart. The main objective here is to seek a common thread, and to work towards obtaining a response gradually.

Kadushin and Kadushin mention a slightly different approach. This takes the silence to be not a trait of the individual, but puts it into the context of the interview: 'Sometimes I guess you feel like talking, but other times, like now, I guess you don't' (1997, p365). They suggest that you can look for a common bond in the silence itself – perhaps, to encourage communication, using something that you don't mind sharing from your experience about quiet situations.

Another approach to the puzzle of a silent interview is to say something to elicit a strong reaction. This could be a statement with which you think the service user is likely to disagree (Trevithick, 2000, p104). It is done in order to move communication forward. Overall it may have the genuine aim of helping the service user to communicate with you, but there are ethical considerations to its use, so it is better to first discuss this approach with a supervisor.

| **Practice issue** |
|---|
| Zadie (social worker) has been asked to visit Mrs Ashbee because her son David has been truanting and causing serious concerns at his school. Mrs Ashbee declines to participate in the interview. |
| Zadie:   I can think of several reasons why you're remaining quiet, Mrs Ashbee. One of them could be that you believe David's teachers are perfectly OK [*pause*] and that the head teacher was right to exclude him . . . [*pause*] |
| In the absence of Mrs Ashbee's views, this theory is a possibility, but Zadie will be hoping that it will draw out Mrs Ashbee's true opinions, so that they can work together on the situation. |

When taking this approach, though, the intention should be to genuinely seek out opinions to further the helping alliance between the service user and practitioner.

## Talking too much?

In an interview, both the extremes of silence and of talking can be a frustration. Here we discuss the situation when you may be unable to focus to ask the questions, or move the interview on because, in your perception, the service user is talking too much.

So what can be done?

First, it is important to appreciate that service users may have a reason for talking, or a need to talk, or be of a talkative nature. A common theme is that drawn-out speech is actually displacement activity – the person is consciously or unconsciously very anxious *not* to talk about some issue, so is instead filling the conversation with discussion of 'safe' material. The talking is intended both to distract you and to leave no space for discussion of alternative topics.

A good response is therefore to try thinking through exactly why the service user is behaving in this way. If, for example, they are talking about everyone in the family except their resident grandmother, maybe there is something about their grandmother they do not want to discuss. You can also assess their non-verbal behaviours for signs of anxiety.

Another reason for too much talking can be an overwhelming need to get emotions outside oneself, and, through repetition, to try to resolve them. This may be allied with a sense of guilt about the experience, so it may be more sensitive here to work with the feelings, putting your other needs on hold.

If you have no apparent subtext to explore with a service user, how should you go about making room in the interview for achieving your joint goals within the limited time available? It may be discourteous to interrupt talking once begun, but it may be possible to set guidelines and priorities with the service user at the beginning of the interview. Agreed guidelines can serve as a basis for mutual reference, should verbal distractions occur.

Should you need to help the service user focus back on the agreed issues, an easy first step is to ask for their attention by speaking their name. In addition, it is possible to use a hand gesture to ask for speaking time. This may also be the moment to acknowledge feelings, with an empathetic remark that shows understanding of their need to talk. From this point, both parties might look again at why they are meeting, and what can be accomplished together in the remaining time available.

An alternative method is to become more structured in the interviewing process, and ask more definite and closed questions (needing yes/no answers); or refer more often to paperwork, perhaps a form that needs completing.

### Reserve or dislike in the interview

This can be a tricky one to handle, not because it is intrinsically hard to manage, but because most people like to be liked. For this reason we have an emotional reaction when we come across a person who appears to dislike us, or with whom we find it hard to empathise.

The first point to make is that you should not take such negative expressions personally. Remember, you will not be organising an interview on your own behalf, but as the representative of a social care organisation.

The service user may have created this collection of potentially negative feelings from previous experiences of the care agency, their experiences with previous workers, or perhaps even from the views of their friends or neighbours. This means that, with the best will in the world, even an admirable practitioner will be bringing with them invisible and accumulated 'baggage'.

There may be other influences at work, too. If you should experience apparent dislike, it may be helpful to check out how this person presents to other professionals. Does the service user perhaps have similar feelings towards all people they perceive as 'authority' figures?

So, the first rule when faced with apparently cool behaviour should be: *don't take it personally.*

A second rule to take on board is that a service user doesn't *have* to like you, or you to like them. It should be possible for you to do your job well without 'liking' entering the equation. Of course, in an interview setting everything is liable to move more smoothly if everyone likes and appreciates everyone else, but it isn't essential. Kadushin and Kadushin tell us:

> Although admittedly desirable, it is not necessary to feel invariably respectful and accepting. It is enough to act respectful and accepting.
> (Kadushin and Kadushin, 1997, p131)

What is important is to keep in control of negative feelings, and to keep them in the background. Further, a social care worker who sees the relationship in terms of service users liking them personally may be a less useful worker. A need for personal liking can sometimes get in the way of forming a professional and effective working alliance.

When faced with apparent dislike, therefore, as yourself: *does it actually matter?*

Finally, however, you may need to reflect on whether there may be some reason for this lack of enthusiasm, a reason of which you are unaware. Such a 'hidden' reason should be considered when not just a one client appears cool, but multiple service users in a variety of interview settings express similar feelings.

In such a case, the reasons for negativity may be related to your interview style or behaviour. Consider, for example: are you naturally abrupt, or could you be perceived as being rude? Do you appear rushed, and do not give a client silence, or time to properly respond? Are you suffering from 'burnout' that communicates itself to the service user? If this is the case, you should consider whether you could make changes in your interview style or behaviour, and then monitor the results. If possible, discuss the issue with a third party, such as your supervisor, or perhaps take a colleague you trust on a joint visit with you.

So the third rule, when faced with apparent dislike, is to check *in case there may be a reason.*

### Working without a common purpose

In these situations, the service user is perfectly happy to talk, and to participate in the interview, but you find that you cannot establish a joint agreed purpose to the interview.

If the service user is an adult responsible for her/himself, and there are no issues, such as mental health factors, that call for further assessment and judgement – then the decisions naturally remain with the service user. This remains the case even though, to an outsider it appears that in doing so they may be acting unwisely, or against their best interests (Norman, 1980). Considering the service user's rights and wishes – as well as carefully evaluating risk, with confirmation of it – will be significant for you in this type of situation.

| **Practice issue** | |
| --- | --- |
| Mrs Kent is in her late 50s, seriously disabled after a back injury, and living alone. Her daughter, genuinely concerned for Mrs Kent's well-being, thinks her mother needs residential accommodation, but Mrs Kent disagrees. During the assessment interview she remains adamant that she can and will be able to continue to cope alone, and is not in need of any more visits from a social care agency – despite evidence that this may not be so. The assessment visit uncovers some issues of safety. | If, as she wishes, Mrs Kent remains at home, who would be responsible if something untoward should happen to her? How would you ensure that her rights and the risks were fully considered? Finally, if you were the worker talking to Mrs Kent, what would you feel were the important issues to discuss with her? |

Here you will need to carefully explore the situation with Mrs Kent, with the intention of identifying together the possible reason/s why she is so sure help is not needed. It may, for instance, be related to her perception of what it means to be a 'service user'; it may refer to her past experiences of seeking help; it might reflect her fear about what will happen to her if she cooperates.

A further approach depends upon you being clear who exactly is your client. You need to listen primarily to the service user, and be clear about who is the priority: in this case, Mrs Kent – not her daughter.

It is worth spending time and energy with service users to talk through the situation. However, rather than seeking to convince by putting up a series of logical reasons, it is often better to look for and resolve the likely *feelings* that are making the service user so sure help is not necessary.

Sometimes, despite your efforts, it may not prove feasible to work towards a service user's cooperation. It may then be necessary to accept and acknowledge that fact, and be prepared, if there are any risks attached to the situation, to alert relevant people.

There will, however, be very different considerations when the person concerned is under the age of 18, or is a caregiver, or is responsible for a young service user, for example when you interview the parent of a child. If the young person is thought to be at risk, but the people concerned deny that the risk exists, or indeed deny any need for social work involvement, then you will need to discuss these issues with your supervisor.

In many situations we meet, the capacity of service users to decide upon issues in their lives may be impaired – temporarily or permanently. Here there may be important issues of capability and consent that are unlikely to be straightforward. The Mental Capacity Act, 2005, which came into force in 2007, applies five principles that will assist you in deciding on whether people have the capacity to consent to decisions in their lives.

The five principles are:

1   Every adult has the right to make his or her own decisions and must be assumed to have capacity to do so unless it is proved otherwise.

    This means that just because they have a particular medical condition or disability, you cannot assume that someone cannot make a decision for themselves.

2   People must be supported as much as possible to make a decision before anyone concludes that they cannot make their own decision.

    This means that you should make every effort to encourage and support the person to make the decision for themselves. If a lack of capacity is established, it is still important that as far as possible you involve the person in making decisions.

3   People have the right to make what others might regard as an unwise or eccentric decision. Everyone has their own values, beliefs and preferences which may not be the same as those of other people. You cannot treat them as lacking capacity for that reason.

4   Anything done for, or on behalf of, a person who lacks mental capacity must be done in their best interests.

5   Anything done for, or on behalf of, people without capacity should be the least restrictive of their basic rights and freedoms.

    This means that when you do anything to, or for, a person who lacks capacity, you must choose the option that is in their best interests. You must also do this in a way that interferes least with their rights and freedom of action.

(Mental Capacity Act website)

When interviewing someone with diminished capacity, and trying to work with them, you must always bear these principles in mind.

## CONCLUSION

Working with people can be complex, and it is doubtful that you will 'get it right' all of the time. Your work with service users is therefore likely to involve balancing rights and risks, especially if you are dealing with people under stress or whose abilities are limited. Common complications in interviewing can be in these areas:

- **Planning**: it is always sensible, even when little time is available, to prepare and plan.
- **Abuse**: it is not necessary for you to accept abuse. Should it continue after you have made your views clear, leaving the interview may be appropriate.
- **Time**: give yourself the flexibility to allow for changes in priorities during the interview. However, if this results in time pressures, it may be best to expect to devote time to service users at a later date.
- **Endings**: be prepared to finish the interview early if there seems to be little likelihood of meeting your joint objectives, or if you feel uncomfortable with that service user.
- **Threatening behaviour and violence**: careful monitoring is sensible, as is awareness of risks. Be conscious of the many factors, such as your role, service users' traits or anxiety that can raise the risk of challenging behaviour.
- **Silence and talking**: if the service user does not appear to want to communicate, use your communication skills and other approaches to find common ground. Talking too much can be an issue in some interviews: you may need to restructure the interview or find ways of recalling service users' attention to concentrate on what you hope to accomplish together.
- **Common purpose**: people may be willing to talk to you but do not see any reason for the interaction. We looked at some issues of balancing rights and risks in working with service users, especially around lack of capacity.

## FURTHER READING

Koprowska, Juliet, *Communication and Interpersonal Skills in Social Work*, Chapter 9.
Thompson, Neil, *People Skills*, Chapter 16.

# Chapter 10

---

# Recording an Interview

---

## NOSSC RELEVANCE

The material in this chapter relates to the following National Occupational Standards for Social Care:

- **Key Role Two**, Unit 9. Address behaviour that presents a risk to individuals, families, carers, groups and communities.
- **Key Role Three**, Unit 11. Prepare for and participate in decision-making forums.
- **Key Role Five**, Unit 16. Manage, present and share records and reports.

*Until it has been properly recorded, even the most successful social work interview is inevitably incomplete. This chapter begins by examining why interview recording is necessary, before going on to look at methods designed to encourage accurate and effective recording of social care interviews. It concludes with a discussion on how to practise interviewing.*

## WHY RECORD AN INTERVIEW?

Recording of social work and social care interviews takes place – but why is this? Why exactly do we need to record interviews? It can be argued that there should be a pretty good reason for you to spend additional time and energy in making a note of what happened in an interview. Although there is some recognition that recording has come to be a shorter process (Kadushin and Kadushin, 1997, p283) there is still a requirement for interview accounts.

There is not just one single good reason why we need to record interviews – there are several:

- It is a legal requirement for some agencies to record interviews.
- A record provides evidence in the case of disputes or challenges between service user and agency.
- Recording of *options* can justify a decision made.
- A case record provides continuity of contact, from one agency worker to another.
- Precise recording may supply evidence for court or other processes.
- A record provides interview details for you to reflect upon, and hypothesise.
- A recording supports accountability for practitioners' time and actions.

Until now, we have mainly considered social care interviews as an interaction between service users and interviewers. Do not forget, however, that (as we discussed in Chapter 3) you will usually be undertaking interviewing not as 'yourself', but as the representative of an organisation. This 'representative' issue is particularly relevant to interview recording: because your activities involve members of the public, your agency needs to ensure that their representatives are acting responsibly, ethically, and within the law.

## DATA PROTECTION ACT, 1998

The Data Protection Act (DPA) 1998 has particular relevance for social services authorities. It introduced a unifying system of rules governing social work records, and access to them – whether files were held on paper, or electronically. Interview records, by their nature, concern personal data, and the recording of personal data is essentially what the Data Protection Act is about. The Act also gave individuals significantly greater rights to access information held about them. It defines two types of relevant data:

- **Personal data** – information about a living individual that is used or processed automatically (e.g. by a computer) or held within a relevant filing system (e.g. manual records system) or recorded with the intention of processing or filing it, *and* which enables the individual to be identified or identifiable.
- **Sensitive personal data** – personal data (as above) that consists of information on someone's racial or ethic origin, political opinions, religious or similar beliefs, trade union membership, physical or mental health condition, sex life, offences (committed or alleged), or proceedings/ sentences for those offences.

---

**The eight principles of the Data Protection Act, 1998**

Recorded personal information should be:
1 Fairly and lawfully processed.
2 Processed for limited purposes.
3 Adequate, relevant and not excessive.
4 Accurate and, where necessary, up to date.
5 Not kept for longer than is necessary.
6 Processed in line with the rights of the data subject.
7 Secure.
8 Not transferred to other countries without adequate protection.

---

It is clear from these definitions that any interview recording is likely to come under the provisions of this Act. Should it do so, there are serious restrictions on what may be recorded, and how – once recorded – information may be stored and accessed. The DPA specifies eight principles (see above).

There are still further restrictions. Personal data may not be held or processed *at all* unless they meet at least one of these six conditions:

1 The person has given their consent.
2 Processing is necessary for fulfilling a contract.
3 Processing is necessary to comply with a legal obligation.
4 Processing is necessary to protect the vital (i.e. life-and-death) interests of the person.
5 Processing is necessary for the administration of justice, activities of the Crown or a government department, or functions of a public nature exercised in the public interest.
6 Processing is necessary in pursuing legitimate interests of the Data Controller or third parties unless this prejudices the rights and freedoms or legitimate interests of the person concerned.

However, *sensitive* personal data may only be recorded and stored if at least one of the above points is met, and *in addition* at least one of the following additional conditions is also met:

1 The person concerned has given their *explicit* consent.
2 Processing is necessary to comply with employment law.
3 Processing is necessary to protect the vital interests of the person or another person.

4 Processing is part of the legitimate activities of a non-profit organisation existing for political, philosophical, religious or trade union purposes.
5 The person has already made this information public themselves.
6 Processing is necessary for legal proceedings, advice, or defence.

Remember, too, that even if information has been appropriately recorded and stored legally, the Act encourages the individual about whom personal data has been written to apply for access to view it.

Knowing that the concerned service user may well read your interview recording should certainly encourage you to involve people more closely in the process. Essentially, the Data Protection Act, 1998 makes accurate recording of social work interviews a legal, as well as a professional, duty.

## ACCURATE RECORDING

Accurate recording of interactions may build a picture and add to evidence for decision making. Lishman emphasises that very accurate records of contacts with services users, observations on emotional states, and details of development are of 'paramount importance' (1994, p37). In such circumstances as domestic violence (Humphreys, 2002, p41), clear observation and exact recording may be vital to help with assessment of risk, or for evidence in court.

### Accountability

Your agency may also justifiably require you to be accountable to them – and the people you see – both for your time and the judgements or actions you make in the course of your work. This concept of professional accountability is particularly important in an organisation conscious of power imbalances, and which wishes to be as open as possible to those who access its services. Such a policy may result in the need for evidence to make clear how you spend your time; or the need to gather evidence of your work, and the time taken to accomplish it. As we said earlier, in the event of a complaint, the written record may also substantiate – or disprove – the allegation.

Justifying a particular course of action (especially for LASSDs) is also an important part of accountability. You may need to record all the alternatives that have been considered, and make open statements about why you had a particular preference. Weighing up the options in your recording is a way of being frank and open about the processes that lead to decision making.

Additionally, even the most dedicated of social care interviewers do not remain in post continuously, or work indefinitely with the same service user.

Practitioners change jobs, and cases. If you have accurately recorded your interviews, it will ensure that any workers subsequently involved with that service user are able to take into account and build upon events of prior interviews (Kadushin and Kadushin, 1997, pp282–3).

---

### Practice issue

Rani was off sick, so in her absence a duty officer had to deal with a crisis on her case-load. Unfortunately Rani had not recorded her last visit to the family, several weeks back, which caused a great deal of additional work for her duty colleague. He was so annoyed that he reported it to her team manager.

---

An organisational policy insisting that your activities are appropriately recorded is consequently perfectly logical and justified. Many agencies support their workers with official forms for interview recording, and it is as well to remember that these are official records that could be used in legal proceedings.

However, quite apart from any requirements based upon the administrative and legal needs of your agency, it is also professionally advisable for you to maintain records: an example would be when interviewing while undertaking private social work. Basic recording will be part of your agency accountability, but for professional reasons it may sometimes be necessary for you to supplement an adequate official record with fuller details.

Typical reasons for a fuller record might include:

■ your learning needs,
■ potential conflict in an interview,
■ accountability.

However, if the fuller record is being taken as a supplement to the official records, you should decide on the confidentiality of these records, and where they should be kept. Ownership can be a problem, and you need to consider the issue carefully in advance if you plan to keep *personal* records (Lishman, 1994, p40).

A fuller agency record will provide a potential measure of protection to you, as an accurate contemporaneous record can give some security against misunderstandings and misinterpretations of your actions.

---

### Practice issue

Alice interviewed a single parent – Joe – who was separated from his partner and their children. The purpose of the interview was to find out the extent of Joe's involvement with his family, and how much practical or emotional support he intended to provide for them. Joe was outspoken in his comments, threatening violence to both his partner and the children. Alice included these comments in a later report to a court. However, through his solicitor, Joe totally denied Alice's account of the interview, accusing her of deliberately making it up in order to deprive him of his children.

As well as being good practice, it was certainly fortunate that on her return to the office Alice had immediately written up her interview with Joe, and had then discussed the report with her supervisor.

---

Finally, while you are gaining professional knowledge it is important for you to be able to demonstrate your abilities and your thinking to a supervisor. A detailed and accurate recording of all aspects of an interview – known as a *process recording* – can be of considerable benefit here, and is dealt with later in this chapter.

## Language

Clarity of language is an important component of communication, (Thompson, 2002, p116) and you should therefore reflect on the style and directness of the writing used in your records. Interview records should be in a vocabulary that service users find easy to understand, and not just because the service user may one day access that file. It should be a basic principle that all written information for a service user needs to be in approachable language (Lishman, 1994, p43). For this reason there should be no use of jargon in your recording, and any descriptions should be presented in a style that the service user can readily accept.

This approach should not be difficult. After all, partnership work suggests that you can always ask service users how they would prefer certain events to be described in the record, and note it with them. We should stress that the involvement of the service user with recording should not prevent the recording of disagreement – if you find you cannot agree on content or phraseology, it is certainly possible to record the fact that you and the service user disagree.

The issue of disagreement leads us on to another important principle of recording, which is always to separate opinion or hearsay from fact. For example, if talking with a service user about their use of alcohol, asking someone to clarify how many bottles of wine they drink per day or per week can be a much more useful statement than writing generally about their use or misuse of alcohol. Even if it may seem an inaccurate estimation, it provides a baseline for further discussions.

(Please remember that tone is all-important in these exchanges.)

| | |
|---|---|
| SW: | OK, we've talked about your issues with alcohol; so, how many bottles of whisky would you say you usually get through in, say, a week? |
| SU: | Oh, not that many. Not more than two or three. |
| SW: | Well, I see five empty bottles over there by your bin; and your daughter tells us that she has seen you getting through rather a lot. Tell me how many you go through in a bad week. |
| Case record: | After agreeing he had issues with his alcohol intake, Mr L said he drank no more than three bottles of whisky a week. However, after discussion, he confirmed that, when he experiences a bad week, he can get through at least seven bottles, and sometimes more. |

In this case, you could then build on the factual statement by asking the service user whether they consider they drink too much, or perhaps whether anybody else has considered that he/she consumes too much alcohol. It may take a great deal of time to write all this into a report, but it is more factually based, and more precise. Consequently the service user will be more likely to accept it, and you will also be able to convey the position accurately to others, should Mr L agree to it.

## HOW TO RECORD THE INTERVIEW

### Notes

For obvious reasons, social work interviews tend not to be recorded in detail while they are happening. Even a very full written record of what went on during an interview will usually be based upon notes. These notes may have been jotted down during the interview, or, more usually, very shortly after it (Kadushin and Kadushin, 1997, p282). In the past, notes may have been scrawled onto a notepad; today they may be typed into a laptop, or personal digital assistant (PDA).

When making these preliminary notes, it should not be necessary to go into much detail, or to write as if the notes themselves were to be the recording of the interview. However, remember that the service user will be observing you writing, and, as you are working collaboratively, you should be ready to share them at any time.

Notes should not be a 'first draft' of an interview recording, but should instead consist of simple nuggets of information, designed to help remind you – when you come to write up the actual report – of the events of that interview. Of course, good practice demands that the 'full' writing of an interview report should never follow too far behind the interview itself; but even so the immediate jotting down of preliminary notes can be of considerable help to you.

Generally, the longer after the interview that you make notes, the more difficult it will be to write them, and the less useful they will be as a foundation for a full record. You need to appreciate that delays in making a record of an interview are almost certain to affect the accuracy of the eventual record. This is because human memory is limited: the longer the period that has elapsed after the end of an interview, the less likely it will be that you can accurately recall its important aspects (Kadushin and Kadushin, 1997, pp282–3). Your memory of the details of an interview fades surprisingly quickly; even postponing recording until the next day can lead to a significant loss. The general principle here must be: *the more crucial the interview, the sooner it must be fully recorded.*

Memory can become confused or overloaded as well, so writing up a record immediately after an interview will *always* be far more effective than writing up the same report only after carrying out further interviews.

While notes should provide sufficient information to jog your memory, certain fixed aspects should always be recorded. Such set details might include date, time, name of service user, objectives of the interview, and perhaps also the location. Whether you note additional points is likely to depend on the circumstances of a particular meeting. For example, during a stressful and emotional interview it would clearly be detrimental for the client to observe you making notes. However, when a service user is providing you with detailed and specific information, they may justifiably feel they are not being taken seriously if a record of what they are saying is not made at the time.

There are other disadvantages to recording during the interview. If you are thinking about what notes to make, and when to make them, you cannot be fully concentrating on either your interviewing or on the service user. Service users themselves may well be disconcerted by unexpected pauses in the interview for you to take notes. Additionally, if they are not permitted to see what is being written, a service user may have a justifiable concern over the nature of the notes (Kadushin and Kadushin, 1997, p280).

One final point: from a service user's perspective, an interviewer taking notes may well feel strange and uncomfortable. Especially if you are writing comments within their 'space', that is, their home, you should work cooperatively, and seek the service user's agreement before taking notes.

### Notes into actual record

Any individual social worker's method of recording an interview is likely to be informed by the specific requirements of their agency, as well as by personal perception and abilities. A worker with an excellent memory will naturally be less dependent upon detailed notes, while someone who has trouble remembering may need to make very frequent jottings.

You should also reflect on the reason why you are making a recording of an interview *before* you begin the process. For example, if the agency needs the events of an interview to be summarised, then you will need to identify the important points of that interview and incorporate them in a short paragraph.

Should no agency guidelines for report length exist, you may be tempted to generate a lengthy description. However, you need to consider the policies of openness and partnership work with service users, as well as the Data Protection Act. As we said earlier in this chapter, Principle 3 of the DPA states that records should be 'adequate, relevant and not excessive'. Unless there are special circumstances of harm or risk, the record of an interview needs to contain a brief description of what took place, details of the decisions reached together, and a note of the joint aims. A full written description in the case file is against the spirit of frankness and evidence-based clarity.

A further point to consider is your record about what you say to the service user. In many interviews, a summary or general outline of your questions will be adequate. However, if there is a risk of harm, it can be sensible to record exactly how you phrased the question, and an exact as possible wording of the reply.

Generally, an interview will be fully recorded some time after the event. Whether based upon preliminary notes or not, that record should contain a series of simple statements, allowing a reader to bring themselves up to speed on the essentials of what happened during that interview, and, if this is relevant, what the social worker observed.

As well as what went on, information concerning future work with the service user may also be appropriately recorded.

Note    Mr Gupta. Hip better. Res. Care?? Chaudri told DN (Jenny?) he needs care?

Record   [date] Visited Mr Gupta by appointment. He appears to be mobilising much better following his hip replacement, but said he is still

> thinking seriously about residential care. He spoke for some time about this, and finally asked me if I knew what his GP (Dr Chen) had said to the district nurse (Jenny? Henny?) because, when the nurse visited to change his dressings, she had apparently told him he should be looked after ... NOTE: Mr Gupta agreed I could talk to the DN regarding his health/nursing needs.

In this instance the worker has developed their notes into a reasonable record of the interview, but they have obviously not used the intervening time to improve the accuracy of their report. Mr Gupta may not have known the name of his district nurse, but the social worker could certainly have found it out, and included it in their report of the interview (perhaps along with the information that the nurse's name was unknown to Mr Gupta).

The lack of later research in this example is intended to illustrate an important point about the conversion of interview notes into interview reports. It should always be understood that, where this is relevant, the record of an interview might be usefully enriched by the inclusion of later factual material. Other examples might, for instance, involve including the names and telephone numbers of relatives, addresses of involved caregivers, and so on.

When writing a report of an interview, you should always remember that, under data protection legislation, a service user might ask to see all agency records that relate to them. Any social work recording needs to bear this in mind. Even confidential information from third parties may need reviewing, to confirm it could be made available to the service user without harm.

## Importance of recording

Social workers may find that recording an interview rapidly and accurately is a laborious task. You may perceive it as of substantially less importance than the interview itself, especially if you have time pressures. In such circumstances, it is hardly surprising that recording of interviews is often delayed, frequently until some time after the event.

However, delay and postponement of interview recording as a strategy is one that you cannot carry out successfully for any length of time. For instance, time management precepts urge that you allow space after an interview for completing the necessary paperwork, of which recording the interview is an essential component; and management checks on your recordings are not unknown.

However, even if a supervisor does not pick up on a lack of recording and demand corrections, there are other potential dangers. For example, as we have already pointed out in the case of Rani, if issues arise in your absence there will be an obvious need for current and accurate records of your cases to be available.

## OTHER TYPES OF RECORDING

Although recording in summary form onto paper or onto a computer is likely to be the main method of recording an interview, there are other methods. Here, we discuss use of video or other equipment, live supervision and process recording. All have a more specialised function, either within a special agency, or within a training role.

### I  Live recording

Live recording involves using a tape recorder, video camera or digital recorder to record the entire process of an interview. Actual live recording can provide important insights into the processes contained in the service user/interviewer dialogue, but it is rarely used for social work interviews.

First, you need to consider both a service user's reaction and yours to the presence of recording equipment. This will have an obvious effect on the dynamics of the interview, as well as on the reactions of individuals. If considering live recording, you will need to think how you can minimise the effects. Should you plan for a service user to be involved, you will need them to have given full and informed consent well in advance. Spending time by discussing the joint benefits, and by talking through any fears, will be an important part of your essential preparation. Service users should sign a form of written consent, and you should also obtain the advance permission of any other participants in the interview.

However, verbal or video recordings certainly have advantages. It is possible to repeatedly replay every part of an interview, examining in detail your actions and interactions with the service user – an examination that should help everyone involved to understand the processes of the interview. Another advantage of recording is that you can gain a perspective on the whole interview, and not simply rely on your later memory of events filtered through your consciousness (Burnham, 1986, p71).

Essentially, video recording allows interviewers to see themselves as they appear to others, and to view the effects of their interview techniques. An actual recording can be viewed later, and you can also transcribe it into print, which can considerably aid analysis.

There are inevitably considerable technical and logistical overheads involved in live recording, which confines its use to specific and probably specialised agencies, or colleges. 'Skills laboratories' (Koprowska, 2005, p39) can help students monitor, change or experiment with facets of their interaction under controlled conditions.

## 2 Live supervision

Generally speaking, live supervision is unlikely to be part of many social care interviews. It can, however, be a key aspect of family therapy work in aiding practitioners' practice (Burnham, 1986, pp71–2). This method of interview recording takes two practitioners: one to work with the service users, and one to observe. A special interview setting can allow the observer to be concealed, perhaps behind a one-way mirror. The interview can also be recorded. As before, full explanations should be given to participants and their consent obtained.

The principal advantage of this measure is that the interviewer can get immediate feedback on their performance; another practitioner selects the issues. A further aspect of the method is the use of breaks, or punctuations. These allow the observer to give feedback throughout the interview, and thereby help it go in therapeutic directions.

As already mentioned, live supervision needs informed consent of interview participants. This method of work also means the involvement of additional workers in the interview process, together with an additional office/studio setting for the interview – a fact that may in itself alter its balance and dynamics.

## 3 Process recording

A process recording is used almost exclusively as a learning tool for new interviewers. You produce a written account of the entire interview, in as much detail as possible. While to an extent this duplicates a conventional interview report, a process recording should contain far more specific descriptions and much more detailed information, particularly about the different processes, the thinking behind your actions and your views about what is behind service users' reactions. An analogy is to think of a process recording as a 'Dr Watson' interview. It seems that Sherlock Holmes, the great detective, sometimes sent Dr Watson to look into things on his behalf. While Watson invariably drew totally erroneous conclusions from his investigations, he always returned with a detailed report that allowed Holmes to produce interesting theories and accurate analysis. Of course, some self-analysis is possible with a process recording, but it is always better shared. Your 'Dr Watson' process recording should contain sufficient detail to allow you and your 'Sherlock Holmes' supervisor to discuss the levels of interaction and thought processes that happened within the interview. This analysis will provide further learning and insight, assisting your own professional development and future involvement with the service user.

However, the process notation is hard, if not impossible, to sustain for the complete interview. For that reason, process recordings tend to be used for beginnings and endings, transition points in the interview, or where you may glean most benefit from close analysis. Uncomfortable parts of the interview fit this category, or particular points – summarising, say, or drawing in a third party – that you and/or your supervisor personally make a learning area.

There are various ways of setting down a process recording: from a free-flowing description, to parcelling out what might be happening into columns across the page. We find the most effective way is to divide a landscape page into four columns:

1   What happened
2   What you thought about what happened
3   What action you intend to take (future questions, future reading etc.)
4   Additional (where you can put theory used, reference to NOSSC key roles etc.)

You may find, however, that colleges have a template for you to use. Whichever method is used, you need to set aside a time at least as long as the interview to do justice to the process recording.

## HOW TO PRACTISE INTERVIEWING

Interviewing, like all other aspects of social work, is a skill that needs practice so that you achieve confidence and consistency. It is also something about which, understandably, workers new to the profession can often feel nervous.

'How is the other person going to react?'
'What if things go wrong?'
'What should I do if something unexpected happens?'

Such feelings are totally natural, reasonable, and to be expected. Experience, and practising interviewing, is the obvious cure. However, while it is difficult, if not impossible, to duplicate an actual interview, it is possible to follow approaches to make yourself less nervous, and to help you feel more knowledgeable about the process before undertaking it 'for real'. Of course, one excellent method of learning about interviewing is to read a suitable book . . .

In addition to reading, the main methods of learning interviewing skills are:

- Observation.
- Role-play.
- Rehearsal of difficult parts of interviews.
- Watching recordings of interviews.
- User participation.

## Observing other social workers

Having obtained permission from the service user, a useful and worthwhile learning experience is to observe an experienced practitioner undertaking an interview with that service user.

However, to get the maximum from such an experience, the observer must first have thought about the concepts involved in interviewing, and so know a little about the processes. They should also clearly identify what they hope to learn from the experience. Check that the interviewer does not mind being asked questions afterwards – and then *use* that opportunity. Most practitioners will appreciate lively questions, rather than a seeming lack of interest.

During the interview, observe how the interviewer uses skills, such as making common ground with the service user, and how they put questions, or bring in other parties to the discussion. Be on the alert, too for all aspects of *non-verbal* behaviour. And, of course, if you are in an observational role it should be possible to absorb much of the non-verbal content of the interview. You can get an idea of areas to consider from the self-assessment form in Chapter 7.

If possible, try to observe several practitioners in this way. The accumulated experience will enable you to compare and contrast different styles of interviewing, and show you how different practitioners vary in their handling of similar areas of enquiry. As an example, observe how different workers introduce sensitive subjects, and what actual words they use to summarise situations.

How practitioners conceptualise goal setting in the interview may also differ from worker to worker. In particular, you can observe what a social worker considers can be accomplished in the space of the interview. This is likely to help you in thinking about your own interview goals, and the place of short-term aims in accomplishing long-term objectives.

Finally, you can speculate on what theoretical perspectives you would bring to that interview, and be able to share this.

### Role-play

Role-play is a well-established and common method of practising interviewing skills. Most social workers will have had experience of this method while at college, or on training, where it may additionally have involved video recording. The main advantage of role-playing an interview is that it is usually undertaken with a peer group, in safe surroundings, and away from actual clients. It may also feel much safer for you, as role-play is not undertaken directly with a service user. The use of role-play in advance of placements may arguably be safer for service users too, as it enables very new interviewers to take on board some basic skills before being sent to practise on 'real people'.

There are several advantages for an inexperienced social worker in following this method. First, it allows you to make mistakes, without risking any harm to a service user. Second, it is useful as a method to experiment with different ways of managing the same interview situation, and over a variety of different interventions. Role-play can also be a very useful way of trying out means of handling the awkward stages of an interview, and has the potential to improve confidence dramatically.

As role-play is usually undertaken within a team, or with a group of fellow students, a certain amount of trust in the audience can counterbalance the anxiety of performing in front of possible critics. Of course, role-play does not necessarily need either an audience or an assessor, so sometimes working in twos and threes can feel a much safer way of handling initial attempts to practise interview skills.

Finally, if you can become relaxed about role-play early in your career, then using this method to increase your skills later on for particular, specialist interviews – such as protection work – will be all the easier.

### Rehearse difficult parts of interviews

This method is really akin to role-play, but links in with more difficult interviewing, or sensitive areas of questioning. It can be an aid when you know that you are going to have to enquire about or challenge in an area that is likely to provoke a strong emotional reaction. A colleague or supervisor can role-play the service user, acting out the emotional response to questioning, and can also give feedback on the language you have selected for the subject. This low-key approach will allow you to modify your language or methods before the actual interview. Speaking phrases out loud to service users is very much easier if you have practised saying them two or three times.

Basically, if you are able to rehearse with a colleague in the secure environment of your office, it will almost certainly lead to greater confidence in your ability to handle the real-life situation.

## Watch videos of interviews

There are some social work interviews on film, videotape or DVD that are well worth consulting. Several television programmes have been made about social work and Social Services Departments, and copies of these programmes may be available to you. Some agencies have a training section that may not only be able to distribute commercial recordings, but may also make in-house videos/DVDs for educational purposes, and some specialist professional videos are also available. An example of an interesting website is Mental Health TV (see Bibliography), where interviews are readily accessible.

What are you likely to learn from watching recordings such as these? One point is that in recorded interviews a criticism of the interviewing style is undoubtedly easier to make, as no personal relationships are involved. Also, as in live observation of other interviewers, watching different interviewing styles can help you in developing your own style and techniques. A video can also provide a good discussion focus for a group to analyse the processes in an interview, especially as it can often be reassuring to watch others making mistakes, and still survive.

## User participation

*What Service Users Want* (see Chapter 6) is a clear statement of the standards that the public expect in their involvement with social workers. Within the profession, there is a growing movement to involve service users in all aspects of social work, and service user participation in social work training is now a degree requirement.

User participation may have a particularly important part to play in heightening practitioners' skills and sensitivity to issues such as diversity, difference or discrimination. When service users share their particular individual experience, it can accelerate the learning process, and make you aware not only of a far greater range of issues, but also their emotional impact.

## CONCLUSION

In this chapter we considered why we need to record interviews. Reasons include:

- Legal and organisational needs, including the need for evidence.
- Accountability for decision making and workers' actions.
- Continuity of contact for the service user.
- As a method of reflecting on or analysing your involvement.

Recording itself needs to be:

- In plain language.
- 'Adequate, relevant and not excessive'.
- Carried out in a timely fashion.
- Supportive of decision-making or analysis of risk.

We discussed other methods of recording, such as taping, live supervision and process recording. The chapter concluded by considering methods that practitioners might use to practise and improve interviewing skills, including:

- Observation of experienced practitioners.
- Role-play with a few colleagues.
- Rehearsal of new techniques or difficult parts of an interview.
- Observation of recorded interviews
- Learning from service user involvement.

All these have a place in allowing you to improve your interviewing skills, or learning new ones, while keeping service users from harm.

## QUESTIONS

1 What is your opinion of a report that states: 'this woman lives in squalor'? How would you rephrase it, or would you not record anything about the environment?

2 You have a court report to write. How will you extract the information on family interrelations from the file?

3 How do you think you might improve your interview recording skills?

## FURTHER READING

BASW Code of Ethics; specifically section 4.1.7.
Lishman, Joyce, *Communication in Social Work*, Chapter 3.
Thompson, Neil, *People Skills*, Chapter 12.

# Conclusion

Social work interviews lie at the very heart of social work and social care.

In this book we have dissected and analysed social work interviewing, and believe we have done so in a way that will encourage you to reflect on your interactions with service users, give you confidence in attempting new ideas and techniques, and help you in working towards consistency in your professional interactions.

In the hope that practitioners will consider and incorporate relevant material into their work, we have tried particularly hard to illuminate points through actual examples taken from social work practice, accompanied by realistic advice. While some of the information included here should benefit even skilled interviewers, its acquisition is essential for the professional development of new or inexperienced workers.

Social work is undoubtedly a challenging profession. It involves working with a variety of people, service users, from all backgrounds; the essence of social work can be seen as helping these individuals change and grow through stressful periods in their lives. Our hope is that *Effective Interviewing in Social Work and Social Care* will provoke thinking; if it also accelerates learning about interviewing, and helps practitioners to be more reflective about their work for service users' benefit, it will have fulfilled its purpose.

# Bibliography and References

Adams, R. (2002) 'Social work Processes', in R. Adams et al. (eds) *Social Work: Themes, Issues and Critical Debates*, Basingstoke: Palgrave.

Adams, R., Dominelli, L. and Payne, M. (2002) *Social Work: Themes, Issues and Critical Debates*, Basingstoke: Palgrave.

Age Concern (2004) *The Impact of Pension Credit on Those Receiving It*, England: Age Concern Reports.

Barr, H. (2002) 'Social Work in Collaboration with Other Professions', in M. Davies, M. (ed.) *The Blackwell Companion to Social Work*, 2nd edn, Oxford: Blackwell.

Berne, E. (1964) *Games People Play*, New York: Grove Press.

Biestek, Felix P. (1979) *The Casework Relationship*, London: George Allen & Unwin.

Bögels, S. (2000) 'Diagnostic Interviewing in Mental Health Care: Methods, Training and Assessment', in A. Memon and R. Bull (eds) *Handbook of the Psychology of Interviewing*, Chichester: Wiley.

Brown, G.W. and Harris, T. (1978) *Social Origins of Depression: A Study of Psychiatric Disorder in Women*, London: Tavistock Publications.

Brown, H. and Egan-Sage, E., with Barry, G. and McKay, C. (1996) *Towards Better Interviewing: A Handbook for Police Officers and Social Workers on the Sexual Abuse of Adults with Learning Disabilities*, Brighton: Pavilion Publishing.

Brown, H. (2002) 'Counselling', in R. Adams et al. (eds) *Social Work: Themes Issues and Critical Debates*, Basingstoke: Palgrave.

Burke, B. and Harrison, P. (2002) 'Anti-Oppressive Practice', in R. Adams et al. (eds) *Social Work: Themes, Issues and Critical Debates*, Basingstoke: Palgrave.

Burnham, J.B. (1986) *Family Therapy*, London: Tavistock Publications.

Cigno, K. (2002) 'Cognitive-behavioural Practice', in R. Adams et al. (eds) *Social Work: Themes, Issues and Critical Debates*, Basingstoke: Palgrave.

Cigno, K. and Bourn, D. (eds) (1998) *Cognitive Behavioural Social Work in Practice*, Aldershot: Ashgate/Arena.

Coleman, J. and Hendry, L. (1999) *The Nature of Adolescence*, 3rd edn, London: Routledge.

Collins, J. and Collins, M. (1992) *Social Work Skills Training and the Professional Helper*, Chichester: Wiley.

Cook, M. (1971) *Interpersonal Perception*, Harmondsworth: Penguin Education.

Coulshed, V. and Orme, J. (1998) *Social Work Practice: an Introduction*, 3rd edn, Basingstoke: Macmillan.

Cree, V. (2002) 'Social Work and Society', in M. Davies (ed.) *The Blackwell Companion to Social Work*, 2nd edn, Oxford: Blackwell.

Davies, M. (ed.) (2002): *The Blackwell Companion to Social Work*, 2nd edn, Oxford: Blackwell.

De Shazer, S. (1985) *Key to Solution in Brief Therapy*, New York: Norton.

Dennis, P.J. and Strickland, D. (2002) 'Who Blinks in Volatile Markets, Individuals or Institutions', *The Journal of Finance*, 57(5), October.

Dominelli, L. (2002) 'Feminist Theory', in M. Davies (ed.) *The Blackwell Companion to Social Work*, 2nd edn, Oxford: Blackwell.

Dickson, A. (1982) *A Woman in Your Own Right*, London: Quartet Books.

Egan, G. (2002) *The Skilled Helper: A problem-management and opportunity-development approach to helping*, 7th edn, Pacific Grove, CA: Brooks Cole.

French, S. and Swain, J. (2002): 'The Perspective of the Disabled People's Movement', in M. Davies (ed.) *The Blackwell Companion to Social Work*, 2nd edn, Oxford: Blackwell.

General Social Care Council (2002) *Codes of Practice for Social Care Workers and Employers*, London: General Social Care Council.

Girdano, D.A., Everly, G.S. and Dusek, D.E. (1996) *Controlling Stress and Tension*, Needham Heights, MA, Allyn & Bacon.

Goffman, E. (1982) *The Presentation of Self in Every day Life*, London: Pelican.

Goffman, E. (1986) *Frame Analysis: An Essay on the Organization of Experience*, New England, Northeastern University Press.

Hardiker, P. and Barker, M. (1991) 'Towards Social Theory for Social Work', in J. Lishman (ed.) *Handbook of Theory for Practice Teachers in Social Work*, London: Jessica Kingsley.

Hargie, O. and Tourish, D. (2000) 'The Psychology of Interpersonal Skill', in A. Memon and R. Bull (eds) *Handbook of the Psychology of Interviewing*, Chichester: Wiley.

Hearn, J. (1982) 'The Problems Of Theory And Practice In Social Work And Social Work Education', *Issues in Social Work Education*, 2(2), pp95–118.

Humphreys, C. (2002): 'Domestic Violence', in M. Davies (ed.) *The Blackwell Companion to Social Work*, 2nd edn, Oxford: Blackwell.

Inhelder, B. and Piaget, J. (1958) *The Growth of Logical Thinking from Childhood to Adolescence*, New York: Basic Books.

Jones, C. (2002) 'Poverty and Social Exclusion', in M. Davies (ed.) *The Blackwell Companion to Social Work*, 2nd edn, Oxford: Blackwell.

Kadushin, A. (1972) *The Social Work Interview*, New York: Columbia University Press.

Kadushin, A. and Kadushin G. (1997) *The Social Work Interview: A Guide for Human Service Professionals*, 4th edn, New York: Columbia University Press.

Koprowska, J. (2005) *Communication and Interpersonal Skills in Social Work*, Exeter: Learning Matters Ltd.

Leadbetter, M. (2002) 'Empowerment and Advocacy', in R. Adams et al. (eds) *Social Work: Themes, Issues and Critical Debates*, Basingstoke: Palgrave.

Lishman, J. (1991) *Handbook of Theory for Practice Teachers in Social Work*, London: Jessica Kingsley.

Lishman, J. (1994) *Communication in Social Work*, Basingstoke: Macmillan.

Marsh, P. (1991) 'Task Centred Practice', in J. Lishman (ed.) *Handbook of Theory for Practice Teachers in Social Work*, London: Jessica Kingsley.

Memon, A. and Bull, R. (eds) *Handbook of the Psychology of Interviewing*, Chichester: Wiley.

Mullally, R. (1993) *Structural Social Work: Ideology, Theory and Practice*, Canada: Oxford University Press.

Nicholson, P. and Bayne, R. (1984) *Applied Psychology for Social Workers*, Basingstoke: Macmillan.

Norman, A. (1980) *Rights and Risks: Discussion Document on Civil Liberty in Old Age*, London: Centre for Policy on Ageing.

Norman, A. (1985) *Triple Jeopardy: Growing Old in a Second Homeland*, London: Centre for Policy on Ageing.

O'Connell, B. and Palmer, S. (eds) (2003) *Handbook of Solution-focused Therapy (Brief Therapies)*, London: SAGE.

Oliver, M. (1987) 'From strength to strength', *Community Care*, 19 February.

Oliver, M. (1996) *Understanding Disability: From Theory To Practice*, Basingstoke: Macmillan.

Orme J. (2002) 'Feminist Social Work', in R. Adams et al. (eds) *Social Work: Themes, Issues and Critical Debates*, Basingstoke: Palgrave.

Parton, N. (2002) 'Postmodern and Constructionist Approaches to Social Work', in R. Adams et al. (eds) *Social Work: Themes, Issues and Critical Debates*, Basingstoke: Palgrave.

Payne, M. (1997) *Modern Social Work Theory*, 2nd edn, Basingstoke: Macmillan.

Payne, M. (2002) 'Social Work Theories and Reflective Practice', in R. Adams et al. (eds) *Social Work: Themes, Issues and Critical Debates*, Basingstoke: Palgrave.

Payne, S. (2000): 'Qualitative Research', in A. Memon and R. Bull (eds) *Handbook of the Psychology of Interviewing*, Chichester: Wiley.

Pritchard, J. (ed.) (2001) *Good Practice with Vulnerable Adults*, London: Jessica Kingsley.

Rogers, C. (1942) *Counseling and Psychotherapy*, Boston, MA: Houghton Mifflin.

Rosado, L. (ed.) (2000) *Talking to Teens in the Justice System: Strategies for Interviewing Adolescent Defendants, Witnesses, and Victims*, American Bar Association.

Sackett, D.L., Richardson, S.W., Rosenberg, W. and Haynes, R.B. (eds) (1996) *Evidence-based Medicine*, Churchill, Livingstone.

SCOPE/Essex Coalition of Disabled People (2002) *The Good Practice Guide: for Support Workers and Personal Assistants Working with Disabled People with Communication Impairments*, London: SCOPE.

Shardlow, S.M. (2002) 'Values, Ethics and Social Work', in R. Adams et al. (eds) *Social Work: Themes, Issues and Critical Debates*, Basingstoke: Palgrave.

Sheldon, B. (1995) *Cognitive-behavioural Therapy: Research, Practice and Philosophy*, 2nd edn, Abingdon: Routledge.

Social Care Institute for Excellence (SCIE) (2004) Resource Guide 3: *Teaching and Learning Communication Skills in Social Work Education*, London: SCIE.

Sutton, C. (1994) *Social Work, Community Work and Psychology*, Leicester: British Psychological Society.

Thompson, N. (2001) *Anti-Discriminatory Practice*, 3rd edn, Basingstoke: Palgrave.

Thompson, N. (2002) *People Skills*, 2nd edn, Basingstoke: Palgrave Macmillan.

Thompson, N. (2003) *Promoting Equality: Challenging Discrimination and Oppression*, 2nd edn, Basingstoke: Palgrave.

Timms, N. (1983) *Social Work Values: an Enquiry*, London: Routledge & Kegan Paul.

Trevithick, P. (2000) *Social Work Skills: A Practice Handbook*, Buckingham: Open University Press.

Trevithick P., Richards, S., Ruch, G. and Moss, B. with Lines, L. and Manor, O. (2004) *Knowledge Review: Teaching and Learning Communication Skills in Social Work Education*, London: SCIE.

## WEBSITE URLS

Acheson Report: 1998 Independent Inquiry into Inequalities in Health Report.
<http://www.archive.official-documents.co.uk/document/doh/ih/contents.htm>
Accessed 24.02.07

BASW website: <http://www.basw.co.uk>
Accessed 09.07.07

Alberta Campus Graduate Program in Counselling
<http://www.abcounsellored.net>
<abcounsellored.net/CAhomepage/apply/skills.html>
Accessed 24.02.07

Data Protection Act 1998 – guidance for social services
<http://www.dh.gov.uk/PublicationsAndStatistics/Legislation/ActsAndBills/
ActsAndBillsArticle/fs/en?CONTENT_ID=4015584&chk=plekuc>
Accessed 24.02.07

Department of Health: Employee checklist for social care staff
<http://www.dh.gov.uk/PolicyAndGuidance/HumanResourcesAndTraining/
NationalTaskforceOnViolence/ViolenceChecklist/fs/en?CONTENT_ID=
4052018&chk=4IafsC>
Accessed 24.02.07

Enabling Support Foundation
<www.enabling.org>, material reproduced with permission.
Accessed 24.02.07

GSCC Skills for Care
<http://www.topssengland.net/>
Accessed 24.02.07

Guardian Unlimited
<http:www.guardian.co.uk>
Accessed 08.07.07

Joseph Rowntree Foundation
<http://www.jrf.org.uk/default.asp>
Accessed 24.02.07

Language Line
<http://www.languageline.co.uk/>
Accessed 24.02.07

MacArthur Risk Assessment Study
<http://www.macarthur.virginia.edu/risk.html>
Accessed 24.02.07

Mental Capacity Act 2005
<http:www.opsi.gov.uk/acts/acts2005/20050009.htm>
Accessed 08.07.07

Mental Health Television, the online broadcast channel with programmes for mental
healthcare professionals and service users
<http://www.mentalhealth.tv/>
Accessed 24.02.07

National Aids Trust
<http://www.nat.org.uk/page/3723>
Accessed 24.02.07

National Occupational Standards for Social Work
<http://www.topssengland.net/files/cd/England/Expectations/ExpectVal.htm>
Accessed 24.02.07

Not Alone. A Guide for the better protection of lone workers in the NHS.
<http://www.cfsms.nhs.uk/doc/lone.worker/not.alone.pdf>
Accessed 24.02.07

Research in practice for children and families
<http://www.rip.org.uk/index.asp>
Accessed 24.02.07

Research mindedness in social work and social care
<http://www.resmind.swap.ac.uk/index.htm>
Accessed 24.02.07, but no longer updated.

Sainsbury Centre for Mental Health ('The Costs of Race Inequality')
<http://www.scmh.org.uk/80256FBD004F6342/vWeb/pcKHAL6UGLUE>
Accessed 24.02.07

Statistic on Race <http://www.guardian.co.uk/macpherson/article/0,,
191672,00.html#article_continue>
Accessed 24.02.07

The Stephen Lawrence Inquiry
<http://www.archive.official-documents.co.uk/document/cm42/4262/ 4262.htm>
Accessed 24.02.07

Victoria Climbié Inquiry
<http://www.nationalarchives.gov.uk/ERO/records/ vc/1/1/index.htm>
Accessed 24.02.07

Working with Diversity
<http://www.workingwithdiversity.org/index.php>
Accessed 24.02.07

## MENCAP-RECOMMENDED WEBSITES

This list is a mixture of sites that give information on tools or products and sites that people with a learning disability have helped to make or enjoy using. These latter websites are included to give some ideas and inspiration about communication!

www.signalong.org.uk
www.makaton.org
www.liberator.co.uk
www.ace-centre.org.uk
www.askmencap.info
www.heartnsoul.co.uk
www.trans-active.org.uk
www.symbolworld.org

www.easyinfo.org.uk
www.easywords.co.uk
www.newhallmemories.org

Accessibility@Mencap.org.uk
www.Mencap.org.uk www.psychology.stir.ac.uk/old/AAC/about
www.photosymbols.com
www.changepeople.co.uk
www.widgit.com

# Index